History's Lost Moments

The Stories Your Teacher Never Told You

Volume II

Order this book online at www.trafford.com
or email orders@trafford.com

Most Trafford titles are also available at major online book retailers.

Printed in Victoria, BC, Canada.

ISBN: 978-1-4269-1968-8 (sc)

ISBN: 978-1-4269-1969-5 (dj)

Library of Congress Control Number: 2009912982

*Our mission is to efficiently provide the world's finest, most comprehensive book publishing
service, enabling every author to experience success. To find out how to publish your book,
your way, and have it available worldwide, visit us online at www.trafford.com*

Trafford rev. 2/5/2010

 www.trafford.com

North America & international
toll-free: 1 888 232 4444 (USA & Canada)
phone: 250 383 6864 ♦ fax: 812 355 4082

Dedicated To The Glory of God
and in honor
of
Laura Millicent Bull Horton
Mount Pleasant, S.C.
2009

Table of contents:
History's Lost Moments
Stories your teachers never told you, Volume II.

Again, as in Volume I,, I thank Vickey Boyd, Sully Witte, and the wonderful folks at The Moultrie News for publishing my weekly column. My wife Millie encourages me and gives generously of her time in proof-reading my work. My parents, Dr. and Mrs. Ira B. Horton, Jr., stand four-square behind me in this venture, ready to lend a hand or money whenever things become overwhelming. Without these wonderful people, and so many others unnamed, these stories of times past would never see the light of day. Any mistakes contained herein are the result of my own oversight. God bless you all, and I am working diligently on Volume III.

Tom Horton
Mount Pleasant, SC
August 2009

Soli Deo Gloria

1

The Man Who Would Have Pre-empted William Moultrie in '76

We're forgiven for not knowing all there is to know about John Armstrong. After all, he's a Pennsylvanian with no ties to the state, and Charleston was the only place that didn't crown him with laurels. Armstrong was accustomed to being indispensable, especially in military matters. But for want of a swifter horse on June 28,1776, we might have celebrated victory at Fort Armstrong rather than at Fort Moultrie!

A quarter of a millennium has worn away all signs on Sullivan's of the struggle by our boys who sought to turn back the mightiest naval armada ever before to drop anchor in these waters. To the engineer's mind, the sand and palmetto log embrasures were indefensible, downright laughable, and quite likely a deathtrap to the patriot defenders.

Who can blame commanding general Charles Lee for cashiering Moultrie and ordering Armstrong to assume the command. Moultrie, 46 years old, was a military novice despite the gold epaulets signifying the rank of colonel. Serving as a captain less than a year on the 1761 Cherokee expedition was a feather in his cap, but hardly the type of resume needed for defending Charleston against the British fleet.

The easy-going Moultrie was a planter, a *bon vivant* known to be lax in discipline but greatly beloved by his troops. Other than his close ties with Governor Rutledge, Moultrie had little else recommending him to the post of danger. After all, wasn't Moultrie the Charlestonian elected to the 1st Continental Congress who refused to serve?

What of Armstrong's record, the man who would pre-empt Moultrie if Charles Lee got his way? Why was Lee insistent that Armstrong replace Moultrie as the guns began to boom that hot June day?

If a continental soldier had impressive credentials in 1776, it was John Armstrong. Born of Scots-Irish parentage in Ireland in 1717, John Armstrong was apprenticed at an early age to a civil engineer. He learned his profession well before coming to the colonies as an agent of the Penn family. Armstrong was as prominent in Pennsylvania for his surveying as was George Washington in Virginia.

By the 1750s, Armstrong was one of the senior representatives of the Penn family in America. John Armstrong's reports to the Penns in London occasionally were passed to the throne.

When prime minister William Pitt directed Britain's interests in the French and Indian War, 1756 to 1763, Colonel Armstrong was the tip of the spear for operations in Pennsylvania. His daring Indian raids earned him the *nomme de guerre*, "Hero of Kittanny." In 1758 it was Armstrong who led the sappers on a dangerous mission to blow up Fort Duquesne, headquarters of the French army. Armstrong was there to second General Forbes' recommendation that the pile of rubble be renamed Fort Pitt. In this fight against the grand French army, Colonel Armstrong became a confidante with George Washington of the Virginia militia.

As an engineer knowledgeable in all aspects of military campaigning, Armstrong exceeded anyone south of Richmond that the colonies could have relied upon. This was the man who had laid out the frontier town of Carlisle, Pennsylvania, the furthermost western outpost. "Old Jack," as some referred to the 59-year-old general, was totally fearless in a fight, and he had that levelheaded engineer's mind so essential in engaging a powerful foe such as Britain.

The dawn of June 28, 1776, brought the dreaded news that General Clinton's British infantry on Long Island (Isle of Palms) would use the ebb tide to ford Breach Inlet and thereby assault from behind the sand fort of the rebels. Simultaneously word reached Lee at his headquarters on Haddrell's Point that Sir Peter Parker had dropped down the channel to anchor right off Moultrie's ocean battery. In a fit of frustration, Lee countermanded Rutledge's authority and ordered Armstrong immediately to take Moultrie's post.

The distance from Haddrell's, today's Live Oak Drive, to the old causeway via Pitt Street is inconsequential. But in colonial times none of these streets existed, and the area was cut through with marsh creek and bogs. By the time Armstrong and Lee reached Moultrie, the show was well in hand. Moultrie's men, the magnificent 2nd Regiment, barely took note of Lee and Armstrong as they entered the unfinished rear sally port. "Steady fire, cool and do mischief!" were the words bystanders remembered Moultrie used to exhort his men to stand to their guns.

Repeatedly General Lee refused to send any more of the gunpowder stored at Haddrell's for Moultrie's use. It appeared that the patriots were getting off one shot for every six by the British fleet. But as the fleet's shells buried themselves deep in the muck of the fort's interior, or went ka-thung harmlessly into the spongy palmetto logs, every one of Moultrie's shells tore gaping holes in Parker's warships. Parker had his breeches blown away by a shell that left the Admiral with an undignified wound.

Archaeological interpretation in 1974 by Stanley South of the Fort Moultrie site reveals a hastily constructed, three-sided log and sand fort with a fourth side facing James Island unfinished at the time of the battle. The parapets were approximately 20 feet vertical, 16 feet wide, and 180 yards long, giving the fort a lower, longer profile than the 19th century edifice we see today. The center of the 1776 fort was a marshy sinkhole flooded a foot or more deep at high tide.

William Moultrie was no engineer, and he wasn't a martinet on parade, but this low-country planter knew a thing or two on June 28. Moultrie knew that if the enemy attacked on an outgoing tide that any attempt Parker made to flank him would lead to British ships running aground. Consequently they'd be sitting ducks for his gunners. If the British came in on a high tide, then their fleet would be pinned between the awesome guns of the harbor's four sides. Moulrie's men stood to their work and the rest is a Charleston legend.

4

General John Armstrong, one of the best engineering minds in the Continental Army, left Charleston with no personal triumphs. He served as a major general at Brandywine and Germantown, and later in the Continental Congress. In his latter years, "Old Jack" helped establish Dickinson College in his home town and served as trustee until his death in 1795.

The Real Pirates of the Caribbean

Click on the television and you see them; flip through the weekly news magazines, and they are there -- swarthy faces with dark eyes glaring from under their rag-wrapped heads. For fun, they behead a prisoner, or two. Otherwise, these terrorists are expert in the disruption of international trade and in creating political instability. Just another night's news from the middle-east? No! All the hype is the newest Disney movie about the pirates of the Caribbean.

And what a whimsical summer diversion these celluloid corsairs offer us from our daily drudge of real destruction, kidnappings, beheadings, and disruption of trade. For a moment these big-screen buccaneers make us forget Al-qada and Hezbollah, but the cold reality is that the greatest of the Caribbean pirates, Jean-David Nau, a.k.a."Admiral Francois l' Ollonais," is the cruelest cutthroat this hemisphere has yet seen.

But Jean-David Nau, or Francois l' Ollonais, is chief among the pirates who plundered and tortured their way to notoriety between 1600 and 1820. Using the name, Admiral l'Ollonais, this French-born freebooter led 3000 renegades, killed upwards of 3000 men who crossed him, and claimed nearly a half-million pieces of eight coins in a campaign of terror spanning seven years, 1660 to 1668, in the waters between Cuba and Venezuela.

Centuries before the term "state-sponsored terrorism" was fashionable to describe thugs who committed mayhem on an international scale, violent and greedy men exploited the rivalry between France, Spain, Portugal, and England over the riches of the New World.

There's no wonder at Hollywood zeroing in upon the age of empire-building where four navies contest every island between Cuba and the Bay of Campeche. Most of the pirates we romanticize sailed with their government's authorization to plunder their sovereign's enemies. l'Ollonais preyed upon Spanish colonists with the blessing and aid of the French governor of Tortuga.

Background on this cruel man is sketchy with most details coming from a former pirate surgeon, Alexander Exquemelin, a crew mate of Henry Morgan. Exquelemin's account, *The Buccaneers of America* (1678), published in Holland, gives a gruesome recounting of Jean-David Nau's rise to fame.

A youthful Nau came out to Hispaniola as an indentured servant in the 1650s. Speculation abounds that Nau, better known by his alias, l'Ollonais, might have been part Algerian. Whether he served his indenture or bolted into the swamps is also a mystery. By his 25th birthday, l'Ollonais and a band of thieves canoed their way to Tortuga, a pirates' paradise. This Tortuga is not to be confused with the chain known as the Dry Tortugas. It's a small island off the northwest corner of Haiti. In the 1660s the French governor there enlisted anyone who'd plunder Spanish shipping in the vast Caribbean Sea.

Unlike the Hollywood movie, however, l'Ollonais preferred small outrigger canoes for his stealthy conquests of merchant ships laden with cacao. What quickly distinguished this pirate from others was his flair for dramatic cruelty which always culminated in barbaric public executions. For his cruelty, l'Ollonais enjoyed another nickname --Fleau des Espagnos (the flail).

The first awareness anyone had of him was a slave insurrection he instigated

on St. Dominique. Soon a dangerous band of runaway slaves and desperadoes were sanctioned by the governor of Tortuga to raid ships that dared to sail outside the Spanish treasure fleets. On his first venture into Campeche he experienced a storm and a shipwreck. Worse yet, his crew mates were slaughtered. Being only slightly wounded, the rascal covered his face with blood and passed himself off as a corpse until he had an opportunity to slink off into the swamp.
l'Ollonais played upon the superstitions of the natives by spreading word that he was resurrected from the dead as a demon.

Dozens of cacao barges anchored off de los Cayos on the north side of Cuba in 1660. l'Ollonais and his pirates looked harmless enough rowing outrigger canoes in the shallows near the flat boats laden with hides, tobacco, sugar, flax, and cacao. Knowing that the first impression in business is the lasting one, l'Ollonais slit the throats of all of his captives except one terrified fellow he allowed to escape to spread the word. The governor of Cuba vowed to track him and hang him. To that end, the governor was thwarted because the Cubans feared l'Ollonais so much that they cooperated with him!

On at least one occasion, a merchant crew abandoned the deck for the security offered by the hatch leading below. Brandishing daggers, pistols, and cutlasses, the pirates clambered aboard and threw phosphorous torches into the hold. Faced with suffocation and intense heat, the pitiful crew exited one by one, and one by one they were decapitated.

Not content just seizing ships, l'Ollonais tried his hand at amphibious assaults of rich Spanish Caribbean ports. He leagued with "Michel the Basque," a fellow rogue who had intense hatred for the Spanish. With nearly 700 buccaneers they invaded Puerto Rico. This 1663 operation earned l'Ollonais the nonofficial title of "Admiral," and "Michel the Basque" styled himself "General de Basco."

The pirate assault of Maracaibo in 1667 was the apex of the wicked duo's reign of terror. Emboldened that they'd seized nearly a half-million "pieces of eight" and tons of cargo, trunks of jewels, and harems of captured concubines, l'Ollonais and Michel the Basque made the largest amphibious landing upon western shores ever made to that date. Enduring heavy casualties because the Spanish defenders knew they'd receive no quarter if they surrendered, the pirates knew that their leaders would allow them "a debauch" if they prevailed.

The most famous Caribbean pirate died as violently as he lived. A raid into Nicaragua in 1668 was the undoing of l' Ollonais. His band got trapped far from their ships by a band of fierce natives known as Indios Bravos.

Ambushed and cut down in battle, this agent of evil was hacked to pieces and roasted over a fire by cannibals. The pirate who once had sliced open a captive's chest and taken a bite out of his heart to terrorize villagers, died unmourned. The pirate who once enjoyed a richer cash flow than did the crowned heads of Europe died with no marker to memorialize him. And the best that Hollywood can do is to amuse us with some zany antics by actors who say "Arrrrgh!"

Southern Dreams Dashed In Peach Orchard Near Gettysburg, July 2, 1863

You've heard of the magnificent courage of Pickett's ill-fated charge at Gettysburg on that hot July 3rd in 1863. His Virginians covered themselves in glory even if they didn't smash through Meade's Union line. But, astute military historians point to a less-heralded battle the day prior to Pickett's charge as being the downfall of Lee's aspirations. The thrust of Lee's offensive on July 2, one day prior to Pickett's charge, was to seize Little Round Top, and the Carolinians commanded by Joseph Brevard Kershaw of Camden led that ill-fated attack.

Ask a southerner when the Confederacy began to fade and odds are that the bloody repulse of Pickett's charge will be his reply. Hearth side historians have long chafed over Lee's strategy at Gettysburg. Pickett's defeat by Meade's Corps on July 3, 1863, captures the popular imagination of high tide for southern independence, but facts borne by lead and cold steel reveal otherwise.

Southern hopes were dashed in a peach orchard off Emmitsberg road 24 hours before the courtly Pickett and his Virginians advanced up the slope of Seminary Ridge. It was this less spectacular assault on Little Round Top by Longstreet's Corps, Kershaw's brigade leading, on July 2, that was the epicenter of Lee's failed campaign. Had Kershaw's Carolinians, along with McLaws' Georgians, seized Little Round Top, then Union General Meade would not have been able to defend against Pickett's furious charge the following day.

Confederate fortune collapsed in a Pennsylvania peach orchard as Camden native, Joseph Kershaw's four South Carolina regiments were decimated by an unexpected, furious Union counterattack. By nightfall of July 2, Lee's offensive had lost its punch, but the sage commander had not lost his will to fight.

Kershaw wrote after the war of the tension he observed between Longstreet and Lee as the two commanders surveyed the fields and slopes before them on July 2. "Old Pete," as Longstreet was known, was opposed to a Confederate attack. If a fight came in Pennsylvania, then make the Federals come after them like they'd had to do with disastrous effects at Fredericksburg. But Lee was insistent. After A.P. Hill and Ewell routed Union forces earlier on July 1, Lee wished to press the advantage.

All seemed quiet at 10 p.m., July 2. Little Round Top appeared undefended by yankees, and the only enemy in sight consisted of an infantry regiment and a battery of artillery. If southern forces could seize the heights, then Meade could be forced farther away from Washington.

Unbeknownst to Lee, the whole army of the Potomac was massing behind Little Round Top and adjoining Big Round Top mountain. Without Jeb Stuart's cavalry to ascertain the enemy's position and strength, Lee went almost blind into his battle plan. Without Stonewall Jackson to handle tactics, Lee truly was without his right arm.

Despite the poor intelligence coming into Lee's headquarters, a reluctant Longstreet told Lee, "My corps is solid as a rock -- a great rock. I will strike the blow and win."

The Kershaw brigade was recruited mostly of upstate farmers between the Wateree and the Congaree rivers. There were few "sons of privilege" in this region; most left a one mule farm to enlist. These were stiff-necked, square-jawed, steely-eyed men who'd stared down death a dozen times before from Manassas Junction to Maryes' Heights.

Longstreet sent word after midnight on July 2 to let the troops sleep a little past dawn. Camped along the Emmitsburg Road near the stone outbuildings and rail fences of the Rose farm, reveille came at 7:15 a.m. Two cooks from each company went in search of the sutler's wagon to procure rations.

Commanders left the foot soldiers with apprehension that this was the big battle that they'd expected since crossing into Pennsylvania. Longstreet's dour demeanor caused concern, yet they marched rout step up the Emmitsburg turnpike, occasionally moving to the side when the cry, "Guns up!", was heard. The rumble of horse-drawn artillery coming swiftly up caused the infantry to stand aside and cheer with ribald salutes to their comrades riding the caissons.

After marching and counter-marching for two hours, Kershaw's brigade was ordered to rest by a rail fence until Lafayette McLaws' brigade came up. Soon, the order was shouted to cross the fence and advance upon the enemy. Joe Kershaw dismounted from his handsome black gelding and marched beside his men in a formation of two columns moving horizontally toward the union entrenchment. Enemy artillery tore gaping holes in the ranks a mile before they reached their foe. Closing ranks from gaps made in their lines, they walked steadily onward without firing.

Union sharpshooters appeared upon their flanks and fired repeatedly, yet

Kershaw's men pushed on. As they reached the slope of Little Round Top, confusion rattled these stalwarts when Perry's Florida brigade broke and ran. The din of battle became horrific as Union soldiers swarmed over Little Round Top. For three hours Kershaw's men held their ground and took terrible casualties amidst a ripening peach orchard.

The fighting became hand-to-hand as Barksdale's Mississippians and Evander Law's Alabama brigade held their ground, too, against unexpected, overwhelming numbers of enemy. Four flag bearers were shot down in succession in Kershaw's brigade when a cry went up to "Lower the colors!" Sergeant Lamb, who had just grasped the flag, yelled back, "These colors don't go down until I go down!" And what was left of the Kershaw brigade rallied on the tattered flag.

Hardly a field officer was left standing as lieutenants and captains sorted out the battalions as best they could while keeping up a steady fire. Slowly the Union line before them began to waver.

No one knew where the command to move to the right flank came from, but the disastrous, faulty command did not come from General Kershaw. The immediate effect was to remove Kershaw's thrust from the developing weak spot forming in Union General Warren's line.

In the fog of battle a mistaken order broke the concentration of force and firepower crucial to seizing Little Round Top. At nightfall, Kershaw brought off his shattered brigade and buried his many dead.

The next morning, Longstreet pleaded with Lee to call off the assault by Pickett planned for Seminary Ridge, saying that the enemy was far too strongly positioned to be displaced by such a small force. Yet if Kershaw's upstate boys had broken through, Porter Alexander's big guns would have been looking down upon Meade from Little Round Top -- and history might have read a lot differently.

William Enston Made A Fortune And Gave It All To The Poor

Andrew Carnegie started it. Ted Turner followed suit. Bill Gates continued it, and now, Warren Buffett's doing it, too - giving away the bulk of their billions to charity. Philanthropy is the noblest tradition of western civilization. Some think the roots of modern philanthropy lie in the selflessness of the Quaker movement in England. Yet others think it began with the preaching of the Wesley brothers. But what about the magnanimous Charlestonian who predates even the Cadbury bequest in England? Could it be that American philanthropy got its incitement from the quiet example of our own William Enston!

Enston, the leading cabinet and furniture maker in Charleston from the 1830s until his untimely death in 1860, predates the international sensation of the Cadbury charitable foundation that started a tidal wave of charitable giving. The Cadbury chocolatiers gave away a fortune in the 1870s for their Quaker-based ideal community for England's impoverished. The story behind the building of the Enston Homes conveys American corporate compassion in a way even the Wesleys never contemplated. The uniqueness of William Enston's bequest is that - he gave it all away upon his death.

Enston Homes, a red-brick, Victorian-styled village of identical two-story cottages, complete with chapel and bell tower, occupies eight-acres on the east side of King Street two miles north of Broad.

A hundred and thirty years ago this King Street extension was part of the Michael Storen farm and was not for sale. But when Storen was told by lawyers Hayne and Ficken representing the Enston estate that funds were in hand to build indigent housing, Storen sold the tract at a low price.

The story of how William Enston got to Charleston is as fascinating as his record of philanthropy. Like so many of America's 19th century success stories,

Enston was an immigrant who arrived in this country penniless.

The earliest memory Enston had was of the Saint Augustine missionary home for orphans a half mile from Canterbury Cathedral in England. For reasons lost to time, Enston spent his youth as a ward of the Church of England. The city of Canterbury was excluded by Parliament from enforcement of the poor laws, probably because the cathedral exceeded the government's provisos for the deserving poor.

Archbishop William Manner-Sutton presided over the Church of England from 1805 through 1828, and despite his being the son of a Duke and a presiding member of the House of Lords, Manner-Sutton took a sincere interest in poor relief. During his tenure church and city officials began planning for the most modern almshouse in the world.

It was two decades too late for Enston, for Heziakiah Marshall, architect for the new housing project did not publicize his plans until the mid-1840s. But Charleston's William Enston was receiving updates from Canterbury and discussing them with clergy at St. Michael's.

As a youngster, Enston was catechized and sheltered by the Saint Augustine mission. They educated him. At age 14 he was apprenticed to a local cabinetmaker.

The next insight we have on Enston's life is that in the late 1820s, about the time Andrew Jackson gained the White House, William, his mother, and two younger brothers stepped off the boat in Philadelphia.

He said that it was due to poor health that he sought Charleston as home just a few years after arriving in Philadelphia. But judging from how quickly the Enston brothers rose to dominance in the cabinet and furniture business here, it may be that this astute craftsman saw an opportunity to succeed the talented Elfe as Charleston's favored furniture designer. Succeed they did for a whole city block, 169 through 173 King Street, became their showroom.

The concept of interior design was still a century away, but William Enston was called in to design and construct furniture, cabinets, and window treatments for wealthy planters and merchants.

Other than becoming a pew-owner at St. Michael's, it doesn't appear that William engaged in much else except work. For a few years he and his wife Hannah lived above 145 King Street. As profits mounted, Enston purchased 118 Queen Street, a Charleston single house with broad piazzas.

When word spread down King to Broad Street on March 26, 1860, that William Enston, age 52, had dropped dead of a an apparent heart-attack, the whole peninsula was stunned. "I bet Enston has every penny he ever ever made," intoned one Charleston merchant. The body was taken by rail for burial beside his mother at the Bible Christian Church on the outskirts of the city. Charleston waited eagerly for his will to be read. When the estate was calculated in excess of $500,000, a hefty sum, disappointment was voiced as many expected his net worth to be in the millions.

By April, 1860, the presidential election and the estate of William Enston were the hot topics locally. Word on the street was that Enston willed all of his estate to charity except for a generous yearly stipend to maintain his wife. Then the rector of St. Michael's revealed that Enston planned to leave the city of Charleston with a model almshouse village similar to the one in the planning stage in Canterbury, England.

Before headway could be made on Enston's bequest, Charleston was was swept into war fever, and care for the poor was subordinated to military mobilization. Four years the war dragged on and Charleston lay in ruins on the fourth anniversary of Enston's funeral. All memory of his noble bequest was lost. The struggle for subsistence consumed everyone's attention through the 1870s.

Reverend Keith of St. Michael's resurrected the noble dream of the humble English-born furniture maker, when in 1876 he teamed with Charleston mayor, William A. Courtnay and real estate agent J. P. Kennedy Bryan to bring the deceased Enston plan to reality.

14

Had not the war intervened, there's no doubt that Enston Homes would have been an even more imposing village than the two block tract it occupies. Each cottage had two rooms, a kitchen, and a small garden. Abundant green space separates the cottages, and in the center of the village is the Episcopal chapel. Hundreds of residents received counsel on thrift, morals, industry, and hygiene in the years 1886 until 1976. Presently the City of Charleston is modernizing the original Enston cottages and building new ones in order to serve the poor again in the noble spirit of William Enston.

A Day of Malice As Lieutenant Governor Tillman Kills Editor of The State

Was it justifiable homicide, or murder? Call it what you will, the gunshot that killed *The State* newspaper editor N. G. Gonzales made for a dark day in Dixie, especially since the triggerman was Lieutenant Governor Tillman! N.G., or "Nanno," had it coming, said Gonzales' detractors, what with those stinging editorials he penned in *The State* that accused Jim Tillman of gambling, swearing, and of being a drunkard.

To the Tillman crowd, it appeared that Gonzales was defaming Tillman in the heartland of his Bible-belt supporters. Jim Tillman, nephew of populist senator "Pitchfork Ben" Tillman, had legions of upstate backers who considered him their champion against the tidewater elites. Such was the political mood on that January 15th, 1903, when telegraph operators in *The State's* Main Street Columbia office tapped out the sensational murder story across the newswires.

The Gonzales name entered into Carolina acceptance when Cuban-born filibusterer Ambrosio Jose Gonzales won the heart of Harriet Elliott, aristocratic daughter of one of the lowcountry's wealthiest planters. Harriet, a pretty, flirtatious girl with a pedigree of Pinckney, Rutledge, and Gibbes' ancestry, was dreaming away her days at Madame Togno's School on Tradd Street when she met the dashing Gonzales in 1856. He was attired in his Cuban liberation army uniform and referred to himself as General Gonzales.

When "Gonzie" was not not off fomenting revolution in Spanish Cuba, he amused his Adams Run in-laws with tales of Pierre G. T. Beauregard, his old boarding school roommate in New York. In the 1850s Beauregard and Gonzales made quick money traveling as agents for the Maynard Rifle Company. When secession swept the South from the Union, "Gonzie" enlisted in the CSA but had a less than glorious career. He always had some swashbuckling scheme involving international intrigue that Charlestonians delighted in, but it was Elliott money that sustained his and Harriet's brood of boys in the postwar South.

Ambrosio Jose Gonzales may have been Cuban born, but no one had greater passion for Carolina society than did he. Three Gonzales offspring , Ambrose; Narciso, who wrote under the appellation of N.G.G., but was called Nanno; and Alfonso all inherited a double measure of hot-blooded temperament.

The boys received their education in the library of Oak Lawn plantation, the country seat of their Harvard-educated grandfather, William Elliott. There amidst moss-draped oaks overlooking a tributary of the Toogoodoo, one of the finest journalists ever produced in this state received a very decent classical education.

N.G. Gonzales spent one year at St. Timothy's Episcopal School in Herndon, Virginia in 1873. There the precocious, 15-year-old flirted with belles several years his senior and boasted in letters home that Virginia girls liked a little brass in their men. From youth it's apparent that N.G. was a cocky boy whose mouth got him into spats that his physique could not extricate him.

By the 1880s, low country readers were accustomed to the initials N.N.G. as Narciso Gener Gonzales' byline in the *News and Courier*. His style is the vinegar and salt prose that his admirers relished. Nanno took on powerful, unregulated banks and the phosphate mining interest, and he railed against the practice of renting out convicts as day laborers.

The Rubicon in Gonzales' career was his failure to get the editorship of *The News and Courier* in the Fall of 1890. Instead he was posted to Columbia to cover the newly elected Ben Tillman and his populist agrarian administration. "Pitchfork Ben" Tillman and his wool hat backers were coarse grist for the Gonzales editorial mill, but when tasked by *News and Courier* to be their man covering the state house, N.G. resigned rather than oblige. How much of his decision was due to disappointment over the editorship and how much was due to his hatred of Tillmanism is unknown.

Ambrose Gonzales, brother of N.G. and a partner in forming *The State* newspaper, tells that Nanno had saved a thousand dollars and planned to purchase a small sloop. Evidently the novels of Robert Louis Stevenson enticed him to consider abandoning polemics and to pursue a vagabond existence as a pearl diver in the Pacific. Instead, N.G. and his brother Ambrose formed The State Publishing Corporation in 1891 with the Gibbes, Richardson, Haskell, Alston, and Coker families as major stock holders. A uniting bond of the newspaper's investors was the Episcopalian, USC, Hampton-ite confederation.

But "Pitchfork Ben" Tillman and his populist reform movement was too strong even for the acid-dipped pen of N.G. Gonzales to dethrone.

Tillmanites sometimes enjoyed sparring with N.G. as they steamrolled their agenda through the state house. The Tillman farmer revolt moderated and soon Pitchfork Ben parlayed his upstate popularity into a U.S. Senate seat.

By 1902 the Gonzales brothers had *The State* on a firm financial footing. Ben Tillman's unruly nephew, George, had recently been thwarted in his bid for the governor's mansion thanks to N.G.'s sarcastic editorials detailing him as a philandering drunkard who gambled away the family grocery money. George Tillman had none of his famous uncle's charisma or ability, and his election as lieutenant governor in 1900 had been a curious coat tail phenomena.

There was no murder motive except humiliation and political defeat, but that January 1903 day around noon when N.G. was walking quickly down Main to Gervais with his hands in his overcoat pockets, he encountered Tillman approaching him from the direction of the state house. Shoving his hands deeper in his pockets, N.G. Gonzales scowled and made a move to the inside of the sidewalk. That was when a shot rang out, close range, and the Lieutenant Governor held a smoking German Luger. Reeling backward against a wall Gonzales glared at Tillman and said, "Go ahead, shoot me again, you coward."

N.G. lingered three days before dying of his wound to the abdomen. Tillman asked for and got a change of venue to Lexington county for his celebrated murder trial. Lexington county had given both Ben and George Tillman their highest vote margin on election night. A favorable judge got the trial postponed a week allegedly to obtain a more favorable jury pool. In the most publicized murder trial in SC history, George Tillman was acquitted of the murder of the unarmed N.G. Gonzales. Senator Ben Tillman paraded about the courthouse exhorting defense lawyer Cole Blease and the jury to "do the right thing." The controversial editor became a martyr to free press, and the Tillman name spiraled into infamy despite the lame duck lieutenant governor's exoneration.

Charlestonians At Center of Confederacy's French Connection

What a shame that southern valor from the Shenandoah to Shiloh was never matched by the bargaining skills of our diplomats. Southern armies scored many victories but rarely had reason to boast of the successes of their envoys at

London's White Hall or the Tuilleries in Paris. Carolina cotton was a hot commodity in European mills, but blockaded ports from Wilmington to Mobile made trade with the South an act of war. The failure of Jeff Davis' delegations in winning trade agreements across Europe proved more vexing for Richmond than did a succession of Lincoln's logger headed generals.

There was one diplomatic triumph, however, amidst a sea of despond in southern trade relations abroad. Known to history as the Erlanger Cotton Bond deal, this financial coup for the South was cobbled together in part by Charlestonians Judah P. Benjamin and Christopher G. Memminger, Confederate attorney general and treasury secretary respectively.

Though the dark clouds of secession loomed for thirty years prior to the firing on Fort Sumter, southerners never gave thought to developing an economic infrastructure that could inspire European parliaments with trust that our triumph of arms would amount to more than agrarian vassal state status.

What southern historians don't often divulge is that southern victory lay in the hands of the European banking community. European bankers' willingness to bankroll Lee's offensives was tied to their locking in southern cotton to French, British, or German textile mills.

Frustrating Richmond's attempts to lure Britain into a cotton alliance was that country's development of the Nile valley as a source of long staple cotton and the state of Madras as an alternate source of short staple. To Judah Benjamin and Christopher Memminger, the CSA's best hope rode with a "sweetheart bond deal" with a a prominent investment company with offices in Frankfurt and Paris. Erlanger and Cie was a corporate name known in all European banking circles.

Erlanger and Cie was in the periphery of the Rothchild banking conglomerate, then the largest private bank in the world. Baron Erlanger was Louis Napoleon's and Empress Eugenie's personal line of credit.

The "sweetheart deal" of the CSA and the House of Erlanger and Cie became even more interesting because of Erlanger's courtship and marriage to the beautiful young daughter of John Slidell of Louisiana. Slidell reportedly was of Jewish descent and Slidell, himself, was the recipient of anti-semitic slurs in the Confederate capital. Judah Benjamin convinced President Davis to appoint Slidell to his post as the CSA's trade negotiator.

Judah P. Benjamin grew up attending Beth Elohim Synagogue on Hassell Street in Charleston. His father Philip Benjamin, a moderately successful merchant at 165 King Street, lived nearby at 15 St. Phillip's Street. The best preparatory school for boys in 1820s Charleston was Rufus Southworth's academy located on St. Michael's Alley. Family friend Moses Lopez picked up the tab for Judah's prep school education.

With Southworth's coaching and Benjamin's ability, it was a sure bet that the boy would continue his studies at Yale. Judah Benjamin's abrupt departure from Yale two years later is still matter for conjecture, but the sharp young man made his way to New Orleans and established himself in law and numerous business ventures.

Friendship with John Slidell of Louisiana proved fortuitous for Benjamin and the Confederacy. Slidell's beautiful daughter, Marguerite Mathilde, became the bride of Baron Frederic Emil Erlanger in Paris. Emil Erlange was a friend of Louis Napoleon, Emperor of France. And Emil's father, the senior partner of Erlanger and Cie, was an itimate with the Kings of Portugal, Belgium, and Spain.

Of all families in the European banking community, none but the Rothchilds and the Erlangers were so closely aligned with royalty, manufacturing and mining, and parliamentary leaders. A handful of Confederate negotiators won over to their cause the young and romantic Emil Erlanger of Paris who was at the time courting Mathilde Slidell, daughter of the CSA's trade negotiator. Slidell's daughters were noted beauties; one became the Baroness d' Erlanger, and the other married August Belmont!

Judah Benjamin and Christopher Memminger were kept informed of the Erlanger Cotton Bond deal through coded letters brought in by blockade runners.

In Paris, a subaltern of Slidell was Columbia attorney, James G. Gibbes. Gibbes wrote much of the legal language of the bond deal, but the House of Erlanger made the terms.

The bonds were secured by southern cotton, much of which was sitting on the wharves of Mobile, Savannah, Charleston, and Wilmington. The bonds were sold at 90 percent face value to dealers in London, Liverpool, Paris, Brussels, and Amsterdam. Erlanger paid 77 percent face value. Wrangling began in Richmond over interest payments, and in Paris over what would happen if the Confederacy failed to achieve independence.

In Richmond Judah Benjamin was critical of the terms struck by his friend, Slidell. Memminger, as Treasurer of the CSA, championed ratification as it was the South's only hope. Judah Benjamin felt like the South was giving away the farm. The Richmond congress debated the Erlanger prospectus along with the casualty reports coming from the Battle of the Wilderness. Benjamin dropped his opposition to the high interest rate and the high fees paid to the House of Erlanger, and the deal was struck. Six million in gold quickly poured into Confederate coffers.

Meanwhile, in European capitals slick talking southern agents reassured investors that should the Confederacy fail in its bid for independence that, of course, the federal government would redeem the bonds. This loose talk prompted the postwar U. S. Congress to enact the 14th Amendment that, among other things, forbids the states of the federal government from assuming debts incurred during insurrections.

For the last years of the Confederacy, the Erlanger bonds provided speculators with a roller coaster ride with many investors making a profit. Erlanger and Cie prospered as planned. The pressure was upon Lee to win one more grand victory, hence the Gettysburg campaign. After 1864 the bonds traded lower each week until they defaulted in 1865. Until their default, the Erlanger Cotton bonds provided the South with its only reliable international currency exchange.

Judah Benjamin fled to London when southern hopes were dashed. Memminger was replaced as treasurer by another Charlestonian, George Alfred Trenholm. Slidell remained in Paris. Slidell's daughter, Mathilde, placed the very first telephone call on the transatlantic cable, a project financed by her husband. In the murky world of international finance, the Erlanger connection is one of the most curious deals ever struck.

Our Town As It Was 50 Years Ago This Month

Pull open the box and snap in the reel; newspapers on microfilm remain the best way yet to travel back in time. In this regard, Charleston is in a select brotherhood, for few cities in our hemisphere have newspapers dating back two and a half centuries. If nostalgia is a yearning for bygone times, then low country life as it appears in the Charleston *News and Courier* in August, 1956, is an elixir for the suburban crush we feel today.

Front page news is supposed to be bold, dramatic, as well as informative. In 1956, the local papers were very much the first bearers of intelligence. Paper boys pedaled bikes and dodged the milk man's truck in the predawn to announce the new day with the thud of a rolled newspaper.

In August of 1956, our front page news certainly didn't herald an apocalypse with each succeeding edition . . . not unless you consider Estes Kefauver's sudden withdrawal from the race for the democratic nomination to be climactic. We were disturbed by fighting over the Suez Canal, and America joined Britain and France in calling for the United Nations to secure Israel with a multilateral peacekeeping force. Eisenhower expressed indignation at how the U.N. was dragging its feet. On page two Ike mentions that he's giving thought to putting Dick Nixon's name on the upcoming Republican ticket.

The story dominating the front pages in early August, '56, concerns the much publicized courts martial of a marine drill instructor at Parris Island. Staff Sergeant Matthew McKeon, USMC, a decorated veteran of two wars, led platoon 71 into the chest deep water of Ribbon creek on a night march the previous July 21. Six marine recruits drowned and Staff Sergeant McKeon was charged with dereliction of duty, failure to follow orders, and drunkenness on duty. The trial drew national attention for two weeks as Generals R.M. Pate and Lewis B. "Chesty" Puller are brought in for the defense.

The democratic national convention opens in Atlanta and the keynote speaker is Texan Lyndon B. Johnson. An early topic at the convention is the desegregation of Alexandria, Virginia, public schools. On the editorial page, noted silhouette artist, Carew Rice laments the loss of the old oaks that lined Highway 17. Rice pens a ditty to illustrate his disdain for the highway department's desecration. A lead editorial by John Temple Graves alarms with its heading of "Fight For Mind of Our Youth Is Taking Place Today."

Charlestonians have always been more interested in section B than in Section A. We've always had our own kingdom by the sea, and most of the time the world passes us by. An interesting feature in Section B tells of J. T. Buxton, president of William's Furniture Corporation, announcing the sale of part of Cherokee Plantation near Yemassee to R. L. Huffines, Jr., for an amount reported to be in excess of $160,000.

A reporter traveled to Orangeburg to be on hand at Jennings Airport when a private plane piloted by Orangeburg businessman, Dick Horne, brought Betty Lane Cherry, the newly crowned Miss U. S. A. and first runner-up Miss Universe returned home to the largest parade Orangeburg has seen since Sherman's army packed out in 1865. State Senator Marshall William's was Master of Ceremonies and everyone wanted a picture taken with the hometown beauty. She deferred questions about possible Hollywood and television offers.

Over in Mount Pleasant the Yacht Club has to cancel its scheduled dinner because most of its membership is planning to be at the Rockville regatta. Mothers beware, the Mount Pleasant Drive-in theater advertises a double feature of "She Shoulda Said No," followed by "Ann Was A Good Girl, But Marky Made Her Do Wrong."

Featured wedding in the Sunday paper is the nuptials of Miss Jacqueline Jo Beeler to Mr. Edward M. Royall, III, both of Mt. Pleasant. The wedding was at Hibben Methodist on Bennett and Hibben Streets. Mr. Robert Royall of Columbia was a groomsman as well as Mr. William Barnwell of Charleston.

Advertisements reveal downtown as a commercial center unrivaled by outlying malls. The Shrimp Ahoy at 122 King Street proclaims itself Charleston's finest nightclub, but the Carriage House on 80 Market Street contends that they are the best for dining, and they offer dancing to the music of Ralph Siswald and the Nomads. Harold's Cabin on Wentworth Street is the place for a deli lunch and perusal of the shelves for exotic delicacies such as chocolate covered ants.

Evan Picone is the designer making a splash on King Street, and Krawcheck's at 311 King advertises a broad selection of designer wool skirts starting at $14.95. In Section B, the New York Stock Exchange table lists the Dow Jones Industrial average at 318 and U.S. Steel is the most actively traded stock at 65 3/8. Daily stock trading equals about 30 minutes of trading volume today.

Real estate ads comprise then as many pages as they do today. The Worth Agency lists 34 Vincent Drive on Shem Creek for $14,675. They also list beach houses on Sullivan's for $17,000 and Ilse of Palms' Ocean Boulevard for $10,000.

The sports section is always popular in these parts as long as the sports editor doesn't range too far afield in his coverage zone. A photograph of the lower-state high school football All-Stars shows Moultrie High's Gordon Darby and Bishop England's Pug Ravenel as backfield stars. Bill King of the St. Andrew's Rocks is also in the picture.

Clemson head coach Frank Howard expresses concern that his top runner, Charlie Bussey, returned from Air Force ROTC summer camp at McDill Air Force Base with an injury that landed him in the hospital. In pro-baseball, Jackie Robinson powered the Brooklyn Dodgers past league leader Milwaukee Braves 3 to 2 with his home run.

The business section is dominated for days by the tobacco auctions in the Pee Dee area. Tobacco baron J.M.J. Holliday is a political kingpin as well as the brown leaf baron of Horry county.

The week in August ends in 1956 with the tension of the courts martial at Parris Island breaking into some soldier humor as Marine General Pate, defending the rigorous training of marine recruits, tells the court that Sergeant McKeon "is a good boy and that he would just recommend a transfer for him to another unit." Defense attorney Emile Zola Berman agrees, but McKeon does not beat the dereliction of duty courts martial verdict. No one here cares a fig what happened in the Suez, and a few begin to sport an "I Like Ike" button on their lapel. That was the way we were in August, 1956.

Curious Place Names Of Christ Church Parish

Crossing Christ Church parish can take all of your lunch hour, not to mention patience, especially if you're caught at a jumble junction such as Bowman Road and Johnny Dodds, or Rifle Range at Ben Sawyer. Since many of us tithe a tenth of our waking time to traffic tie-ups, one way to ease the stress is to let the historians help with a bit of diversion. The next time you're caught in traffic east of the Cooper, ponder the origin of the picturesque place names the early parishioners coined for these parts.

Officially the name Christ Church was applied in 1690 to the new Anglican parish stretching from southeast of the Wando to the headwaters of Awendaw Creek.

England's most famous Christ Church is the one in Oxford, the great cathedral and anchor to the college by that name. John Locke and several of the proprietors were Oxford-educated. Almost every colony England claimed by 1770 had a Christ Church parish, for England planned to rule her empire from an Oxford - London axis.

Henry Compton was Bishop of London in 1690 and he personally approved the name Christ Church for this parish east of the settlement of Charles Town. Compton previously was Bishop of Oxford before being elevated to the see of London. As he was selecting and approving of the naming of our parish, Bishop Compton was educating the Stuart princesses Mary and Anne, daughters of James II.

If Cainhoy is your destination, then Highway 41 offers more history than hassle by the time you get to Laurel Hill. Time has erased all but a few clues that this was the stately plantation of Peter Bonneau, M.D., surgeon, planter, and signer of the ordinance of secession. Still visible from the highway are 200 year-old oaks of the avenue leading to the columned mansion. Tradition holds that in 1865 the Bonneau mansion was the headquarters of Union Colonel Beecher.

Over the course of weeks that he was billeted there, Beecher received a letter from his wife imploring him to burn the house of "that secessionist." The fiery deed was done. By the 1890s courting couples carried picnic hampers in buggies to frolic among the ruins that to them were as ancient as the acropolis in Athens.

Not far from Laurel Hill is knoll of loblolly pines that is known as the

Phillips tract. During reconstruction this land was seized for back taxes and transformed into a freedman's community, one of those "twenty acres and a mule" settlements you read about in American history.

Before the Phillips' family acquired this land it was the seat of the Rutledges. In the early 1700s, John Rutledge, M.D., of England married Sarah Hext of Boone Hall. Edward Rutledge, Signer of the Declaration, was born here, and probably, too, John Rutledge, the first chief justice of the supreme court. Leave it to the pines to whisper the glories we have forgotten.

Cainhoy is as rich in lore as is old Mount Pleasant. One story says that centuries ago the ferryman was named Cain. But old surveys tell another tale. A 1709 map depicting the broad path from Thomas Island to the Wando has the words "cane hay" on the west bank. Harry Guggenheim, owner of a 16,000 acre plantation in the 1930s, possessed an old plat that showed this area as "Cane hay." In colonial times travelers from St. Thomas and St. Denis parishes waited on a ferry here to take them to Daniel Island from whence they'd proceed by horseback to the settlement of Calais on the west side of that island.

Moving toward the upper reach of Christ Church parish and the headwaters of the Wando, there sprawls the breadbasket of Charleston county, better known today as Awendaw. Gone are the old-timers who can recall that the best cornbread in the South was called "Awendaw bread." Grain was raised from Awendaw creek clear up to Hellhole swamp.

On Rifle Range Road, moving northeast from the intersection of the Isle of Palms connector, lies the Liberty Hill community, another of the postbellum freedman settlements that dot the coast from Beaufort to Wilmington. Liberty Hill for years was known as the source of cut flowers sold by the flower ladies at the corner of Broad and Meeting Streets. Nearby was the sweet grass that these ladies harvested for their intricately-woven baskets.

Coming into Mount Pleasant by way of the Ravenel Bridge, gaze out toward the Wando-Welch terminal on your left. From Remley's Point to Hobcaw

Creek there were shipyards lining the river from the earliest days of the colony until the Confederate era. George Dearsley built brigantines and other large square-riggers at his yard as early as the 1690s. Benjamin and Andrew Quelch, nephews of Dearsley, expanded the shipyard and continued it into the mid-18th century as one of the colony's greatest commercial enterprises. The sloop of war "Colonel Rhett" was built there in honor of the Charlestonian who defended Mount Pleasant in the French invasion of 1706.

On Wakendaw Creek early settlers built a shipyard and settlement known as Libby's Point. In time the name became Linn's Point, and in the 1960s a very old wooden ship's prow was uncovered in the mud. It appears that there were as many as twenty small settlements east of the Cooper by 1740.

Matthew's ferry may have been the forerunner to Remley's point. In any event, the name was corrupted to Mathis Ferry by the 19th century. William Matthews operated a ferry house, tavern and inn on the Wando River. A wagon road connected William Matthews' tiny settlement with Shem Creek opposite the Haddrell's Point ferry operation.

On Shem Creek, the area's first industrial park, there were numerous mills and boatyards. Addison's Shipyard on the south bank of Shem Creek built ironclads for the Confederacy. A gun emplacement nearby frequently drew fire from Union batteries on James and Morris Islands.

Of course, the name Mount Pleasant has nothing at all to do with the idea of a mountain. Outside of London there is a Mount Pleasant that gave rise to the name of Motte's and later, Hibben's plantation. Therefore, abbreviating the word "mount" is historically incorrect.

For those who have an abiding interest in the origins of place names in South Carolina, a journal is produced annually by the English department at USC, and it's available at most libraries.

Meta Morris Grimball's Diary Reveals Charleston As It Was, 1860 - 1865

The issue a historian has with an old diary is not that it's the consequence of one person's imperfect grasp of the momentous as distinguished from the mundane. Fortunately for all who have a passion for moss-draped oaks and stately homes set amidst cotton fields, there's scarcely a better glimpse into the affairs of one of the lowcountry's aristocratic antebellum families than the diary of Meta Morris Grimball, wife of planter John Berkeley Grimball of The Grove plantation in lower St. Paul's parish.

The Grove with its stately white clapboard house and adjacent slave street, its barns and fields composed a feudal village, as structured and orderly as a fiefdom in old Saxon England.

The squire, in this case, John Berkeley Grimball, was vassal to the political hierarchs of his state. Mister Grimball, as his wife Meta referred to him, was accustomed to traveling to Liverpool to confer with his cotton factor. Southern cotton brought considerably higher profits from English mills than from New England counterparts.

Life between Willtown Bluff on the Edisto and Adams Run on the Ashepoo was placid in the spring of 1860 when Grimballs, Barnwells, Heywards, and Lowndeses gathered for rowing on the river, and grand plantation dinners.

Racky, the sky terrier, darted playfully about her adoring master. Racky was a gift from Grimball's cotton factor in Liverpool, a token of esteem between an English banker and Carolina planter. Meta Morris Grimball and her husband of thirty years reared four sons in this cotton culture of the Carolina low-country. Hardly was there contemplation that anything could disrupt this tranquil kingdom.

But war talk and gloom did descend upon this agrarian paradise. New Year's Eve, 1861, parties were canceled as sons of the gentry reported to their militia units. The weather furthered the gloom by being wetter and colder than was seasonal.

Meta's concern for her sons was superseded by her desire that each serve in a fighting unit. John resigned as a midshipman at the Naval Academy and received a commission in the South Carolina navy. Lewis, having just completed medical school, sought a commission as a field surgeon. Young Berkeley was an officer with the Sumter Guards, a unit Meta describes as" a sedate body under command of John Russell, a book seller on King Street." She later on describes this unit as having only four men besides her son who were fit for duty; the rest were sick, or drunk. Meta's sons William and Arthur served on Morris Island and were eaten alive by mosquitoes. Mister Grimball took a boat out there to take them money so that they could purchase vegetables for their mess. Despite being an agricultural-based economy, the South never developed a proficient quartermaster corps.

Between December, 1860, and April, 1861, our state discovered that fine-looking uniforms and a spirit of bravura did not a field army make. Dysentery and typhoid broke out among the ranks in the encampments with young men laid to rest weeks before the guns of Sumter boomed.

Southern confidence soared when Pierre Beauregard arrived to take command of the state's troops encircling Fort Sumter. Meta Grimball's diary reveals a pathetic love story involving Beauregard that was circulating at the time the general arrived. When Beauregard, a swarthy, handsome Creole graduated from West Point, he was wildly in love with General Winfield Scott's daughter, Ginny. "Old Fuss n' Feathers," as the cadets called General Scott, was not about to let his only daughter be courted by a swarthy fellow who spoke with an accent. Beauregard learned that General Scott never let Ginny see any of the letters he'd written to her. Ginny died shortly after learning that Beauregard was engaged to another girl. Such a "doomed romance" seems almost too symbolic for the opening events of the South's "lost cause."

The surrender of Sumter called for celebration in the city. A letter that Major Anderson sent his wife in Kentucky just before the battle was opened in the Charleston post office and read as a matter of security. In it Anderson said, "My government have shamefully abandoned me, and I shall now fight and die like a man." It's clear that he meant to die by his guns, but that fate was denied him.

The Grimballs continued to receive interest on bonds paid from a New York investment houses right up through the commencement of hostilities. National mail and commerce moved unimpeded until two weeks following Sumter's capitulation. A copy of the radical newspaper, "Abolition World" proclaimed to the North that South Carolina had handled the secession crisis in an honorable manner.

Meta Grimball reveals that the mood in Charleston was that the Sumter victory was our state's contribution to the confederation, and that local men were reluctant to volunteer for service beyond South Carolina's borders. Officers campaigned for election on the basis of fighting in Virginia, or remaining in the state. Colonel Johnson Pettigrew's regiment was the first regiment from here to volunteer for Virginia duty.

The Manassas Junction victory in July, 1861, was considered a full rout of the enemy. But the Grimballs and all Charleston went into mourning for Henry Middleton of the Hampton Legion and Bernard Bee. The funeral for Bee was the largest seen in Charleston in years. Soon, however, military funerals were the order of the day at Magnolia.

By August, 1861, typhoid fever spread along the Carolina coast adding another horror in addition to the fear of invasion. By September, the Charleston boys serving in Virginia were writing home that they were freezing at night on guard duty. A group of fathers went up and took clothes and returned saying that 20,000 men were ill from exposure, and that South Carolina's soldiers were the poorest equipped of the Confederate forces in Virginia.

By 1863 the Grimballs had removed to Spartanburg and taken refuge in a wing of St. John's college. The CSA was having a problem with counterfeiting of its currency, perhaps a federal sabotage effort. General Bee's widow lost her two children to the dyptheria that spread through the upstate in 1863. For a hundred pages Meta Grimball's reflections offer the most plainspoken account of the war we're likely to read.

The hundred-page transcript is in the possession of the southern studies department of the University of North Carolina, and the University has graciously made the entire diary available on-line. Check it out.

Old Greenwich Was An 18th Century Georgian English Village

Four quaint street names, a park, and two grave stones are what remains of an English colonial village situated on the east bank of the Cooper, very reminiscent of old Greenwich which lies southeast of London. Few can recall our lost Greenwich, pronounced "grennidge," a Georgian village complete with a common, an inn, a tavern, and a glorious vista of the harbor and the steeples, gabled-roofs, and wharves of Charles Town.

Prior to the revolution an enterprising tavern and mill owner sold off half of his harbor-front property as lots in a new township named after a river hamlet in his native England. Jonathon Scott, the owner of Scott's tavern on Shem Creek and Scott's mill higher up the creek, envisioned a bustling commercial town rising from the east Cooper bluffs.

And why shouldn't Scott expect a glorious future for his new village of Greenwich in 1763? To confirm his loyalty to newly crowned King George III, Jonathon Scott named his recently cleared sandy wagon paths after 18th century

English political icons.

Scott's Greenwich of Christ Church parish stretched from present day Morrison Street to McCants and endured approximately seventy years until incorporated into the village of Mount Pleasant in 1837. The street names Scott selected remain as he named them: Pitt, King, Bank, and Queen. Alternative names he might just as well have chosen are Chatham, Fox, or Burke instead of Pitt and George and Charlotte instead of King and Queen. Bank Street most likely celebrates the growing confidence the English placed in the powerful financial regulatory institution then taking shape known as the bank of England. Why Scott chose these particular names is no mystery, however. He was loyal to his sovereign and wished to perpetuate the ideals they championed.

William Pitt, the elder, 1st Earl of Chatham, was the brilliant architect of victory in the Seven Years War, 1756 to 1763, a war that saw Britain seize much of Canada from the French. Pitt did more for extending the empire than anyone since Elizabeth. From well-connected commoner to aristocrat within the royal circle, this old Etonian and grandson of one of the world's richest men, Thomas "Diamond" Pitt, advanced quickly in the circles of power. His accelerated rise was due partly to his Eton classmates, Charles Pratt, Lord Camden, and George, Lord Grenville, top advisors to the king. Another Etonian and confidante of Pitt was Henry Fielding, the novelist.

Young Pitt became a political disciple of Lord Cobham and a political enemy of Robert Walpole. Pitt's fiery rhetoric earned for him the unofficial titles, "the voice of England," and "the champion of commerce." As champion of commerce, Pitt was open to discussing ideas that we today would term as free trade. Pitt championed colonial interests in parliament so effectively that had Britain allowed colonial parliamentary representation, it's doubtful the colonies could have had such clout at they already had in men such as Pitt, Burke, Barre, and Fox. Interestingly, Pitt's faction in parliament were labeled "the boy patriots" a generation prior to the usage of that term in the American colonies. William

Pitt's staunch defense of colonial commerce and trade would have appealed greatly to the industrious Jonathon Scott, a man already engaged in trade, taverns, a ferry service, a mill, and land development.

Intersecting Pitt Street in Scott's Greenwich is King Street, named for the thirty-year-old monarch, George III, of the House of Hanover. "German George" as he and his two forebears were known, suffered from a debilitating illness known as porphyria, and he was beginning to act in a disturbed manner around the 1760s when Scott named the principal street leading to the harbor after this monarch.

Knowledge that George III was ill was confined to a close inner circle. His inconsistency in handling the thorny American economic demands frustrated numerous olive branch peace overtures from colonials. Still, for at least three years after the commencement of hostilities, George Washington offered a toast at his mess table to George III and damnation to parliament.

Charlotte of Mecklinburg-Strelitz, consort to George III, possessed the qualities of beauty, refinement, grace, and regal bearing that for so long had been unremarkable in the Stuart and earlier Hanover women. Some boastful Tories exclaimed that her blue blood pedigree was superior to her husband, of the royal house of Hanover. Charlotte is remembered by Scott's tribute of Queen Street.

The idea of Bank Street in our Greenwich as an honor of the powerful central bank of Threadneedle Street in London is conjecture, but there are no records of Bank as a family name in this area in the 18th century. In the early 1770s there was a banking crisis in England that caused the sudden reduction of credit in the colonies. Merchants from Savannah to New York sought to sell down their inventory, and by 1772, England and her colonies were in a panic. The Bank of England rose to the occasion with pioneering techniques in controlling currency and specie. The Bank of England was an innovative economic organ the likes of which had never been seen before in national politics. Great hopes were placed in the expectation that the Bank could rein in

34

autonomous corporations such as the East India Company, the Russia Levant
Company, and Hudson Bay Company.

The Bank of England remained a privately owned entity until after World
War II, but its alliance with the economic arm of the government stabilized
English commerce which was soon facing transition from outmoded mercantilism
to the emerging ideals of Adam Smith.

Scott's Greenwich was a miniature of any of the coastal villages ringing
England from Padstow to Poole to Steyning. Scott's Snuggery was a cozy inn
and tavern located somewhere within the confines of this little village. A village
common of at least ten acres was maintained for grazing livestock and the
gathering of firewood. Two 18th century grave stones rest undisturbed in the
village cemetery on Carr Street.

The revolutionary war did not produce a renaming of these old streets with
more more politically attuned names from the federal era. Pitt Street would have
become Jefferson or Franklin Street; Bank could have been renamed Commerce
Street, and King and Queen, of course, George and Martha!

Charleston's Thomas Pinckney Remains The Forgotten Founding Father

Clearly Thomas Pinckney is the forgotten founding father, the one
overlooked amidst Charleston's Signers, Delegates, and Defenders. William
Gilmore Simms refers to Thomas Pinckney as the "last of the giant oaks, one of
the "godlike few." Those are grand words for the Pinckney some scholars refer to
as the "forgotten founder." Soldier, governor, diplomat, presidential candidate,
and friend of Washington and Lafayette, this handsome, erudite man won

grudging respect for America in London, Paris, and Madrid.

Where is a modern day Plutarch to chronicle the lives of the noble Americans the way the Plutarch told of Crassus, Caesar, Pompey, and Cicero? Surely Charleston's Thomas Pinckney personifies the virtue and none of the vices of those noble Romans.

This particular Pinckney was selfless to a fault, because his service to the young republic ruined his chances for amassing fortune through his plantations and law practice. He never wavered when his country called him, whether in military duty, state craft, diplomacy abroad, or quelling riots locally. If Tom Pinckney had lived in Saxon times his name might have been "Pinckney the lesser" because he stood in the shadows of his more renown older brother Charles Cotesworth Pinckney and their cousin "Constitution Charlie" Pinckney, the framer credited with advocating the radical concept of federalism.

The makings of this noble Charlestonian begins no doubt with his mother, Eliza Lucas Pinckney. No male issue from this worthy woman could skirt the archetypal noblesse oblige of that grand age. Examine his upbringing; this Charlestonian was destined to great service from birth.

Pincheni, Pinkini, Pinqueny, or the anglicized Pinckney, all connote that the forebears of this Carolina surname were in no way subjects of English rule. But Thomas Pinckney, the elder, was a mighty man in Carolina in the 18th century, and he stood high in the esteem of Crown authorities; so high that by 1753, Thomas, the elder, was made agent for the colony Carolina and removed with Eliza and the two boys to London. The duty of crown agent was to facilitate commerce between the plantations and the urban merchants. Young Thomas and his brother, Charles Cotesworth, lived amongst lords and ladies in Surrey, the genteel side of Adamesque London.

The Pinckneys even considered selling their land holdings in Carolina and resettling permanently England. Thomas, the father, returned alone to Charleston on business in 1758 and promptly contracted a fever and died. Thus did the fortunes of two countries shift with the sting of one insect.

As Cokie Roberts attests in her book, <u>Founding Mothers</u>, Eliza Lucas Pinckney returned to manage the lands of her husband as successfully as she'd managed the holdings of her late father while he was away and she was just a teenage girl. In fact, few men in the colony possessed the business acumen of this capable woman. Her boys were left behind with a governor to carry out their late father's wishes for a complete English gentleman's education.

The boy who would be our governor, America's first ambassador to the Court of St. James, and federalist candidate for president, among many of responsibilities, was schooled alongside future lords, earls, and a duke or two at Winchester in London. Where his older brother stood high in latin, young Thomas excelled in Greek, so much that even during the turmoil of the American revolution he kept the Greek poets in his saddlebag while on campaigns.

Eliza vetoed Harrow as the school for her sons because it was known to persuade young men of connection into the Anglican priesthood, and her sons were to be prepared in the law and state craft. Hazing, known as fagging, was rift in English schools and the Pinckney boys were toughened to slights, insults, and brutality by boys of the upper forms, or grades. Young Edward Rutledge, whom Tom Pinckney called Ned, was there, as was William Henry Drayton and some of the Middletons. A coterie of young Charlestonians became the playful, radical fringe of Whig politics in 1760 as the young Hanoverian, George III, and his consort, Charlotte of Mecklinburg-Strelitz, ascended the throne. During the colonial crises of the stamp taxes, well-known artist John Zoffany sketched young Thomas as a defiant rebel gesturing during a debate.

While at Westminster, the boy who'd one day be a major in the American revolution and a major general commanding the southern department in the War of 1812, first learned military drill and the manual of arms from grizzled, retired army sergeants of His Majesty's army. Tom Pinckney took fencing lessons while his fellow low country schoolmate Thomas Heyward attended the debates at parliament where Pitt championed the colonial cause.

As his older brother Charles Cotesworth had done, Thomas went up to Oxford, to Christ Church College, then a bastion of aristocratic "Whiggism." The university was at a low-ebb of scholarship, as the high-jinx of the boys attested. The great Edward Gibbon was there as a don. William Blackstone lectured on jurisprudence. No record of his marks exists, but Tom Pinckney was passed on to the Middle Temple of the Inns of Court in London where the brightest lads read law.

Thus the man who one day, as our minister to Madrid would negotiate the Treaty of San Lorenzo, or The Pinckney Treaty, that gave America land rights to the west bank of the Mississippi, Thomas Pinckney was ever ready with sword or legal argument to serve his America.

As a captain of continentals, Tom Pinckney recruited Orangeburg distric, thereby depriving tory interests of many able-bodied men won over to the patriot cause. On a secret mission for General Benjamin Lincoln, Pinckney escaped capture at the fall of Charleston in 1781. As a major of infantry at Camden he had his leg shattered by a musket ball and was taken prisoner. Upon his parole, his wife, Elizabeth Motte Pinckney, nursed him to health at her family plantation, Fort Motte on the Congaree. The British burned his plantation on the Ashepoo.

Upon the war's end, chaos reigned briefly in the streets of Charleston and Thomas Pinckney, alongside Colonel William Washington, sabered rioters in Broad Street in what is remembered as the "Fallonite uprising" one frightful night in December, 1782. He endured the snubs of George III at the Court of St. James as our nation's first minister there. Soldier, governor, congressman, ambassador, and one who foreswore wealth to serve his country, Thomas Pinckney, of lower George Street, is forever one of "the godlike few" of Carolina's sons of destiny.

It Happened Long Ago On Historic Old Belleville Road

There's still a joy in finding an unhurried rural route where motoring along at a sedate speed unwinds much more than just miles from the odometer. If that quiet country lane also happens to be one of the oldest and most historic roads still in use since colonial days, then it's worth the ride of 81 miles to discover Old Belleville Road in Orangeburg and Calhoun counties.

In 1740, roads leading from Charleston were few and travel was dangerous. Old State Road, Highway 176, was at times no more than a path through lonely pine forests. The oldest road maps reveal very few byways leading from this thoroughfare. But Old Belleville Road was the best-known byway north of Charleston in the 18th century. Weary travelers had been on the road for two days by the time they reached this intersection with Old State Road. A few of the coaching inns along the State Road still stand, looking remarkably like they did in years past. Most likely this important intersection of two routes also boasted an inn and tavern, a well, and a blacksmith's forge. The nearest settlements of size were Lewisfield, today's St. Matthews, a mile or so to the northeast and Orangeburgh, approximately ten miles to the west.

Passengers stretching their legs at this thriving intersection learned that Belleville Road got its name from the imposing plantation belonging to Colonel Moses Thomson on the banks of the Congaree River ten miles northeast. Belleville was one of several imposing homes with landscaped lawns located on the bluffs of the Congaree. One account of Belleville describes it as a frontier version of Versailles.

Upriver by two miles, Rebecca Motte's stately home, Fort Motte, occupied a hill called Mount Saint Joseph. Thomson's Belleville overlooked McCord's ferry, an important link for waterborne commerce linking with Congaree with the

Saluda River basin. A few miles higher up the Congaree lay Fort Granby, located on the outskirts of what has become the city of Columbia. In the Revolution the three communities were at the heart of the British struggle to control the upstate.

History buffs recall these place names and their fame. Belleville, Motte, and Granby have long ago descended into the sands of time. McCord's Ferry lies beneath the massive supports for the U. S. Highway 601 overpass of the Congaree. But Belleville Road winds its way from the center of downtown Orangeburg to Highway U.S. 176. There its path is interrupted by newer roads. It picks up again above St. Matthews and threads its way to Thomson's old fields near the present-day Fort Motte community.

Riding the black asphalt of today's Belleville Road offers many of the same vistas afforded those earlier travelers when German and Swiss settlers spoke English with guttural accents. Today's route has changed little since Robert Mills' atlas was published in 1820. In the 1760s, pine pitch was transported in barrels to barges at McCord's ferry and floated to the coast for export to Bristol.

Lord Rawdon and General Cornwallis used Belleville Road as a strategic pass to the High Hills of Santee and Camden. Moses Thomson rallied his Raccoon Rangers and led them from Belleville south to Sullivan's Island where in June, 1776, these upstate patriots prevented Clinton's army from crossing Breach Inlet and enveloping General Moultrie that glorious day he defeated the British fleet. Four years later, Thomson was captured at his Belleville plantation and taken by Belleville and Old State Road to Charleston for a miserable imprisonment in the provost dungeon beneath the Exchange Building. He was paroled and sent home, only to be arrested again and marched back to imprisonment in Charleston.

The lieutenant-governor of Georgia, John Treutlin, was brutally murdered by Tories in 1781 at the intersection of Belleville Road and Old State Road.

In the dark days of Charleston's occupation by the British, it was Governor John Rutledge's secret plan to hide his wife and children on one of Colonel Thomson's many fiefdoms that comprised the massive Belleville estate. However, the illness of Mrs. Rutledge and the suspicion of Tory surveillance on the Congaree dissuaded Rutledge from this plan.

In December, 1781, the Gamecock, Thomas Sumter, passed down Belleville Road with his mounted militia and two cannon as he encircled Lord Rawdon's encampment located at Orangeburg.

In the 19th century, two families owned large portions of Belleville Road from Orangeburg to where it intersects with Old State Road. One family was the Jamisons and the other was the Hoffmans. Doctor Van Jamison of Pennsylvania settled in this area after the Revolution. His medical skills and knowledge of homemade remedies made him a Godsend to these rural people.

Doctor Jamison selected a hill three-hundred feet above sea-level for the construction of his country home, White Hill, overlooking Belleville Road. The steep hill was impassable in rainy weather until the highway department cut deep into the clay to lower the road bed. This hill can be seen just before Belleville Road crosses I-26 today. Evidently this was the ocean shore thousands of years ago, because Jamison discovered a deep vein of old oyster shells, many intact, just fifteen feet beneath the surface. By 1810 he had a lime mine and kiln that produced 30,000 bushels of lime a year, a quantity that he could have doubled had transportation from the area been better. Jamison sold much of his tract to the Tyler family, but the vast extent of his former property makes up the unincorporated settlement that still bears his name today.

Sherman's army ravaged the farms of Belleville Road in February, 1865. But the fertile soil was soon back in cultivation, minus slave labor, by spring.

Julius Hoffman, just down from Jamison, discovered that the spring water that bubbled up on his property possessed a pleasant taste and seemed to promote all-around good health for those who drank it. Hoffman set up a water bottling operation, a spa of sorts, and a pavilion which operated until the 1890s. Wagons with painted signs boasting Hoffman's Bottled Water were a common sight for decades in the 19th century.

Today's Belleville Road is just as delightful a drive as it was 250 years ago. The road named SC-29 on the Interstate overpass remains incognito to outsiders. Don't look for an on-off ramp, either. They keep this one strictly for themselves up in Orangeburg and Calhoun counties!

Likable Ike Was A Reluctant Candidate, October, 1951

We'll always remember Ike as the unflappable old soldier whose grin seemed as much a fixture of his two-term presidency as did the ever present golf clubs. The Kansas farm boy with a plowman's gait became militarily squared to the cadence of a West Point drillmaster's bark. This cadet football jock graduated as the oldest member of his class of 1915 and rose steadily through army ranks to the pinnacle of military command. In 1951, the man who'd been architect of Operation Torch in North Africa and Operation Overlord in north Europe, as well as postwar allied commander of SHAEF and NATO, and president of Columbia University desired only quiet retirement and a few rounds of golf.

His detractors say that he stalked the 1952 republican nomination as cleverly as any seasoned politician ever did before him. The evidence, however, reveals Eisenhower as the most reluctant candidate in American history, a man cornered between duty and destiny.

It was 55 years ago this month, October, that Ike realized the futility of resisting the juggernaut of speculation about his candidacy. He'd said repeatedly that he didn't want the nomination; he denied being either a republican or a democrat; and he'd already turned down feelers by both parties in 1948. Why did the great men of politics, banking, and industry not leave him to the joys of his memoirs?

Ellis "Slats" Slater, millionaire liquor executive and longtime friend of the general, invited Eisenhower to the annual get-together of the Bohemian Grove Society, a gathering of wealthy republican males held on an estate in the red wood forest north of San Francisco. The midsummer retreat of the men of industry, finance, and the republican party has taken place yearly since 1870. Some of the most powerful men in the nation revert to their youth, live primitively in huts, and engage in raucous revelry.

Unbeknownst to Ike, General Albert Wedemeyer, then military advisor to Senate republican leader Robert Taft, was also on the guest list. In a series of skits and pranks, Wedemeyer and republican-hopeful, Bob Taft, were portrayed as silly, while Eisenhower emerged as the smooth, cool operator.

Since no one speaks of the goings-on of the Bohemian Grove conclaves, it's still speculation as to what transpired, but Taft's candidacy for the presidential nomination took a nasty spill in the red wood forests. The powerful men at Bohemian Grove gave Ike a rousing sendoff. But Eisenhower didn't take a hint.

The Bohemian Grove group had yet another motive for their gathering of notables among the red woods. Earl Warren of California was gaining momentum among western republican delegates eyeing a recapture of the White House in 1952. But the eastern establishment did not believe that Earl Warren, or Taft could carry the swing voters necessary for a republican victory.

The most powerful of the "barons of Bohemia" was former president Herbert Hoover, the man known simply as "the chief." Hoover feared two things about the coming election of 1952. One, Bob Taft couldn't be elected dog catcher on a national ticket. Two, democrat Adlai Stevenson was not imbibing deeply enough of the internationalist-interventionist view of foreign policy.

Big business boys such as Henry Ford, Bernard Baruch, Bob Woodruff, Lewis Maytag, Jock Whitney, and Charlie invited Ike to dinner at posh clubs from Manhattan to Chicago. Each appealed to the five-star general's sense of patriotic duty. Ike was noncommittal.

The Cold War and the raging Korean War made Ike's military credentials outweigh his naiveté in politics. At each tête-à-tête, Ike reconfirmed his 1948 stance with the pat refrain, "I'm flattered, but I'm simply not interested."

Eisenhower's detractors maintain that he was coy as a debutante. But behind the scenes the Eisenhowers were reconciling their marriage amidst rumors of Eisenhower's alleged affair with his pretty English wartime driver, Kay Summersby. When excerpts from General Patton's diary mentioning Eisenhower and Summersby turned up in the hands of a Taft campaigner, Henry Cabot Lodge, Jr., moved swiftly to secure a political appointment for the man, and that was the end of the matter. Mamie told her friends that she was not interested in her husband pursuing the nomination.

The closest friend Eisenhower had in those days was General Lucius Clay, who incidentally was the man Secretary of State James F. Byrnes was seeking to head up The Citadel upon the retirement of General Summerall. He had the ear of his wartime chief. Clay was speaking privately with Lodge, Baruch, and Hoover. Ike was their man, and the only one who could give confidence to the emerging military industrial complex and instill fear in Stalin.

General and Mrs. Eisenhower flew to Paris in early October, 1951, to visit to celebrate Ike's 61st birthday on October 14th. He gruffly told the press, "They know where I am if they want me." Joining them on this trip was General Edwin N. Clark, a retired West Pointer and Harvard law grad currently working as an international business consultant for defense contractors. Clark had been an advisor to Eisenhower during the four years he'd served as president of Columbia University and was a growing power in the republican party's liberal northeastern wing. Robert Taft represented the diminishing conservative faction that was seen as doomed and losing out to an Adlai Stevenson candidacy in 1952.

All night, October 13th, Eisenhower and Clark sat up in a Paris hotel working on an acceptance speech to the the draft movement of the eastern-

44

industrial wing of the republican party. Mamie and Clark's wife played canasta.

Ike's words, "I consider myself a liberal; I also consider myself a republican; and through the years when I have voted, I have voted republican. If given the nomination, I will wage an aggressive campaign." On October 14 the news that Ike would run went coast to coast.

The Eastern Establishment got their man; Herbert Hoover got his revenge, and the republican party made inroads in an "all democrat" south by picking up Virginia, Florida, and Texas. Ellis "Slats" Slater intimated to Ike that the Bohemian Grove fellows preferred the staunchly anti-communist Dick Nixon as running mate to Senator William Knowlton of California. You know the rest of the story of October, 1955.

Make Time For Tales Of Old Moncks Corner

Highway clutter conceals old Moncks Corner as much as concrete monstrosities mar old Mount Pleasant. But a trip up the road is worth the trouble because the little town they call "the Corner" still has hidden treasures aplenty. Traveling back through time requires no small amount of imagination these days, not to mention patience with the intrusion of the present into our sense of the past.

Some sunny Saturday you should make your way up East Bay onto Morrison Drive, skirting by Magnolia cemetery onto Highway 52, or the Dual Lane, as we once called it. Big box stores with texas-size parking lots intrude where mossy cypress trees complete with knobby knees and alligator-laden lagoons once lent mystery to the all-day buggy journey to "the Corner." The Corner was how Charlestonians referred to the town on the headwaters of the

Cooper named after Thomas Monck in the early 1700s.

The road that leads by The Elms plantation and the black water of Goose Creek conceals much mystery and lore that is disappearing beneath asphalt. No one remembers when dark-skinned men poled dugout bateaux and glided silently through water-oaks, myrtle, cedars, and wild wisteria. The road north, a sandy, broad-path, was shaded by ancient trees draped with spanish moss. Genteel folks hardly came this way; they took a steamboat up the Cooper to Stoney Landing. Of those hardy enough to come up by road, the mounted travelers had it easier than did stagecoach passengers. Cantering to the Corner was a day's ride past sites of the most romantic legends of the colonial Old South.

The road you're traveling bumper to bumper today was once the Cherokee Path that predates the coming of the English colonists. It winds upward to Oconee and the Six Nations. The colonists adapted the path to parallel the Santee River up to the Congaree. Local tribes carried pearls, bright shells, and deer skins north and westward in a trade that reached to the Mississippi Valley in a complex trade arrangement that predates the coming of the white man. Today, Highways 6 and 176 retrace parts of these old Indian paths.

A site along Highway 52 worth examining on your way to old Moncks Corner is The Elms that once belonged to Ralph (pronounced "Rafe") Izard. He was one of the most prominent of the "Goose Creek men" who came here from Barbados. The Elms was home to the most beautiful woman in the colony, Izard's wife, Miss Delancey of New York. Years later, her collateral descendant from New York became Wellington's quartermaster-general at Waterloo. The Izards withdrew to Europe to avoid the bitterness of the Revolution.

These "sugar men of the West Indies," royalist descendants of the cavaliers of Charles I, were contrary in intentions politically and religiously from the early crowd that settled Albemarle point under the old puritan, William Sayle. The Goose Creek men included surnames of Broughton (pronounced with a distinct "out" sound), Middleton, Drayton, Daniel, Boone, Moore, Izard,

Grimball, Ladson, Schenking (later shortened), and others. These moneyed elites from England, by way of an exile in Barbados during Cromwellian times, desired high church Anglicanism and the establishment of a medieval fiefdom in Carolina complete with titles of aristocracy such as Cassique and Landgrave.

Another spot off Highway 52 worth checking out is Yeaman's Hall, the seat of Sir John Yeamans, the most powerful of the Barbadian aristocrats to come out to Carolina. Sir John, an early governor of the province, was the son of a Bristol merchant executed by Cromwell's men in the Civil War. John Yeaman fled with the family silver to start life anew in the West Indies. He was the man who introduced African slavery into the colony, a custom that foreshadows three centuries of Carolina history. The Barbados men did everything in a grand fashion, as opposed to the thatched cottage farms of the puritan followers of William Sayle. Saint James Goose Creek was their house of worship where God, King, Church, and Parliament were emphasized in that order.

Passing over the creek whose bends reveal an uncanny resemblance to a goose's neck, you are moving through old Fairlawn Barony. Fairlawn was the seat of Sir John Colleton, great-grandson of the original Lords Proprietor by that name. This makes the young man one of the true cavaliers who came out to Carolina, as distinct from the numerous homegrown aristocrats who developed early on here.

By the 1680s, Fairlawn Barony was owned by Joseph West, a powerful London merchant whose family established a trading post at Pine Top on the Wateree. They later renamed the settlement after their London friend, Lord Camden. West sold the land that is now Moncks Corner to James Le Bas, a Huguenot who had lost everything in a slave uprising in Santa Dominica. By 1729 the Corner had devolved to John Vicaridge. The village that sprang up was called Epsom, after a memorable place in England.

Thomas Monck purchased 1000 acres in 1735 surrounding the two roads where the Cherokee path split, thus the corner in Epsom became Moncks Corner.

Some say Monck referred to the town as Mitton, and later as Milton. There were four taverns and five stores at this great stop on Charles Town's major route northwest.

The biggest mercantile operation in Moncks Corner was that of Simeon Theus, but Moncks second wife, Mary St. Julien Monck, kept a large general merchandise store that priced its goods the same as those sold in Charleston. In later years, her descendants claimed that she really didn't run the store herself. The St. Juliens owned considerable land all the way up the Santee to the Eutaws, a series of limestone springs and underwater caverns, a place where Indians worshipped their deities.

The town of Moncks Corner became a market town where the planters of the Santee poled their crops down river on rafts and bateaux. There were barns for storage, taverns for celebrating, and inns for stacking six or eight strangers to a room. You won't have to worry about lodging as you motor up to the Corner. In a later column, we'll return to Charleston through old Wadboo Barony and the Silk Hope Plantation Road. Be sure to check out the Berkeley County Museum while you are in Moncks Corner!

A Night of Terror Near Old Moncks Corner

Who can blame us for not putting a historical marker near Wadboo Creek on state road 402 up in Berkeley county. After all, not far from where the blacktop route crosses the snake-infested stream, there lies a wooded knoll where 500 of our finest patriot fighters were routed by Bloody Ban Tarleton's dragoons around 3 a.m. on April 14, 1780. The affair can't accurately be described as a battle, for our hardy horsemen skedaddled, defenseless and unmounted, into the murky swamp. Even Colonel William Washington and General Isaac Huger fled into the black bogs of Wadboo swamp to escape the slashing swords of Tarleton's loyalists.

But one fearless Frenchman, Major Pierre- Francois (Paul) Vernier, commanding Count Pulaski's cavalry, gave all an example of how a Frenchman dies in war.

Dying well wasn't what the gallant Vernier had on his mind that April night spent amongst crickets and bull frogs near the Cooper River, a mile from Moncks Corner. Vernier commanded the horsemen of Pulaski's famed Polish legion. But, hunkered amidst 700 horses, men, saddles, stands of arms, and lounging troopers, General Isaac Huger, the patriot general, let his attention lapse for an hour or two of much needed sleep. Only a small guard was posted on the causeway leading to Wadboo Bridge, thereby leaving Huger's bivouac wide open. The miracle of the Battle of Biggin Bridge was that the complete rout was not their annihilation.

It was uncharacteristic to leave themselves prey to a night-attack. This incident that came close to paralyzing patriot resistance can be explained in one of two veins: either the soldiers of Huger, Washington, Horry, Jameson, and Vernier were exhausted and derelect in carrying out their night patrol, or, more likely, they were contemptable of their foe being able to accomplish a surprise night maneuver. A bloody, demoralizing half hour of chaos taught the survivors that Tarleton was a wily foe.

The affair at Biggin Church was the first of two great clashes of arms at or near the holy edifice. Ban Tarleston, easily the greatest British cavalry leader in the south, had been stalking "Billy" Washington for 72 hours, using as a base the Quarter House tavern, a well-known hangout thought to have been located at the northwest corner of where I-26 intersects Dorchester Road.

Tarleton's Legion were the elites of the loyalist forces. Ban Tarleton was an Oxford-educated dandy who recruited tough New England horsemen and armed them wih the finest blades and swiftest mounts. They wore a distinct green jacket and white breeches and were known for lightning strikes on a battlefield, keen reconnoitering, and providing a screen for troops on the march. Bloody Ban Tarleton had disdain for the rebels, contemptible dogs he called them, and slashing and hacking them to pieces was a chilling, persuasive warning he brought on behalf of his sovereign.

We've come a long way in weapons and tactics since the 18th century, but don't underestimate the ability these mounted warriors used to keep tabs on their enemy. They may not have had hovering predator drones and AWACS in the sky, but they did have the human net of never-sleeping eyes focused on their adversary. Flying squads of Tory horsemen swept areas known to be frequented by patriot militia. Unlikely eyes, the eyes of slaves, draymen, and even children became reliable informants. Loyalists and patriots alike knew that ten-percent of their number would change sides in a heart-beat if offered a handful of silver.

On the afternoon of April 13, 1780, the outer perimeter of Tarleton's force picked up an African man with papers on his person. They brought him in for interrogation. "Well, well. What have we here?" the intelligence officer must have exclaimed, for the scribbled paper was a troop disposition from Brigadier General Isaac Huger to General Lincoln in Charleston.

Tarleton's orderly book gives this account; so does the journal kept by Lieutenant Allaire who rode with him. But orderly books sometimes fall into enemy hands, so the story of the African bearing a message may have been a ruse to protect a more sinister source. Tarleton had little time to decide whether the information was valid. He was a "hell for leather" commander seeking to impress his superior, Sir Henry Clinton, and the opportunity to catch the entire rebel cavalry napping near Moncks Corner was a dog's chance not to be missed.

"Boots and saddles" was sounded by the bugler, probably standing in Dorchester Road, and men poured out of tents with harnesses and accoutrements.

50

Intelligence revealed that Washington's legion had moved just hours earlier from Middleton plantation across the Ashley to the headwaters of the Cooper, near Biggin Church. Huger and Washington together presented a golden window of savage opportunity -- the kind that superior tacticians seize with alacrity.

Tarleton ordered strict silence and utmost speed. Sabers, carbines, and bridles were muffled, and guidons, not voices, were used for commands.

It was long past midnight at Biggin Church, located on road 402, a left turn off Highway 41. Biggin was named for Biggin Hill outside London. The Moultries were great landowners here. Several hundred patriot, or whig militia were quartered inside the stout brick walls of the church, and some were in tents on the grounds.

A mile away, near the river bridge, lay 500 of the best horses and troopers in the patriot army, not to mention ammunition wagons and rations. The guards either went to sleep, or were contemptuous of a night attack.

Screaming cavalrymen on thundering horses with booming pistol shots burst upon our sleeping heroes. Half-dressed men ran barefoot into the night-shrouded swamp. Washington and Huger abandoned their headquarters tents, sidearms, and papers.

It was the better part of valor to scamper and live to fight another day, but it was a humiliation and embarassment, too.

French born Paul Vernier, commanding Pulaski's cavalry, stood ground and fought with pistol and saber, almost alone amongst his allies. He was cut up badly and dropped to his knees crying for quarter when a green-jacket sabered him behind his right ear. Vernier was dragged off to a nearby cabin and roughly laid on a table where he cursed the Americans for running and cursed his captors for sabering him after he'd surrendered. Tarleton's roughnecks poked at Vernier and mocked him in his suffering until he expired a short time later.

Two and a half weeks later, on May 11, 1780, Charleston fell to the British, the greatest defeat of the patriot side in the Revolutionary War. But Ban Tarleton met Colonel Washington on another field where this vile score was settled.

Bill Pinckney Of Dalzell Was The Original Drifter

It matters not that their songs made mention of Harlem, Brooklyn, and Atlantic City. When the Drifters sing "Up On The Roof," we don't conjure images of tall apartments in New York, and when they harmonize "Under The Boardwalk," none visualize Atlantic City, the place the song was written for! Two generations of southern collegiates reaching from W & L to The Citadel have tapped their Weejuns to the Drifters' melodies. What we loved about the Drifters, and love still, is that coffee-rich baritone, bass, and tenor blend that percolates uniquely from southern black men raised on old-time gospel songs.

Like everything in the 1950s, music was in transition. First there was the jitterbug craze and then the boogie-woogie beat. But it was the slow-shuffle shag, the dance craze originating at the Beach Club at Ocean Drive, affectionately known as OD, that began a new music craze. You don't have to be music ally-inclined to realize that 2:2 time in the spiritual, "Amen" and the 2:3 time of the southern favorite "Amazing Grace" is a beat that evokes sweet surrender. No music defines our low-country more completely than does that of our own Bill Pinckney and his Original Drifters. Their story is a tale that begs retelling.

When they make the documentary of Bill Pinckney's life, the camera will pan the back streets of Dalzell, South Carolina, as they looked in the depression years. Today, Dalzell is out the back gates of Shaw Air Force Base, and the Sumter county town that a poor black boy would have known seventy years ago does not exist. But the Baptist Church that he attended still stands, and the central feature of the Drifters is their love of gospel music.

Sharecroppers' sons didn't go to college back then, but they did enlist in the Army. Bill Pinckney volunteered for one of the Negro regiments of the segregated American military. Bill Pinckney saw Europe. Bill saw Normandy, St. Lo, Bastogne. He traveled with celebrities -- Patton, Bradley, Eisenhower. And he came back with souvenirs -- scar tissue, purple hearts, bronze stars, and presidential unit citations.

Segregation wasn't the only reason Pinckney left South Carolina for New York in the 1950s. The war had given thousands of blacks a promise of a new life. Brooklyn and Harlem were their destinations. Pinckney went north to play baseball in the Negro Professional League. What's amazing is how many blacks from here made up neighborhoods in Brooklyn, and how many Baptist churches sprang up on street corners there. Bill played ball and sang in the choir.

Street-corner gospel quartets and jive singers were everywhere in the black boroughs from Queens to Long Island. Radio station WWRL had a disc-jockey, Tommy Smalls, with a show-name of Doctor Jive, "Live with Doctor Jive from three oh five to five three oh at 1600 on your radio dial!" This is the ground -zero of soul music.

Doctor Jive brought street-corner groups into the radio studio and let them perform live. If they got call-in response, Doctor Jive arranged a gig at Club Apollo, or the Cotton Club in Harlem. From then on, fame was your destiny, if not, you'd a drive a delivery truck.

It wasn't Bill Pinckney, but his friend Clyde McPhatter and the Dominoes who got the live appearance on Doctor Jive's live radio broadcast in 1953. It was the beginning of the sweetest sounds ever heard on a rock-'n-roll station. Clyde was a Durham, North Carolina, fellow who was searching for his American dream.

Clyde McPhatter was fired from the Dominoes and soon pulled together some back-up singers to shuffle around behind his booming lead. McPhatter

already had the name "Drifter's" in mind when he asked Johnny Moore of the
Hornets, two brothers named Thrasher, and Bill Pinckney of The Mount Lebanon
Gospel Singers. Ill-advisedly, Clyde sold the name to the Drifters to a slick
manager named George Treadwell. Treadwell was a trumpeter and husband of
singer, Sarah Vaughan. After performing at the Apollo one night, Treadwell
fired the entire group starting with Bill Pinckney for asking for a larger pay
check.

Immediately Treadwell hired a new set of Drifters, five kids singing doo-
wop, as they called it. They were called the Five Crowns with lead singer, Ben E.
Nelson, soon to become famous as Ben E. King. Another recruit was Lover
Patterson. Treadwell became famous with Ben E. King and The Drifters. "There
Goes My Baby" was the first hit to air King's rich baritone voice.

But Bill Pinckney was not to be left behind. The original band members
united behind his leadership and formed a counter group called The Original
Drifters. There were lawsuits between the groups and as to who owned the name
and songs. For a few months Pinckney caved in and called his band The
Harmony Grits. He performed with Ray Charles and Solomon Burke. But
Pinckney's enormous popularity stuck with the Drifters name, and George
Treadwell lost Ben E. King to solo status and others to the draft.

Rudy Lewis, a 28 year old tenor, was boosting Treadwell's Drifters ahead
of Pinckney's Original Drifters with new songs such as "Some Kind of
Wonderful," and "Up On The Roof." On May 21, 1966, the group had a studio
engagement to record 'Under The Boardwalk" when a phone call to Lover
Patterson broke the tragic news -- Rudy was dead. He'd died of a cafe coronary
in his sleep. What could they do? Hastily, a phone call was made to former band
member, Johnny Moore, and he stood in to sing lead on the now famous "Under
The Boardwalk," but the tempo was slowed to reflect their sad mood that day.

Atlantic Record label offered Bill Pinckney's group a contract to do songs
that he had collaborated on with the Drifters before the split. Southern colleges

gloried in the sound of Bill Pinckney and The Original Drifters. The Old Folly Beach Pier swayed many a night, as did Art's Seaside at IOP, to this glorious sound. Both bands stayed in circulation and stayed in litigation. Our General Assembly made the Dalzell native South Carolina's Ambassador of Soul. A deeply religious man, the elderly Pinckney remains connected to his church and gospel music as well as his glory days with the Drifters.

Napoleon's Sister-in-Law Was An American Hussy

Americans care little about Napoleon Bonaparte beyond their fascination with his military romp across Europe. His motto, "Audacity, audacity, always audacity!," still rings through the corridors of military schools, and his grand restructuring of French society is worthy of notice. To us, Napoleon is a man who should have consulted a realtor before selling his Louisiana Purchase for a trifling 80 million francs in May of 1803. Looking through the "little corporal's" day planner for May, it's obvious that the for sale sign on his Louisiana property was not the only entry that month.

First, there was the renewed hostility with Britain. But what caused acid reflux for the ruthless reducer of the Vendee, the victor of Rivoli and Marengo, is that his bumbling brother Jerome had gotten himself involved with a strumpet. For the man who conquered Cairo and forced humiliating settlements upon the legacies of Charlemagne, Napoleon could not accept in his royal household a harpy from Baltimore named Betsy Patterson.

The question is not why Jerome Bonaparte was smitten Betsy Patterson in 1803, but rather, how did an American teenager, daughter of a gunpowder and weapons merchant, get entangled with Napoleon's immature brother? There's no evidence to sustain the cock and bull story that Jerome was here on a secret mission seeking another source of explosives from William Patterson, a Scots-Irish immigrant who made a fortune supplying munitions to the patriots in the Revolution. Historians guffaw at the thought that France, purveyor of the finest firearms in the world, would seek anything from our neophyte munition industries.

The accepted version of Jerome Bonaparte's introduction to the sixteen-year-old heiress from Baltimore is really the stuff of pulp-fiction paperbacks. Being the youngest of the Bonaparte siblings, Jerome's childhood was spend in poverty as his widowed mother endured shifting fortunes in the French Revolution. Jerome received little formal education, and the sporadic discipline meted out by his desperate mother was insufficient to produce a resourceful young man. Napoleon intervened and installed his brother in a boarding school. A year later, the boy was put to sea as a midshipman.

Following a "show the flag" cruise to the Antilles, Jerome's frigate plied the American coastal waters and put in at Baltimore for refitting in one of its numerous ship yards. News spread quickly that a brother of the great Napoleon was on-board the French frigate, and soon the elites of Baltimore were queuing up to host this thin, dark relation to Europe's brash, new ruling family.

William Patterson didn't encourage his high-spirited daughter to romance the French tyrant's sibling. The scheming was all Betsy's idea, and that's the way it was for the rest of her status-seeking life. Speculation is that this Irish colleen bewitched hapless Jerome with a forwardness that no European gentle woman would approve.

Baltimore was abuzz with rumors of a pending Bonaparte marriage taking place in their midst. Would Napoleon himself come, or send a delegation? Would Betsy Patterson soon become princess of Bavaria or Lombardy?

Papa Patterson did the wedding up right. Betsy was Presbyterian, but her father advised her to become a Catholic. Her wedding to Jerome Bonaparte was performed in the Cathedral of Mary, Our Queen of Baltimore with Archbishop John Carroll officiating before the notables of the central Atlantic states. No Bonapartes attended; they didn't even respond to the invitation!

Jerome had abandoned ship and was technically AWOL, plus, under French law, his marriage to Elizabeth Patterson was not valid because he was a minor at age eighteen. To make matters worse for the newlyweds, Jerome received a summons to return to France immediately without his woman. He was the dithering Bonaparte, and he dallied a year, living off the generosity of his father-in-law.

News reached Baltimore in march, 1804, of Napoleon's sudden arrest and execution of the Duc d' Enghien for allegedly plotting his assassination. Two months later the little big man crowned himself emperor of the French. In Baltimore, Jerome summoned his courage and sailed with pregnant Betsy on her father's yacht to Europe. But no European port would allow Elizabeth Patterson to debark. Jerome entered through Ostend and made way overland to face his furious brother. He didn't realize it, but it was to be his last glimpse of his pregnant bride. She sailed for London and waited for Jerome's beckon.

Betsy's day neared and she gave birth to a boy who had the brooding countenance of a miniature Napoleon. She named her dark offspring Jerome Napoleon Bonaparte in a desperate attempt to soften her famous brother-in-law into acceptance.

Archbishop Carroll, a friend of Pope Pius, pleaded to no avail the legitimacy of the ceremony in Baltimore.

The imperial Napoleon vented his wrath upon his brother, but Jerome was soon made an admiral and a general and given command of the army in Silesia. An envoy of Emperor Napoleon arrived in London with an annulment and pension, together with a "get out of town" pronouncement. Within months Jerome was King of Westphalia and regally married to Princess Catherine Frederica of

Wurtemburg, a blue blood but no beauty like Betsy Patterson.

Pitiful, forsaken Betsy returned with child in tow to her father's mansion. Jerome was called by all "the little prince." He attended Harvard, and that institution bestowed a B.A. and a law degree upon their royal grandee.

"Bo" Bonaparte never deigned to practice law. Instead, he and his socialite mother traveled to Rome and lived for years near his aunt, Pauline Borghese, sister of the now deposed Emperor. Princess Pauline and "Queen Elizabeth" as she teasingly referred to herself, did everything but hang out a sign offering young Jerome as an available suitor for a royal marriage. Elizabeth denounced America all the while writing her elderly father in Baltimore for more money to sustain her lavish life-style.

Finally growing dejected with Jerome's dwindling prospects, 'Queen Elizabeth" returned home and saw Jerome married to a well-to-do Baltimore girl. He became a colonel in the American army, and his son, Charles Joseph Bonaparte, became Secretary of the Navy for Theodore Roosevelt. Betsy Patterson lived to be 94, an embittered old woman who clawed her way into the footnotes of history.

Bull's Treaty Between Warring Carolina and Cherokee Nations

"Look on my works, ye Mighty, and despair! Nothing beside remains." So goes Percy Shelley's tribute to the crumbled monument that once proudly honored Ramses II. From ancient Egypt's crumbling ruins to callow Charleston's colonial remnants, succeeding generations bury with time the great deeds of their mighty men. Occasionally, myopic historians recover a moment worth displaying again.

58

Such a forgotten moment for Charlestonians is the Cherokee Treaty hammered out between two powerful nations in September, 1761. The forgotten historic place is the ancient cabin of William Bull on the banks of the Ashley; its brick and tabby foundation still stands today.

Two men could hardly be less alike than Attakullakulla, Chief of the Seven Nations of the Cherokee empire and Lieuntenant-Governor William Bull, *de facto* king's counsel and executive for the colony of Carolina. Husking off the ten generations of forgetful descendants and a snowballing succession of momentous events, time has dimmed the luster of this diplomatic achievement that represented a first on these shores -- the recognition of the interests of one's rival as central in the construction of lasting peace.

This forgotten treaty is unique in that it recognized the needs of both parties as an avenue to lasting peace. Earlier Indian treaties had been a diplomatic continuation of the whipping that had occurred on the battlefield. Bull was a prototype of the modern statesman.

Two-hundred and fifty years later, two men could hardly be more alike than the proud Cherokee "emperor" of seven nations and the tidewater son of landed-gentry who upheld royal authority and anglicanism in this corner of the British realm. Each man was a force to contend with. Each had powerful allies who, collectively could annihilate the other. But the Cherokee chieftain and the Carolina governor were men of principle, devoid of the guile.

The Cherokee War of 1760 scorched the Carolinas from the lower Savannah to the Saluda and beyond. The French and Indian War that engulfed the mid-Atlantic colonies might have passed us but France and Spain manipulated the grievances of the Creeks to the west and the Cherokees to the northwest, all to our woe.

The upper reaches of the Keowee and the Lynches rivers were laid waste by "screaming savages, their faces painted red and yellow." Settlers upstate barricaded in crude stockades feared their demise through the winter of 1760. We know this area as Clemson, Greenville, Spartanburg and Greenwood. As far as the Congaree the shrieks of the warriors of Attakullakulla's seven nations brought a terror never known before or since in Carolina.

Governor Lyttleton, the newly arrived head man sent here from Whitehall, had no time for cordials at the Exchange. The Carolina militia was stretched beyond its capability with repeated deployments to rescue besieged stockade encampments.

Charleston overflowed with refugees from upstate. Even that influx of the destitute brought unrest as these dissenters were loathe to obey the curfews and customs of this very English city. Settling the Cherokee issue had a twofold urgency, protecting the upstate and ridding the city of the influx of fiercely independent hill folks.

Lyttleton produced results; he cobbled a deal with the governor of New York and received on loan a regiment of heavy dragoons. These battle-tested veterans secured the Congaree basin near Colonel Moses Thomson's Belleville plantation.

The Charleston militia and upstate rangers moved to root out Cherokee bands in the state's northwest quadrant. Lyttleton was successful beyond his expectation. Attakullakulla sent his deputy, Chief Occonostota, in full battle regalia to treat with the governor at the Council Chamber on the corner of Meeting and Broad. What a sight the painted warrior made in the city that so feared him!

The Gazette exalted Lyttleton and the Library Society, then a forum for the landed-gentry, gave him a banquet that a conquering Caesar would have relished. Lyttleton was soon made governor of Jamaica and was off to greater fame in that sugar cane kingdom. But his treaty here was short-lived. Lyttleton gave short shrift to the concerns of the Cherokee natives and the white mans' encroachments. In fact, Lyttleton was downright arrogant, and within months the war blazed anew.

Lieutenant-Governor William Bull once again proved that Carolinians preferred homegrown leadership over the grandees that London sent out. Bull again dispatched the Charleston militia upstate. He, if not a protégé of William Pitt, at least was an admirer of that British statesman, and recognized that lasting peace requires honest brokers who are willing to give and take.

Through intermediaries such as Charleston's legendary Indian agent, Colonel John Stuart, Bull gained the ear of Attakullakulla at his capitol city of Chota, near Vonore in eastern Tennessee. Bull pledged security to "Little Carpenter," as Attakullakulla had been known since youth, if the great man would cease hostilities and come to Bull's home, Ashley Hall plantation, on the banks of the Ashley River.

Ashley Hall was situated on the ruins of an ancient Indian city. A high burial mound contains remains of the chiefs and warriors from centuries before the white man arrived. Attakullakulla threw caution to the winds and came with just a handful of advisors and warriors.

Bull did not bring them into the city proper as Lyttleton had done with Chief Occonostota. That would have been too reminiscent of the colonists' perfidy only months previously. Instead, the great men met in the stockaded cabin that had been Bull's father, Stephen's first dwelling on the Ashley, built sometime in the 1680s. There Attakullakulla and Bull dismissed all but their interpreters and they eventually passed the peace pipe. Bull lavished the Indian emperor with imported presents, and the chief from over the hills reciprocated with embroidered textiles that stunned the English colonials. These were no savages, these red men of the hill towns.

Bull made allowances for Cherokee hunting rights, and he pledged severe retribution for white infringement. The men parted more as brothers than adversaries. The finest tradition of American-style diplomacy was inaugurated in our Carolina low-country. The treaty lasted 15 years until British agents roused hatred anew amongst the Cherokee. Bull and Attakullakulla had passed on to their happy hunting ground by then. The foundation of the cabin still stands as the base for a home at the bend in Ashley Hall Road today. Where is our Shelley that will commemorate in verse the legend of these two noble men?

The Papers Of Anita Garibaldi Among Treasures At USC

Let's start with the assumption that some readers may not know what rumors about Anita Garibaldi to toss and what fantastic tales to divulge about this hot-blooded latin insurrectionist. For not since Bizet's Carmen scorched opera stages from Sienna to Salzburg has a spitfire such as Giuseppe Garibaldi's raven-haired, Brazilian-born 'Nita so captivated the western world. And why shouldn't a comely Brazilian republican-radical- turned-Italian- insurrectionist still enthrall us with her exploits just as she charmed her beau Garibaldi, cock of the risorgimento?

Anita Ribeiro Garibaldi's legend lives on alongside her husband's in countless articles and books. Now fact can be culled from fiction without roaming library shelves a half a world away. The place to peruse the records of these star-crossed revolutionists is neither Salerno, nor Catania. The Garibaldi papers are housed in the Thomas Cooper Library Manuscripts Collection at USC!

Take one Sicilian manuscript collector with a hankering for our southern climate, and you have Anthony Campanella. Find a university that accepts priceless gifts upon terms that they'll never be traded, loaned, or auctioned, and you have The University of South Carolina. Stories of fiery Anita thrill us wherever they may be found, but having the mother lode of material centered in Carolina's Thomas Cooper is a history writer's rapture.

As we await new works on these icons of Italian unification, we owe ourselves another titillating glimpse into this woman's soul. To say that the Thomas Cooper Library has the papers of Anita Garibaldi is a bit misleading, for Anita couldn't read or write. She dictated her correspondence, a trait that makes her even more intriguing.

The name "Anita" was a nomme de guerre bestowed by her common-law husband, Giuseppe Garibaldi. Baptized Ana Maria de Jesus Ribeiro da Silva in Laguna, province of Santa Catarina, Brazil, this child of an impoverished fisherman came of age reverencing the Holy Virgin and cursing the Spanish landlords.

Like her kin, Anita married young, probably at age 14. Legend has it that in 1839, soldier-adventurer Garibaldi sailed into the harbor near Laguna and glimpsed a pretty girl cavorting among fisherman on a dock. Garibaldi couldn't take his eyes off of the dark-haired beauty with her long tresses flying as she flirted with the men.

We're left to ponder what transpired on the waterfront as Garibaldi's ship gathered provisions, but at nightfall, the pretty Anita left husband and home forever behind as she sailed with this mysterious Italian soldier of fortune. Her cuckolded young husband must have been the butt of savage humor in the village that night! Anita spent the first of many nights wrapped in the arms of the dangerous revolutionary she said always smelled of gunpowder.

The Garibaldi fellow that whisked Anita away was one of the 19th century's great political radicals. His passion was the overthrow of monarchies and replacing them with republican-styled governments. His mentor was Giuseppe Mazzini, and his tactics were those of the Carbonari, the guerilla bands that plagued the monarchs of northern Italy and Spain.

When Mazzini's movement faltered in Italy, Garibaldi traveled to South America to hone his skills as a soldier. It was as a mercenary in the uprising of Rio Grande do Sul against Brazil that he first laid eyes upon this fiery girl whose hatred of aristocracy rivaled his own.

Anita fought alongside her husband on horseback, on foot, and at sea. She wore a brace of pistols, swore like a sailor, and rode bareback like a gaucho. Somehow the two romantics managed to emerge from the fray unscathed.

The western world was awash with the forces of social change. Argentina, Brazil, and Uruguay were undergoing insurrection. Anita followed Garibaldi across the Andes and bore him two children during his revolutionary campaigns.

In 1848 another wave of revolutions swept across Europe and the Garibaldis made haste for Sardinia to fight with Charles Albert's forces against Austria. Giuseppe and Anita, with infants in tow, made the strangest guerilla band ever seen.

Regrettably, Charles Albert's army was not of the same zealous nature as were the Garibaldis regarding the ouster of Austria from northern Italy. It took the Hapsburgs of Austria less than a year to send Charles Albert's Sardinians reeling westward. Anita followed her husband and his red-shirted band through the hill country southward to unite with Mazzini in an attempt to bring republicanism to Rome and the papal kindom.

She was pregnant and carrying a sick infant in her arms as the horses traversed washed out paths through rugged country. Her horse slipped and threw Anita hard upon the stony soil. Remounted they rode on, but soon Garibaldi was ambushed by forces loyal to Pope Pius IX. In the ensuing shootout Anita fought back, wheeling her horse from side to side and firing a revolver with one hand as she clutched her sick child with the other. This image of her has been preserved in an equestrian marble statue on the highest ridge of the Janiculum, looking down upon Rome.

Exhausted, anemic, and exposed to the hardships of guerilla war, Anita could not go on. She wouldn't allow her husband to hide her away in some remote village, for she felt that her own life was nothing compared to the the cause of republicanism.

In the night of August 8, 1849, amidst the sound of guns, the 29 year-old wife of Giuseppe Garibaldi died in his arms from complications associated with her fifth pregnancy. Her four surviving children watched mutely as their mother was buried in a hastily dug grave. Garibaldi removed her red scarf and draped it over his shoulders. Anita's scarf had been the diaper of their first child born in an Argentinian campaign, and it became a trademark of Garibaldi a decade later when he and his red shirts liberated his native Sicily.

The romantic stories of Giuseppe and Anita Garibaldi were enormously popular in the American South prior to the War Between the States. Many southern women saw themselves as rebel heroines in the mold of Anita.

Thanks to Anthony Campanelli' generosity, the world will make a path to the Thomas Cooper Library to reacquaint with these romantic nationalists whose memory is perpetuated by freedom-loving people worldwide.

Olivia Laurens' Grand Journey To The Upstate, 1825

Who's been up the Interstate to Greenville recently? What does it take, three hours on cruise control and most of your morning?

Greenville is rather a mundane trip, but if only we knew what adventure it used to be, we'd opt to see the road as our ancestors did. Olivia Laurens' travel diary from the summer of 1825 gives a glimpse of what a trip from Charleston to Greenville used to involve when roads were rough and accommodations were rustic.

Caroline Olivia Laurens was a twenty-year-old heiress of the Ball family who married her distant cousin, Henry Laurens, Jr., heir to the estate of Henry

Laurens, former president of the Continental Congress. Except for some Allston or Heyward unions, this was as moneyed a marriage as ever contrived in old Carolina. When Olivia and Henry set out on an upstate trip, it was more a noble progress than a buggy ride. They possessed the finest coach, the best carriage horses, and the most dignified outriders of anyone.

Olivia's journal, previously unpublished until the South Carolina Historical Society produced it in serialized fashion in its quarterly publication in 1971, begins on Monday, May 23rd, 1825, in Charleston at the city dock at the foot of what is now Calhoun Street. Olivia, Henry, infant John, and servants depart the majestic Laurens home with all its gardens, outbuildings, and citrus grove located at the foot of Laurens Street and the intersection of East Bay. Unfortunately the decaying mansion was pulled down in the 1940s.

None of us would begin our trip to Greenville by shoving off into the Cooper River bound for Clements Ferry. The hour-long ferry ride was prelude to connecting with their sailing yacht that would convey them upriver to her family plantation, Limerick, where they disembarked for a leisurely luncheon. They awaited the tide and floated upriver to the Laurens' beautiful plantation, Mepkin.

The day which began at the city dock at 8 a.m. wound down with the 7 p.m. arrival at the Mepkin dock with plantation servants all arrayed, eleven hours to go 25 miles!

They rested a day before their overland journey that would be a four-month sojourn from the malaria-prone Lowcountry. Henry took in a leisurely deer hunt early the next morning and killed a fine buck before changing into traveling clothes for the coach journey to the upstate.

Charlestonians were fond of escaping to Pendleton, Paris Mountain, Table Rock, and Greenville in those early days. The two-hundred and fifty mile distance was a week's ride for a horseman, longer than that for a coach, and ten days time for a postal letter. The sights and scents were invigorating to those afflicted with heat, humidity, mosquitoes, and malaria.

Olivia and family rolled out of Mepkin's sandy lane at 7 a.m on Wednesday, May 25. Well-wishers including "Dr. B. (perhaps Beaufain) and Frederick" accompanied them on horseback fourteen miles, as far as Wadboo springs. The spring was not only a curiosity, a deep, clear pool thirty feet across, but it was the perfect natural rest stop. Their route so far was what we'd call Highway 6 heading to Eutaw Springs, but the Santee-Cooper project of the 1930s submerged part of their road under Lake Moultrie. So far the trip has been a lark, picnic hampers and open-country.

They averaged 4 miles per hour over the rutted road. Carriage innovation had not risen to the level of coil-springs; rather, they rode on stiff scissor-springs. The worst nightmare was to lose a wheel, causing occupants to be pitched headlong into the road. All sorts of evil lurked in the swamps and dense woods, everything from desperadoes to lawless squatters. A coachman riding shotgun was a customary practice through the 18th and 19th centuries.

Leaving Wadboo for the Eutaws around noon, they rumbled northwest along the Santee basin passing old plantations now underwater due to Santee-Cooper. The next rest stop was Eutaw Springs, a geological marvel that Indians once used as a sacred site. Carriages stopped at the Eutaws for its crystal pure, cool water. Gushing water pumping upward through limestone caverns passed through craggy formations to emerge through a hill several dozen yards westward. Indian braves used to swim the subterranean channel. The Revolutionary battlefield was a quiet woodland paradise situated nearby. Olivia snacked on delicious artichoke hearts near the spring. All is underwater today.

From Eutaw to The Rocks plantation home of Captain Peter Gaillard was but a short ride. Laurenses and Gaillards needed no letters of introduction which travelers often carried when venturing out of their parish. This area was a nexus of Huguenot homesites with surnames of Gaillard, Simons, Tresevant, among others long familiar in the Charleston season of balls and assemblies.

Gaillard was a host extraordinare, taking his guests on a tour of the local

area and honoring them at table. It was hard to push on from here into more
unfamiliar country.

The next stop was Felder's farm about twenty miles distant. This area
should correspond to Parler crossroads, a mile northwest of where I-95 passes
through Santee. Their host takes a liking to Henry and invites him to a deer
stand the next morning. Southern travel made allowances for necessities like deer
hunting and trout fishing along the way.

It was by now Friday morning when they departed Felder's at daybreak
headed for Houseman's tavern, twenty-eight miles distant. It was their fifth day
on the road and they were and day and a half out of Columbia township on the
Congaree. Measuring along Highway 6 puts Houseman's in the vicinity of St.
Matthew's, then called Lewisfield.

On the way the dappled grey went lame and had to be swapped for a spare.
The route became sandier and steeper. Carriage occupants had to get out and walk
as the horses strained and the drivers cracked the whip.

At Houseman's a welcomed sight was meeting their friend, Major Garden,
son of Doctor Alexander Garden of Charleston. A chance meeting of old friends
at a road tavern was added cause for an evening of fiddle music, port wine, and
laughter. Join me next week as Olivia's party makes a grand entrance into the
muddy little town that had once been Colonel Taylor's cotton plantation, but now
was the political compromise resulting in our new state capital. Greenville is
another seven days of adventure yet to unfold.

Olivia Laurens' Grand Excursion To Greenville, 1825

Going to Greenville by way of Columbia is so commonplace that no
modern travel-writer would bother to write up the experience. We set the cruise

control and relax as the miles blur by, for we can breakfast at home and luncheon at Vince Perone's. But what a difference a century and three-quarters ago do make. Olivia Laurens' travel journal from May, 1825, published in the South Carolina Historical Quarterly in 1971 gives perspective on getting from here to the upstate when fashionable Charlestonians sought cooler climes in piedmont villages such as Pendleton and Greenville.

Few families could match Charleston's Laurens family in wealth, so when Olivia, husband Henry, Jr., and their infant son, together with servants embarked on a four-month holiday to the upstate, it took them almost a week just to get as far as the new capital, Columbia on the Congaree. Their carriage rolled along rutted roads at four miles-per-hour, and every 24 miles or so, they turned in to a rustic road house, sometimes respectable, sometimes suspect. Their journey began on Highway 6 and continued northwestward on Highway 176.

Near what became St. Matthew's, the travelers rested at Housman's stagecoach inn. By coincidence, they met a family friend, Major Garden, up from Charleston on his way to the capital. The next morning at 6 a.m. they and Garden parted Housman's. Coach horns, the crack of a whip, and trotting horses conjure a romantic getaway more than do car horns, screeching tires, and our V-8.

Pulling the sand hills from Housman's to the Congaree required Olivia and her infant to step out of the carriage and walk as the driver urged the straining horses in the heat of May.

It was customary for travelers, upon approaching a city, to refresh themselves for a day or two at a road house, clean themselves, the carriage, and their equipage in preparation for making a grand entrance.

Olivia doesn't dwell as do other diarists of the day about Columbia's legenday small-town beauty. Emma LeConte's diary recounts Columbia as one of the prettiest towns in America with magnificent hill top views in every direction! In 1828, the city was three-decades old, laid out on a grid that covered what once had been the finest short-staple cotton plantation in the state. Moving the capital from Charleston satisfied increasing numbers of red-soil aristocrats with names such as Calhoun, Pickens, Richardson, and Taylor. These were men who mistrusted the tidewater elite as the ones who'd capitulated in the revolution. They were correct not to tie the State's fortune solely to the whims of the Lowcountry.

Columbia was a grid of six streets by six streets laid over two hills and, a valley. Olivia's entourage stayed at Clark's Hotel, next door to the court house. Clark's was the home away from home of the legislature, and since the original state house was a clapboard, two-story structure hastily built, the Clark's Hotel was often where the early business of the State transpired.

South Carolina College was nearby and the boys dined at Clark's, fewer than 50 of them and the half-dozen, or so, faculty. After dinner entertainment for the Laurenses on Saturday, May 28, 1825, was a half mile stroll to Taylor Hill to watch the sunset reflected in the Congaree. It's still a magnificent sight.

At 3 a.m. Sunday, Olivia heard the stage horn sounding. As the stage rolled up, the driver helped the wife of Senator John C. Calhoun to disembark. They learned that earlier in the evening the stagecoach lost a wheel and passengers were thrown into the road.

Crossing Broad River by ferry, the Laurens' carriage rolled northwest along what we call Highway 176. These Charlestonians had been traveling 5 days, yet they'd covered just 120 miles. The best overnight had been Peter Gaillard's home, The Rocks, at Eutaw Springs. Henry Laurens, Jr., had been on two deer hunts as guest of his hosts. No mention in is made of money trading hands at the inns, so the cost must have been negligible for the Laurenses.

Above Columbia the roads worsened, and the nature of the people living along the road coarsened. Nowhere was there the gentility associated with that part of the state encompassed by the parishes. This was dissenter country and composed of stern-faced men and women of either German or Scots-Irish origin. To these sandhill folks, Charleston represented inherited wealth, hereditary power, and churches ruled by bishops.

One wayside upstate inn had a dwarf on the porch and a bear chained in the yard. Olivia's crowd turned back to stay in one they'd previously rejected.

By June 4th, the jostled occupants of this custom-made carriage caught sight of the hill that are harbingers of the Blue Ridge. After all, they'd traveled 11 days to get to the village named Laurens after their namesake.

It was at 11 a.m. on June 4 that Olivia and family entered the village of Greenville. She exulted that they'd ridden all morning since leaving the Goldsmith farm without losing their way once! The crossing of a swift branch at Davy Ford required all occupants wading across as the driver feared the carriage might be swept downstream. Such were the perils of travel upstate!

They made straight for Doctor John Crittendon's Greenville Hotel, and it is clear from Olivia's delight that this establishment was the most genteel place she'd seen since departing the low-country.

Wading barefoot in the Reedy River was a frolic for these salt-water marsh dwellers. The next day was Sunday, and Greenville had no church buildings, but an ecumenical service was held at the court house, which, along with the Greenville Hotel, comprised half of the public buildings in the village. The masonic hall was the most majestic building, and a masonic parade was the biggest event. On Monday, they went "Paris Mount" to sketch a waterfall.

Lowcountry names abounded in Greenville; Allston, Bee, Dawson, Huger, and Harleston are a few of the names she mentions. Dinners, picnics, teas, and horseback rides in the country whiled away day after day for Olivia Laurens and her young family until early October when it was time to make the arduous journey back. But all felt renewed and as if they'd been in a far away wonderful land.

71

More Than 220 Years of Excellence At The College

Could there be any other place where the expression "the college" is as definitive as it is here? Everyone knows that "the college" refers to the oldest municipal college in the country, the College of Charleston. From Walhalla to Wadmalaw, the expression " my child attends the college" evokes images of the cistern and Randolph Hall. We are used to students ambling across George Street, and graduation where young women wear long white dresses and carry a single rose.

While the College dates to 1785, the discussion of chartering one here began as early as 1723. Reverend Thomas Morritt wrote the Bishop of London regarding an Anglican foundation here for an English-styled college. But fifteen years prior to Morritt's futile attempts, James Childs, a utopian idealist, planned a village complete with its own college on the west branch of the Cooper River northwest of here. Childsbury lasted but a few decades and no college was ever built. Today, a few unearthed bricks are all that remain of a village consisted of several streets and a tavern. Childs' dream of an American Eton on the headwaters of the Cooper were never realized.

Charleston men possessed wealth that matched or exceeded that of their New England brethren, but lacked the Calvin-inspired, Puritan penchant of New Englanders for school houses. Realizing the acute lack of free schools, Lieutenant-Governor William Bull recommended to the General Assembly that a public school system be established for the upcountry and that a public college be chartered for Charleston.

Thus, the most capable and accomplished men ever to affix names to one piece of paper in South Carolina assembled at the state house at Meeting and Broad on August 26, 1785, to sign the College of Charleston charter. William

Moultrie, Daniel DeSaussure, David Oliphant, Daniel Bordeaux, John Rutledge, Thomas Heyward, Jr., Thomas Bee, David Ramsay, Ralph Izard, Arthur Middleton, Gabriel Manigault, Charles Pinckney, and Charles Cotesworth Pinckney were among the notable men pledging their support to what is now the tenth oldest college in America.

Among these names were men who'd already pledged their all in the cause of the revolution. There were governors, declaration signers, soldiers, Oxford and Princeton men, and several who'd soon be hammering out a national constitution.

As with any great undertaking, there were the out-front movers generating public acclaim, and always there were behind-the-scenes subscribers who quietly maneuvered the idea into being. Benjamin Smith, vice-president of the Library Society bequeathed £500 for the building fund, the first donation of size. Then John McKenzie gave £1000 and donated 800 leather-bound books. The renown craftsman, John Prue, a master cabinetmaker, gave substantially to get the process rolling. Miles Brewton gave generously, and lady, Mary Ellis, donated substantially, making her one of the first woman philanthropists.

Henry Laurens had long been chiding his fellow Charlestonians for their obstinacy in developing a fine educational system.

Beating the drum for a quarter century was the Charleston Library Society. The board of the Library Society urged on numerous occasions that higher education be established for this colony which possessed so many fine minds honed in England to the classics. Lectures, debates, and scientific experiments attracted Charleston's literati regularly to the Library Society.

The history of the location of the College is as fascinating as is the story of its financial struggle. The ten acres situated within George Street to the south, Coming to the east, St. Philip Street to the west. and Boundary (Calhoun) to the north. This land was originally deeded to Henry Hughes in 1672 as part of his plantation, then considerably beyond the walls of the new Charles Town built in 1680. John Coming bought this parcel from Hughes. Coming's wife, Affra, sold

the land to General Thomas Pinckney. Pinckney's son sold the land to the
Commissioners of the College.

The deed describes a marsh on the northwest quadrant and Captain John
Harleston's land as bordering on the southwest. On the southeast side there is a
footpath connecting it to the Broad Path, as upper King Street was known. Close
by was the Glebe House, still used by the College. It was the parsonage for St.
Philip's, a gift to the church by Affra Coming.

The year 1785, the year of the College's charter, was a daunting one for the
region and for the western world. Though the colonies had achieved
independence, the framework of government known as the Articles of
Confederation was collapsing. So, too, was the solvency of state governments, a
matter of grave concern. Bitterness toward former loyalists was tearing families
and townships apart. Former Lieutenant-Governor William Bull, a loyalist
residing in London, sought unsuccessfully to regain title to vast properties he
entrusted to his nephews in Carolina. The year 1785 was hardly a time to lay a
college foundation!

So, in time of uncertainty, it is testimony to the faith of the combined
clergy of Charleston that the fledgling institution opened its doors. The presiding
Episcopal bishop, the Huguenot pastor, and a Catholic priest made up half of the
initial college faculty. Such a liberal notion hardly prevailed elsewhere, certainly
not in Boston. From the College's establishment, the religious issue was moot; it
would be ecumenical.

Abroad, 1785 was frightening in what it portended. The Austrian-born
Queen of France, Marie Antoinette, found herself accused of a tryst with Catholic
Cardinal Rohan. Reputedly she sold her favors for a diamond crucifix that the
Cardinal possessed. The scandal was the last straw for the floundering monarch,
Louis XVI. James Watt and Matthew Boulton first fired up their great steam
engine in Papplewick, Nottinghamshire. With the coming of the French
Revolution and the age of steam, the western world would never again be the

same. Charleston would not be the same, either.

The ten acre campus had been dense forest, field and pasture land, a potter's field, a barracks and parade ground during the Queen Anne's War, and lately, in revolution, the site was a staging area for munitions and troops moving in and out of the defenses higher up the peninsular. Under the able leadership of its first president, Doctor Robert Smith, a Gonville and Caius , Cambridge man, the little college by the Broad Path developed into the proud reputation that it possesses today.

Indian Fighters Made The Best Civil War Generals

There's something about the way they struck a pose for the camera, their flint-hard jaw and steely eyes that stare right through you. The drooping mustache, the arms folded, and a holstered .44 revolver completed their rakish air. There's just a rawboned look about them that mocks danger. Most were West Point grads who rose through the ranks to their Civil War commands, some Union, some Confederate. But their initiation to the savagery of war came through the Comanche, Apache, Arapahoe, and Sioux. The great battlefield commanders of the Civil War were, for the better part, hardened Indian fighters.

Andrew Jackson's administration created the 2nd Cavalry Regiment and posted these horse soldiers to the Great Plains to quell uprisings of the Shawnee, Pawnee, and Cheyenne. Wagon trains rolling across Kansas toward the Platte River were being attacked by plains indians.

For nomadic, bronze-skinned warriors shooting up wagon trains was holy war. These pioneer palefaces despoiled their land and violated their squaws. To our ancestors, trekking west was a manifestation of destiny. The red man was a savage who, in their mind, could never be assimilated. The army cleared the Santa Fe Trail of hostile tribes. The 2nd Cavalry Dragoons kept open the corridor to Oregon and California. Looking back, this unit served as the incubator for the leadership of the future Confederacy.

The elite 2nd Dragoons traveled light, moved swiftly and braved heat and blizzard to defeat their wily foe. Their battles raged across Kansas, Nebraska, and Colorado. The Dodge expedition of 1835 became a textbook operation of American-style warfare studied at West Point by R. E. Lee, U. S. Grant, A. S. Johnston, and dozens of names made indelible by the future War of Secession.

In fact, most Civil War commanders worth their spurs were seasoned Indian fighters tested by arrows on the banks of the Brazos or the Cimarron. Phil Sheridan, George McClellan, Earl Van Doran, and J.E.B. Stuart were just a few comrades who lived rough from saddlebags and did remote western tours lasting from 36 to 60 months.

They valued their four-legged mounts above everything else; South Carolina's Nathan "Shanks" Evans rode an Irish-thoroughbred foaled in Kentucky from a Sweepstakes winner. That horse. "Bumblebee," won prairie derbies and rode down many a Comanche brave. These were the days when Army officers didn't depend upon government-issue, especially if the officer hailed from the moneyed families of the antebellum south.

"Shanks" Evans was a cavalry commander of the famed 2nd Dragoons during the bloody Indian wars of the 1850s. A native of Marion, South Carolina, this Randolph-Macon and West Point Class of 1848 graduate kept a journal of his army life, and much of it is incorporated in Jason Silverman's "Shanks: The Life and Wars of General Nathan G. Evans, CSA" (C.2002: Da Capo Press).

Activated in 1836 for frontier service, the 2nd Cavalry was inactive for a decade prior to its controversial reactivation in May, 1855. Bringing the regiment back to duty during the Kansas-Nebraska, free-state, slave-state struggle was an inflammatory act on the part of the Franklin Pierce administration. Many critics said that Secretary of War Jefferson Davis "pulled the wool over" Pierce to get an all-southern regiment into service. Davis stacked the command slots with his own favorites, all West Point grads like himself, and all known to favor the Southern nullification.

The cadets in Shanks Evans' class, or just below or above him at West Point, constitute the nucleus of both armies in the terrible War of Secession. Bernard Bee; T. J. Jackson; Kirby Smith; George McClellan; Fitz-John Porter; Ambrose Burnside; George Pickett; Henry Heth; and more than a dozen other boisterous boys matured in the ranks from plebe to first classman high up on the Hudson. They made fun of the bad food, walked tours, struggled with impossibly hard academics, and endured all the harshness of army life while preparing for all types of warfare. That they would ever be foes never crossed their minds in 1848.

Over mugs of sugarless black coffee by campfires and bivouacs as far afield as the Nebraska prairies to the Rio Grande, these men regaled each other with heroics of their latest Indian fight. They laughed over how the Indian never understood the concept of distance, how a mile meant anything from a day's journey to a stone's throw. "Ride with me a mile, maybe two," was a standard cavalry joke. It was Indian for "pack your bags, soldier, you'll be days on the trail!"

The 2nd Dragoons was an all-southern regiment. The flower of southern martial minds constituted the leadership, thanks to Secretary of War, Jeff Davis' maneuvering. Commanding with rank of colonel, was Albert Sidney Johnston, the foremost southern man of rank at that time. The executive officer was a veteran of the Mexican War and countless Indian fights, Lieutenant-Colonel R. E. Lee. Adjutant, with rank of major, was William J. Hardee, perhaps the greatest tactician of mounted warfare in this hemisphere. Captain Nathan "Shanks" Evans was one of the company commanders.

On one deployment from Fort Leavenworth, Shanks Evans lost the heart of a pretty girl he was wooing when his classmate, J.E.B. Stuart quickly won her affections! Shanks was able to assuage his chagrin by winning a huge sum of money on his horse, Bumblebee, beating all comers in the Army Derby. Don't you know these commanders joked about these exploits over black coffee from Fredericksburg to Gettysburg. What a tragic thing it was for them to have to turn on one another in the 1860s.

The Indian fight that cemented many of these men as blood brothers was the Great Comanche War in the fall of 1856. Comanche warriors were surprised and defeated in bloody hand-to-hand fighting at the Choctaw River.

Shanks Evans killed the Comanche chief and captured the eagle feather standard reverenced by the enemy. The standard was a seven foot banner of woven eagle feathers and red flannel. He brought the relic back to Marion, and the South Carolina legislature presented him with a gold hilt sword. Evans was mentioned in the newspapers of 1856 as a hero. These Indian fighters a decade later roamed the hills of the Shenandoah in pursuit of a less wily foe than the Arapahoe of the 1850s.

The Day After Christmas in 1906

How could it have been the best of times if they had no bowl games on wide-screen tv? Charlestonians didn't know, and they wouldn't have cared how we ring in New Year's. They had their own way of winding down the old and ringing in the new year. Here's a sampling of our town as it was on December 26, 1906, as revealed in *The Evening Post* of that date.

78

What's unsettling today is that from Baghdad to Belfast, from Afghanistan to Gaza, there's death and division. Peace on earth, or chaos and death? On this date 100 years ago, The Evening Post's front page reported on continuing racial unrest along the Mississippi from Memphis to Yazoo. Fifteen to twenty were killed and many more sustain wounds in gun battles near railway lines that deny blacks passage or employment. There's talk of all-out race war breaking out around Crawford, Mississippi. A week before in Crawford a railroad conductor was shot and killed and vigilantes take bloody revenge. The governor has called out infantry and artillery companies. Meridian is in a state of emergency. Train depots have been burned and employees attacked. Chaos prevails in a 500 mile stretch along the Mississippi River, and similar race riots break out across Texas.

Internationally, the British and Belgian exploitation of the Congo causes a twinge of conscience here at King Leopold's shameful plunder of that region. The London Exchange is boasting of millions to be made there in rubber extraction. Leopold has an emissary in Washington whose mission is to stay Teddy Roosevelt's hand in curbing American investment in the Congo. When money meets morality,odds on, money wins every time. Historians today estimate that 4 to 6 million Africans were exterminated by Leopold's policies and ruthless agents. The basis for much of the British monarchy's enormous fortune today is tangled in this calumny in the Congo.

Up in Columbia, Christmas Day is marred by H.D. Smith's body being found crumpled at the foot of the stairwell of his Assembly Street boarding house. He was a 60-year-old timber agent for the Southern Railroad. No foul-play is expected. Locally, quite a few Charlestonians are fined and some are arrested for raucous behavior in Market Street on Christmas night. Drunken, disorderly behavior, and the exploding of a particularly large firecracker called a torpedo produces several arrests. One prominent fellow pays a fine of five dollars. Five bucks is quite a stiff police fine in 1906 because a three-month, home-delivery, subscription of The Evening Post costs just $1.50

Charlestonians are interested in a military appropriations bill that will greatly increase personnel in coastal artillery forts along America's perimeter. A recent Army inspection reveals that Fort Moultrie's big coastal guns did not pass maintenance inspection. They have not been properly greased, nor are they in firing order. Around the nation, 14,000 soldiers are posted in coastal artillery bases in 1906, and the report maintains that 35,000 soldiers is the White House target. This is all part of the "big stick" approach mentioned with Teddy Roosevelt's name.

Weather statistics in downtown Charleston, measured at the Custom House, reveal a cold, crystal clear Christmas in 1906. The high is 40 degrees and the low is 24. Humidity is 72%, and the winds blow from the north at 10 to 15 mph. Columbia's temperature range on Christmas in 1906 is 26 to 32 degrees. Despite the briskness, thousands of Charlestonians are seen hustling about King Street loaded with presents!

On Christmas day up on Marion Square, The Citadel pulled out all the stops at the president's quarters to help Colonel and Mrs. Asbury Coward celebrate their Golden wedding anniversary. On Christmas Day, 1856, Coward, handsome in dress grays, recently degreed from The Citadel, responded "I do," to Reverend John Bachman's proffered question of "Do you take this woman, Eliza Blum, etc., etc." A gala celebration and ball was held 100 years ago at The Citadel with many distinguished names represented on place cards. Asbury Coward, the man Robert E. Lee called one of his best regimental commanders, also served as The Citadel's president in the reunification era.

Society news made The Evening Post, "The" newspaper of choice for many Charlestonians, and in December, 1906, even Mount Pleasant is abuzz with house parties and boys returning from Clemson and Carolina. Cambridge Trott, Alex Mitchell, Charlie Trott, and Edward Fitzsimmons return after exams at Clemson.

R.N. Royall reports spending Christmas in McClellanville at the home of Andrew Dupree, Mrs. Royall's father. Miss Mattie Silcox writes that she's home from Winthrop. Eugene Johnson says that he'll be attending a party at Freeman plantation, and the Misses Gailliard, Margaret and Irene, welcome Miss Virginia Seigneious of Orangeburg to their Wentworth Street home for a series of holiday balls.

One of the best stories in the December 26, 1906, Evening Post recounts the visit here of the Honorable Edward Strobel, prime minister for the King of Siam (now Thailand). Strobel is a native of Charleston. He has a suite of rooms in the elegant St. John's Hotel, rebuilt 70 years later as the Mills House Hotel. Strobel is a Harvard and Harvard law graduate. He served as Bemis professor of international law at Harvard before being picked as advisor to King Chulalougkora. He is listed as serving as assistant head of state and prime minister of Thailand. Born here in 1833, his parents were Maynard Strobel and Caroline Davis. He was Class of 1877 at Harvard. Evidently Strobel returns regularly to Charleston and gives lavish entertainment at the St. John's on Meeting Street.

Kerrison's announces its annual sale at 80-82 Hassell Street by promising the finest clothing and home furnishing. The William Minnis Company at King and George Streets heralds gourmet groceries and candies, including a new shipment of Whitman's chocolates. Carolina Savings Bank boasts assets over two million dollars! Lawrence Pinckney Real Estate Company, 36 Broad Street, phone number 378, will loan you the money to purchase a home from his numerous listings! Certainly many of the same concerns and similar passions prevail today, but Charleston is still a timeless, pastel-tinted town rising between two tidal rivers in a southern paradise.

Colin Powell Wanted Career in New York's Garment District

Colin Powell's worst critics said that he was the result of what occurs when an army major gets affirmative action. His biggest admirers said he could have had either party's nomination for president in year 2000. But after looking at what he's accomplished, who can deny that the man from "Banana Kelly," South Bronx, has paid his dues.

Colin Powell has never liked his first name. His father saw the name on a packing crate the day his son was born. Powell pronounced it the British way, Kah-lin, until his college years. In his biography under education, he lists a B.S. in Geology from C.C.N.Y. , and he cites an M.B.A. from George Washington with a follow-on stint as White House fellow in the Nixon administration.

This Jamaican kid born in Harlem, reared in South Bronx, spent 35 years in the Army, serving as platoon leader in Vietnam tour one and as battalion commander and as a division operations officer in tour two. He lists command experience as an infantry battalion commander in Korea, as a regimental commander in the 101st Airborne and as brigade commander of infantry. Of course, he was Chairman of the Joint Chiefs of Staff during Gulf War One, and they remember him at the Pentagon piping in Calypso music on Friday afternoons.

A few other notations on Powell's resume mention things such as Secretary of State for Bush 2 and National Security Advisor for Bush 1. Curiously, his resume does not cite his position as assistant sales manager for Jay Sickser's wholesale business in New York's Garment District in the early 1950s. But then, if Jay Sickser hadn't had children to take over that business, Powell believes he never would have attended City College of New York and further matured into the national leader he has become.

Jay Sickser was a shrewd merchant. Powell and the childrens' garments wholesaler teamed up to make an interesting pair in the commercial district of South Bronx. Collie, as Jay Sickser called Powell, learned yiddish and eavesdropped on buyers' conversations. He reported information gleaned from buyers to Sickser who'd close the sale. For two years the duo racked up big sales, but as Colin Powell finished high school, his inquiries on becoming Sickser's business partner met with the first blunt lesson of his life. This family-owned business would stay exclusively with Sickser's children. With an arm around the 17-year-old boy's shoulder, Sickser said, "Collie, don't put too much hopes in the store. Go to college and get all the education you can."

Though Luther Powell arrived in America on a banana boat, his son Colin never lacked the nicer things. Powell's memories include little of what the hit Broadway musical "West Side Story" portrays. Nor was it the violent blood feud depicted in the movie, "Fort Apache, The Bronx." Colin Powell belonged to a neighborhood gang, but it was not the dangerous kind. His gang consisted of Puerto Ricans, Jamaican Blacks, Chinese, Italians, Poles, and recently arrived European Jews. They hung out on at San Fiorino's Shoe Repair Shop, and zip-guns, drugs, and sex eluded them to their dismay. His crowd didn't have the guts to be "gangstas," they feared their old man. Rap music was years away; these Bronx kids listened to fast-beat Caribbean tunes. Caucasians were minority in Powell's world, that is, until he headed uptown to attend C.C.N.Y.

Luther and Maud Powell brought their two children up in the Episcopal faith of their Jamaican upbringing. Modestly, Colin Powell admits that he doesn't meet the stereotype Americans hold of black men. He's tall, but he's awful as a basketball player. The only basketball team Powell ever made was his church team, and that was because his father was senior warden and coach. Even so, Powell sat on the bench. He ran track one year, just enough to letter, at P.S. 39.

In nothing did Colin Powell stand out from the crowd. His grades were below average. Math and science almost kept him from a high school diploma.

Maud Powell, ever the attentive mother, arranged for extra-help, but Colin just wasn't interested in school, or anything else.

Once on a church youth trip, Colin and two other boys disgraced themselves by sneaking off and buying a six-pack of beer. When accosted, Colin redeemed himself by assuming full responsibility for the grievous sin, thereby displaying that he had not one rebellious gene in his make-up.

The comfortable life that his immigrant parents provided for him and his older sister, Marilyn, was being frittered away by Colin until he got that afternoon job at Sickser's. For the first time in his 17 years he was getting praise and reward for something he enjoyed. Jay Sickser, a man older than Colin's father, began to treat Colin as a colleague. They made quite a pair in the competitive commercial district of South Bronx.

Even the guidance counselor at P.S. 39 was dubious when Colin announced that he intended to apply to university. He had not shown much stick-to-it discipline, save for the two years at Sickser's. But those years of work and words of praise meant the world to the kid from Kelly Street.

Two acceptance letters arrived in one week to Colin's relief and his parents' shock. NYU said he could attend, but their tuition was $750 a year. C.C.N.Y., an open university chartered for immigrants, welcomed Colin, and their tuition was $10 a year in 1953.

This university that's graduated the likes of Felix Frankfurter, Upton Sinclair, Abe Rosenthal, Robert Wagner, Abram Beame, Ed Koch, and 8 Nobel Prize winners had no idea that the black boy from the Bronx would be at the top of their list of distinguished alums.

A week after enrolling, Colin shunned the expensive fraternity scene for the R.O.T.C. program. Colonel H. C. Brookhart, a highly decorated West Point graduate just back from the Korean War, was the Professor of Military Science at C.C.N.Y., and he mentioned to the lanky Powell that he should try out for the school's elite drill team, the Pershing Rifles. The rest is well-known American legend. Colin Powell took to military training like an eagle takes to flight; the military was even more exciting than selling baby prams at Jay Sickser's!

The World-Renown Inns of Summerville A Century Ago

Before the Caribbean became our playground, Charlestonians summered amidst the pines and azaleas of historic Summerville. Evidently there's been a settlement high up the headwaters of the Ashley for as long as there has been a Charleston. Summerville is our oldest resort town, so it comes as no surprise that our most acclaimed inn is tucked away in the pine forests of this historic village of clapboard cottages festooned with flower boxes. But a hundred years ago Summerville boasted four nationally-acclaimed inns, and the moneyed set returned year after year to these sylvan settings where pines whisper and flowers bloom incessantly.

For two-hundred years it was the dreaded marsh vapors that sent coastal dwellers inland. The best prescription for avoiding the tropical disease malaria was escaping to the aromatic pine forests. The earliest inn of record, the Postern, dates to 1818. Brown's Hotel dates to 1823, and it evolved into an even grander facility known as the Dorchester, a haven for Charlestonians coming up on one of the four trains a day that serviced the town.

Summerville was once a gateway to the western quadrant of our state. Everyone from peddlers to preachers went from there prospecting westward. Not known for its refinements, Brown's was a memorable snuggery for travelers. Its metamorphosis into the Dorchester Inn brought a higher class clientele and a reputation for its cuisine.

There's no guarantee that Summerville would have remained just another lovely, obscure southern village had not a team of health specialists chosen it as one of the world's two finest health resorts. But, at a health summit in Paris in 1889, international medical specialists conferred upon Summerville an accolade that catapulted its status as a resort to rival that of Sarasota, or Britain's Bath and Germany's Baden.

Seizing upon the new-found notoriety, deep-pockeded Charlestonian investors, George and Frederick Wagner, partnered to develop what they envisioned as the finest resort in the South. They determined that they'd call their establishment The Pine Forest Inn, and they billed it as a grand lodge upon a manicured estate offering elegant accommodations and recreation. These King Street merchant princes of Charleston's gilded age purchased 22 acres on the edge of Summerville for the enormous sum of $9,000 in the spring of 1889. On this wooded property the Wagners laid out golf and croquet courses, lawn tennis, and bowls.

Adjoining their property was the experimental tea farm of Dr. Charles Shepard. The only tea farm in America just happened to coincide in timing and location with one of America's greatest inns. The combined effect of tea shrubs interlaced in Oriental fashion with blossoming plants produced a memorable stroll. The tea was distinct and even garnered approval from discerning Brits. The scent of Shepard's garden was an aromatic adornment to the halcyon bliss afforded by the Wagner's Pine Forest Inn.

The builder was Alexander Baird, and the Wagners secured him for construction of the edifice that some described as Summerville's Biltmore. Though not as grand, nor as costly, the Pine Forest Inn delivered the sort of elegance that guests of the Biltmore expected. The main building was four stories tall, and it boasted a 40 x 38 foot parlor furnished to receive the world's aristocrats.

The Wagners visited resorts around the South and returned determined to go one better on any hotels within range of here. They put in a library and reading room with the latest periodicals brought in by train from New York. The wine cellar had no equal.

One approached the grand entrance by way of a wraparound porch 185 feet long and 17 feet deep. Inviting, cushioned rockers were arranged in communion with porch swings and tea caddies. The entrance hall was 47 x 24 feet, with tall ceiling, and dazzled the eyes with crystal chandeliers, mirrors, and polished heart-pine floors. In season, the hall blazed with cut azaleas.

No wonder Presidents Teddy Roosevelt and William Howard Taft declared their wish to return again and again!

The latest Edison Improved Electric Plant delivered heat adjustable to each room. The adjoining wings gave the place a stately southern mansion effect. In fact, the West Wing Suite was continuously on reserve for the entourage that accompanied Ann Morgan, the sister of financier, J.P. Morgan, kept the west wing on reserve for herself and her entourage.

The Pine Forest Inn served the finest roast duck in the South, and the Inn boasted of a separate dining room for the personal staff that accompanied their guests. French chefs and German bakers were on the premises, and fresh cuts of meat rolled in daily on the train from New York.

Log burning fireplaces were framed by Italian marble mantels and hearths. Rich pine paneling hugged the walls which were ringed with leather-tufted chairs. The quiet, discerning wait staff blended into the background.

Tucked away amidst oaks and pines were cottages for those desiring seclusion. Acres of roses surrounded the Pine Forest, establishing a breathtaking bank of color. Numerous arbors, trellises, and shady bowers provided intimate rendezvous for tea and tranquility. The delicious silence apart from the faint murmur of the breeze through the pine boughs was itself worth the Inn's tariff. A week was a brief stay at the Pine Forest. Some guests wintered there yearly. A French baroness built a cottage situated next to the Inn gates.

Northern industrialists used the Pine Forest as a base from which to scout local properties to purchase as shooting preserves. Several Charlestonians made fortunes selling the tax-burdened properties of their deceased relatives. There were rooms at the Pine Forest where such hushed negotiations could occur.

The Pine Forest had competition, however. Not far away was the Squirrel Inn and Wisteria Inn. The Carolina Inn was known for understated elegance. Efram Zimbalist, the renown violinist, brought his family yearly, so did Elizabeth Arden. Guests could fox hunt, fish for black bass, shoot dove or deer, or relax at gaming tables with interesting guests.

What brought all of this grand entertainment to a close? The automobile, the Great Depression, and the new resorts of south Georgia and north Florida killed it. But nose around old town Summerville, you will find elegance and charm in abundance!

Mount Pleasant As It Was in the 1940s

A friend of this column who desires no mention provides us with fond memories of what a small town Mount Pleasant was in the 1930s and '40s. Before there was a Johnnie Dodds Freeway, and before metropolis-sized subdivisions ringed Georgetown Highway, there was a grey asphalt two-lane road that sloped from the toll bridge that we called Grace. Many true Charlestonians travelled the bridge to summer in Mount Pleasant where the breeze was cool and the living was easy.

With no by-pass, Georgetown Highway wound around in two-lane fashion and was named Coleman Boulevard in the 1960s. The scenic ride from the bridge to Shem Creek resembled a page from Field and Stream magazine more than the side-by-side strip malls that compete for attention today.

A tomato-packing shed occupied the spot on Shem Creek where the bank currently is. The tomato packers discarded the green tomatoes and tossed them by the dozens into the marsh. As the tide rose, those tomatoes floated up along the sandy beach that fronted the Old Village. Villagers referred to the hard-packed beach as Bay Street, just as their elders had done. Another landmark was Hay's wharf that jutted out into the harbor between Venning and Hibben Streets.

Shem Creek was home to just four shrimp boats then. Captain Magwood's seafood processing shed was the only semblance of the coming food and beverage industry. No large shrimp boats existed on Shem Creek prior to 1940.

Sixty-five years ago Pitt Street was a bustling town-center. Wacker's Drug Store was a popular meeting place on Pitt Street. After catching up with friends at Wacker's, you'd stroll across Pitt Street to Coleman's Hardware. Coleman's survived into the 1980. It might take him 30 minutes to find the item, but Mr. Coleman always had what you went there for.

King's Store was the imposing two-story frame structure now occupied by an elegant inn and restaurant. And when Mount Pleasant Academy relocated, the village post office moved into its vacated site. There's a fitness center on the spot today, but in the 1940s villagers made two stops a day there to check their mail boxes. There was no door-to-door delivery until the 1950s.

Wacker's Drug Store was the original pharmacy on Pitt Street. It had booths and a soda fountain, but it was a dark place inside and half the size of today's Pitt Street Pharmacy. Then as now, the drug store was a popular hangout for the youngsters. Wacker's back door opened to Doctor Frampton's back gate, and many was the time that the good doctor reached over the back gate to deliver a prescription for a patient he'd just treated.

The business district of the Village continued much farther down Pitt in the 1920s. The northwest corner of Pitt and King Streets had a wonderful German bakery that filled the neighborhood with the smell of fresh bread. That street corner was known as station number 4 on the trolley route running between the

Isle of Palms and Mount Pleasant. Patjen's store was around the corner on Church Street.

A sound we don't hear around the village anymore is the old dinner bell of bygone years. The brass bell from the Mabel, an old farm produce boat, was mounted on the porch of one family and its melodious peeling summoned the children home to dinner more quickly than any cell phone could in our time.

Each home had its own well, some went quite deep to avoid the briny taste. The town supplied water by 1935. Town water meant that there could be upstairs bathrooms, for wells seldom could produce enough water pressure to put water on the second floor.

Another noticeable difference in the way that people lived sixty-five years ago is that there were several generations cohabiting in almost every house. Families usually had one or two elderly family members residing with them. A day nurse to sit with someone cost around seven dollars weekly back then. Retirement complexes would have been considered science-fiction here in the 1940s!

Walking on up Pitt Street, the folks of the '40s knew the Darby Building as the Baptist Church. Quite a few village romances sealed their nuptials in the former Berkeley county court house turned church. Over on Whilden Street, the Saint Andrew's Episcopal Church served as a chapel-of-ease, or convenience, for Christ Church on the Georgetown Road. Pew rent went out of fashion around the year 1910.

One wealthy family living in Mount Pleasant in the 1940s, was the Osgoods, of northern industrial fame. Their mansion on the harbor in some ways resembled a Mediterranean villa. Mrs. Osgood named her home Alhambra and the lush garden surrounding it, Pierates Cruze.

Upon entering the Osgood house, one couldn't help but notice a medieval knight's suit of armor gleaming in the front hall. The Osgoods held socials and dances for the soldiers manning Fort Moultrie and invited the young ladies of the neighborhood. Mrs. Osgood often reclined in her hammock near the harbor and listened to opera on the radio. Today, the home is long-gone and only a few reminders of the villa's fabulous garden bear testimony to the elegance that once was.

Simmon's Street marked the boundary between the town and the country, for beyond that point were farm fields. Creekside subdivision was a large farming area. Mount Pleasant was known, too, for having some of the largest pecan groves in the country.

The area's black community enjoyed a wonderful pavilion called Riverside Park at Remley's Point, and weekend dances were big events in the 1940s. In the winter of 1939 - 1940, Big Bands such as Cab Calloway and Duke Ellington performed there. The white community would go to listen and watch the dancing.

The town got along fine with a volunteer fire department with Jim Frampton as the volunteer chief. Walking the sandy beach in front of the oak-shrouded antebellum homes was a lazy summer day's past-time. Soft-shelled crabs were there for the taking, and a neighbor could be seen casting a shrimp net at low tide. My friend assures us that nowhere could have been pleasanter than this town was in the 1940s.

Charleston's Historic Battery Dates To War of 1812

No landmark signifies our city to visitors more so than does the oleander-lined sea wall and artillery park which we call The Battery. For 195 years this seawall-fortress has been a promenade for lovers, a must-see for tourists, and a last ditch of defense from invaders of every stripe and hue. So long has the seven

acres of high ground been the focus of downtown that most of us have lost sight
of the park's origins. Fortunately for us 21st century Carolinians, the city fathers
recorded the history of The Battery in the Charleston City Directory of 1880.

The early settlers called it White Point for the mounds of oyster shells that
the natives discarded there. The desolate place was a wash and beyond the pale of
the early settlement in the 1680s. Cut by tidal creeks and littered with refuse, the
mud bank served as Charleston's Tyburn with a gallows standing forlorn, a
chilling warning to pirates.

Our battery didn't play much of a role in the revolution. The Granville
Bastion, a patriot fort, was a hundred yards north. Only a few homes had been
built along an oyster shell lane they called South Bay. Palmetto logs walled in by
planks, the same idea they'd used at Fort Moultrie, formed the early seawall
beginning at the Granville Bastion and continuing southward.

With increasing numbers of Charleston sailors being seized by the British
navy on the high seas in 1811 and with John C. Calhoun as one of the "war
hawks" in Congress, Charleston prepared for another war with Britain. An
embankment was constructed here and armed with the heaviest guns ever before
seen in the city. Eventually the term "city battery" was shortened to "the battery."
And when the War of 1812 ended three years later with no action in our area, the
guns disappeared, but the name forever stuck with the seven-acre promontory.

William Crafts supervised the construction of the second sea wall built of
stone ballast carried over by English trading ships. This wall was securely in
place by the hurricane season of 1820.

Shortly after the dismantling of the big guns of 1812, three wealthy
Charlestonians, Ravenel, Holmes, and Siegling purchased land belonging to the
former sites of Forts Broughton (pronounced with an "out" sound) and Mechanic.
The gun embrasures were leveled and magnificent harbor front houses were
constructed. They then asked that Fort Street, a wagon path for supplying the
several gun batteries, be widened and renamed South Bay. Of course, it's South

Battery today.

South Bay homeowner James G. Holmes was the first to make a motion to the city fathers that the old gun park be made into a beautified public place. This was in the early 1830s. Too bad for them, though, as the early expenditure of money and effort was blown away in the hurricane of 1854. The east sea wall was completely washed away, and the rebuilding of it is the edifice we see today, completed sometime in 1856.

This new half-mile of promenade became the most celebrated vista of any antebellum American city. Hoop skirts, parasols, carriages, and gentlemen in top hats and tails grace hundreds of engravings made in the late 1850s. Charleston then was the sultry, romantic mecca for fiercely independent landholding elites.

The White Point park as we know it came into being on a piecemeal basis as the city acquired parcels of real estate in various transactions. Major Miles and city alderman Gourdin acquired in 1848 the Moreland property and cottage just south of South Bay Street and west of King Street all the way to the Ashley River. Many locals saw this quiet transfer as the key bargain in the whole matter. The entire tip of the peninsula, all fifteen acres, that the first settlers called White Point now was in city possession.

But the guns of April 1861 replaced the tranquility of parasols and top hats in the park as the city fathers sold half of the fifteen acres to raise money for turning the other half into gun embrasures twenty feet high. From here the big guns poured explosives into a doomed Fort Sumter. From White Point to Cummings Point the Union broke apart amidst a thunderstorm and a cannonade that April day.

Pictures as late as the 1870s reveal that the debris of the Confederate era had not been fully cleared away. But the earthen gun embrasures were leveled and the streets cleared. Young oaks symbolized peace and strength and were the gifts of William Gregg and William Ravenel, nearby residents. The dilapidated old bathing house was pulled down in 1880, thereby giving a clear view of the harbor. It stood in front of the present Fort Sumter House.

A victory for White Point was the prevention of a pavilion here, as these amusement parks were becoming the rage at the turn of the century. Dignified Charlestonians were not about to let that happen, but there were the progressive newcomers who saw a pavilion as the modern thing to do. A fountain was put squarely where an arcade had been debated. And city ordinance forbade any political oratory and prohibited military parades here. The Fort Moultrie monument was unveiled in 1876 as our centennial event, and three years later, the William Gilmore Simms bust was installed.

To our everlasting gratitude, the city fathers rejected the temptation to join the popular municipal trends and to maintain the old city charm that countless generations of Charlestonians have drawn inspiration from.

Maybe you got engaged there, or perhaps a pigeon or seagull visited your picnic, but you never forget your visits to Charleston's famed waterfront battery and its White Point Gardens, and a stroll around Colonial Lake is the most solace one can have in a suburban setting anywhere.

The Independent Republic of Horry

Swamps so thick with briers that a crow couldn't fly over it because his shadow would get entangled in the underbrush. That was the wisecrack of one wag describing Horry County in the 1800s. Most Charlestonians know little of Horry save for the Grand Strand and Murrell's Inlet. Horry's history is different from any other part of South Carolina, unique in its own accent, its lifestyle, and its history.

As early as 1521 Spanish dons were regaled with tales of a mysterious land its natives called Chicora. The adventurer d'Allyon enticed an enterprising captive they called Francisco Chicora to sail back to Spain with them in 1521. This sly Indian may be responsible for many Spanish explorers coming to our coast. He spun fabulous tales of wigwam kingdoms and mounds of pearls existing in Chicora's land.

Rugged individualists seeking nothing more than to be left alone by cantankerous bishops and kings came to settle in the impenetrable wilderness that separated the settlements on the Cape Fear from those of the Waccamaw.

Isaac Marion, a relative of the Swamp Fox, dwelled in a framed cabin named Boundary House very near the North Carolina - South Carolina border, not far from the ocean surf. It was here that the rider bearing news of the Lexington - Concord battles stopped to rest in 1776. Isaac gave him a fresh mount, food, and spirits to continue his mission to Charleston.

Named for Francis Marion's fearless subaltern and fellow Huguenot, Peter Horry, the county is one of the first wave of new counties created after the Revolution. Stammering Peter Horry amused his comrades in battle with his inability to enunciate either curse or command clearly, but he never erred in the crushing blow of his Hanger sword. Horry and Marion used the difficult terrain of this area as swampy hideaways to regroup.

Fast-forward to 1985 when Conway-native-turned- Bowdoin-College-English-professor, Franklin Burroughs, made his epic week-long float down the Waccamaw River from its headwaters in North Carolina to its mouth at Winyah Bay. Burroughs' delightful story of his solo-canoe journey entitled "Horry and the Waccamaw" repopularizes the legends of this forgotten, but historic backwater. Burroughs and historians Catherine Lewis and Charles Joyner have elevated the stories of Horry County to the deserving status that it rightfully holds.

The first established settlement in this tanglewood and bog of old Chicora is the Little River community just a short distance from the North Carolina line.

In an effort to buffer Georgetown from marauding Indians, the royal government gave out land grants of fifty acres for every person who'd brave the harsh conditions. More likely, these were single men, trappers and free-spirits. Some may have been on the run from the authorities. Unlike other settlements in South Carolina, these 18th century rustics came down from eastern North Carolina rather than up from Charleston. Hence, the distinct twang of the Horry accent is altogether different from other intonations.

Lore has it that the Little River folks were fiercely independent and were no respecters of distant authority. They made their own entertainment and they made their own rules. The justice of the peace needed to be a burly man fast with his fists. One account in Catherine Lewis' "History of Horry County" tells of an 18th century Justice of the Peace and an ornery, drunken cuss getting into a brawl near a tavern. The no-holds barred fight, complete with combatants gouging, biting, and kicking, took a time-out for lunch and libations before resuming with a death blow to the J.P.'s antagonist by mid-afternoon.

No county delights more in its backwoods' repute than does Horry. Place names divulge an earthiness as well as a sense of humor among the earliest citizens. Crossroads with colorful names such as Hardshell, Hell's Neck, and Free Will contrast with communities named as Shoo Fly, Playcard, and Drinking Gully. Pole Cat Bay is just upstream from Wolf Pit Bay and Buzzard's Bay. No trace of old world pretentiousness can be found here.

The earliest map shows a village called Kingston situated on a bend of the Waccamaw River about 25 miles inland. Alexander Skene and Chief Justice Robert White laid out this river-front town prior to 1735 in an effort to serve the timber and pine pitch trade with Britain. The earliest names mentioned in settler deeds, names such as Alford, Bellamy, Causey, Dawson, Grainger, Sarvis, and Vereen still survive on land deeds today.

Kingston was centered around a knob hill called Bear Bluff. Legend has it that a settler killed a bear and barbecued him right on the spot. The Reverend

George Whitefield made a sweep through this unchurched land and spent New Year's Eve there in 1740.

Whitefield recalls much ribald bantering between the men and women, and the very suggestion that any be baptized brought laughter. Finally one woman brought her infant to Whitefield for baptism, more to shut him up than to dedicate her child to the Lord. By the time Whitefield withdrew to his room, the tavern was full of revelers and dancing continued till the wee hours. The evangelist shook the dust from his shoes as he left Kingston.

In 1785 a prominent Charlestonian named Robert Conway moved up to the Waccamaw region and settled in Kingston. Conway became one of the largest landowners in the area and soon was the representative of Horry in the new General Assembly in Charleston. Within his lifetime the town of Kingston was renamed Conway.

In 1860, Horry citizens opposed secession from the Union. Though most owned no slaves, they realized that the coming war was about states rights. When the war commenced, Horry boys enlisted *en masse* in the 10th South Carolina Volunteers, and a large percentage of them lie buried in the red clay of Chicamauga.

Today, the fiercely independent Horry folks keep their reputation for festivity and old-time ways alive with the Gallivant's Ferry Democratic stump meeting. Democratic party candidates who want their vote must first come have a plate of chicken bog and then belt forth a fiery speech from the porch of Holliday's Store. Horry County still adds flavor to South Carolina history with its defiant, and occasionally irreverent, behavior.

Louisa Susannah Wells Says Good Riddance To Charleston

Strange as it seems today, there was a time when Charleston was a hostile place for conservatives. When loyalty to the crown and tithe to the bishop defined conservative belief, those faithful monarchists who refused to buckle to the new republican ways were tarred and feathered by Whig mobs. Some of the finest folks in Charleston were forced to flee. The entire congregation of the Scots Presbyterian Church left, including one Tory belle, Louisa Susannah Wells, who kept a journal of this dismal time.

Louisa Susannah Wells, daughter of prominent Charleston physician, John Wells, and granddaughter of noted bookseller, Robert Wells, was one amongst several hundred affluent, literary-minded Charleston loyalists who succumbed to taunts and threats.

The list of exiles in 1778 reads like a who's who of Charleston. Surgeons recognized by the Royal College of Physicians, lawyers trained at Oxford and the Temple Bar, booksellers representing London and Edinburgh publishers, ministers with connections to Canterbury; the list bears mute testimony to bitter civil war that seared families asunder during our revolutionary struggle.

Louisa Susannah Wells was a frolicsome teenage girl, daughter of Charleston's most respected surgeon. Grandfather Robert Wells owned a book store on Tradd Street, and the Wells literary circle reached to Philadelphia, London, and Edinburgh.

Carolina Day, June 28, 1776, that day so odious to her and her family, was the beginning of her misfortune and the onset of her bitterness toward Charlestonians. That was the day local traitors fired on the British fleet sent by King George to uphold royal authority. Louisa could never forgive her family's former friends. She and her Scots Presbyterian church friends chose to abandon

Charleston forever.

The Wells slipped out of Charleston one or two at a time over a three-year period. This cultured family that had corresponded with Hume, Burke, and Wilkes, and Franklin, Rush, and Garden severed all connections with this proud, but rebellious city that had been their home for generations.

Along with Uncle Robert Rowland, cousin Charles Elliot, and flirtatious Miss Frances Thorney, Louisa sought passage on the brigantine, Providence, formerly the L'Esperance. They stayed in town with the Roupelles until winds and tides were favorable to board the Providence, then lying off Fort Johnson. Ship master, Richard Stevens, was known by Tories as a discreet captain capable of eluding French, American, and British privateers who seized anything afloat as prize money.

Afraid of employing a harbor pilot, Stevens arranged for a free Negro sailor to navigate the tricky passage across Charleston bar. Stevens' thinking was that this man would be less suspicious of his ship which reported Rotterdam as her destination. Louisia mentions that Charleston pilots deliberately steered suspected Tory ships into dangerous shoal water to wreck them. For this reason Captain Stevens picked his pilot from among knowledgeable free blacks on the waterfront and slipped him a hundred Congress dollars to expedite Providence across Charleston bar.

Poor Louisa Wells nearly fell out of the skiff ferrying her out to the Providence. Upon climbing up the ladder to board the ship she dropped her shoe in the water and watched as the ribboned slipper sank from view. But gallant Captain Stevens jumped overboard and rescued it in a wet show of chivalry!

The Providence was becalmed for two days; part of that time they anchored off Fort Moultrie. Louisa looked out on the decaying, spongy palmetto logs that were pocked with rusting iron cannon balls. She saw the blue liberty flag with the crescent. It was a grim reminder that the mightiest empire on earth had been rebuked by a small band of determined rebels. As her ship bobbed helplessly offshore, she began to suspect that they'd been hoodwinked by their pilot whose name was Bluff. Perhaps even he had led them upon treacherous sandbars.

On the afternoon of July 1, 1778, the breeze filled their sails and Providence heeled on a larboard tack and all gave a hearty Hurrah to King George, and damnation to Congress. With that denunciation, Captain Stevens hurled a ballast stone into the sea. "When that rises, I return." All bid good riddance to Charleston!

With a stiff southwesterly, the Providence made 150 leagues in 72 hours. Stevens debated with his eleven passengers about hoisting Irish colors to avoid capture. The green flag with bell and harp was deemed less safe than the Thirteen Stripe they all detested. If captured by American privateers, their biggest worry was being hauled into Boston or Philadelphia, as these Whig ports were known to treat American tories the harshest.

Pitching seas caused cabin furniture to become flying missiles that caused injury to Louisa's shipmates. Safety lay in keeping to one's curtained bunk day and night. When calmer seas permitted, the eleven passengers entertained each other with bizarre tales. Louisa's tale took the prize for the macabre. Right before she sailed from Charleston, a gravedigger had accidentally cracked into a coffin of an adjoining grave in one of Charleston's downtown churches. To the digger's horror, the body of the young man, George Woodrup, had turned sideways and placed his head under his hands, as if asleep. The man had been buried alive!

The good ship Providence did not make it safely to Rotterdam, for the odds of one hostile force, or another taking them was too great. Imagine their chagrin when they were hauled over by a privateer flying the colors of their beloved sovereign, George III. The captain of the HMS Rose wouldn't believe their story that they were loyalists fleeing American persecution.

Miss Wells and her party were escorted into New York harbor as a British prize. New York was then under British General Cornwallis' authority. She remarked at what a poor presentation New York made from the sea as compared to Charleston's mile long row of three-storied dwellings on Bay Street.

Fortune began to smile again on Louisa and her companions once the Admiralty Courts heard their claim. In two months she was on board another ship traveling in convoy to Portsmouth. This time the Sexton of the Scots Presbyterian Church of charleston was her dining partner, as were other members of the Charleston church who refused to breach their loyalty to royal authority. Louisa married a newspaper publisher and moved to Jamaica, one of many noble citizens driven from this city for their conservative political beliefs.

Swedish Feminist Frederika Bremer Comments on Charleston

Frederika Bremer wasn't the pretty face that Gloria Steinem was in her prime, nor was she as strident as Betty Freidan in The Feminine Mystique. But she championed the European notion of gender equality. But in 1850, when American minds were occupied with manifest destiny, free-soil, or slave state annexation, the notion of women's suffrage was a half-century away. Still, the Swedish writer, Frederika Bremer, had to overcome the strong objections of her northern hosts to extend her American tour south of the Mason-Dixon.

That Bremer came to Charleston in spite of the remonstrations of New England literary notables such as Channing, Emerson, Longfellow, Lowell, Alcott, and Whittier is testimony to her independent mind. That Frederika enjoyed Charleston and its people above all stops on her American tour bears evidence to our ancestors' cordiality to contrary viewpoints.

Frederika Bremer was a Swedish novelist whose publishing success brought her to the attention of the fiery liberal English writer, Harriet Martineau. Martineau was one of the torchbearers of feminism and abolition, as well as a collaborator with the political economist, John Stuart Mill. Martineau cultivated friendships with such diverse thinkers as Charles Darwin, Thomas Carlyle, and Charlotte Bronte. Martineau had visited Caroline Gilman at her Charleston residence, and Martineau recommended that Bremer add Charleston to her proposed American tour.

Arriving in New York in 1850 with letter of introduction, Bremer soon had entree to the flower of New England's literary circle. From New York, Bremer traveled to Boston and met James Russell Lowell. Lowell's wife was kin to Caroline Gilman in Charleston.

Lowell was one of the founders and early editors of Atlantic Monthly magazine as well as of the prestigious North American Review. Gilman periodically sent some of her essays, many dealing with the emerging genre of juvenile literature, to Lowell for publication. Word of Bremer's fascination with our new republic spread from Boston to Charleston's "Brahmins" through Caroline Gilman, whose drawing room at 11 Orange Street was a gathering place of local bookish women.

Two of Gilman's Charleston intimates were Mrs. John Holbrook, wife of the nationally noted medical professor, and Mrs. William Howland, wife of a prominent local businessman.

Gilman, Holbrook, and Howland were determined that this visiting literary savant would visit Charleston. They sought to dispel the northern notion that all southerners were fire-eaters and shallow of intellect. Overcoming the negative influence of the likes of Emerson, Alcott, and Channing was no easy matter, but Mrs. Howlands' earnest solicitations prevailed.

Bremer boarded a steamer in New York and endured a week-long, storm-tossed voyage to Charleston, arriving at City Wharf on March 28, 1850. She thought Charleston looked so very European, much more so than did Boston or New York. Instead of proceeding straightway to the Howland's stately home on Lynch Street, later renamed Ashley Avenue, Frederika checked herself into a small hotel and acclimated herself to the city and its strange slave culture.

Bremer's diary reveals an almost instant attraction to the scents of orange blossoms and the salt air. But she was repulsed by the turkey buzzards who inhabited the Market Street area so thickly that one had to walk around them. Vultures also perched on rooftops and gazed expectantly down upon the venders.

The Africans Frederika encountered were colorfully dressed, especially the women, each with a bright bandanna wrapped artfully around their head. Their spoken language was unintelligible to her, but she found them jubilant, not sullen as she'd anticipated.

Bremer called upon Mrs. Howland for tea to ascertain if staying at her home would be an agreeable affair. She was still ill at ease around these southerners who so casually accepted slavery as a fact of life.

The coterie of ladies awaiting Frederika at the Howland mansion quickly quieted her apprehension that southern women were vain and idle adornments to their outspoken husbands. The wisteria adorned piazza that opened upon an enchanted walled garden was backdrop to Bremer's first taste of the famed southern hospitality she came to admire. It took her less than an hour to decide to accept the Howland offer of accommodation.

Immediately Bremer picked up on nuances of old-south lifestyle. In the Howland home the white children and the slave children ate in separate rooms, but played arm in arm. Nowhere in Bremer's notes does it appear that she saw the seamier side of slavery, the notorious "sugar house" on the east side where unruly slaves were beaten into submission, or the shackles that bound recaptured runaways.

Instead, she saw the paradise side of Charleston. Charleston gardens then boasted banana trees as decoration. Frederika said the taste of this fruit was more like biting into a bar of soap than the succulent delicacy fancied by these semitropical denizens.

Evenings on the lamp-lit piazza spent in the company of friends were the pleasantest of times in Frederika's American tour. The African boatmen rowing on the Ashley River singing as they rowed made for one of her happiest memories here.

A week or so into her visit, Frederika accepted an invitation to visit the country seat of Joel Poinsett north of Georgetown on the Little Peedee River. The Howlands advised Frederika to take a steamer rather than venture over the rough roads.

Poinsett and his lady lived in a simple country home they named Casa Blanca after their residence as Minister to Mexico. Frederika was met by her charming host and taken by buggy over flat pine lands to the river estate where they were the only white folks for miles in any direction. She was amazed that the Poinsetts had no locks on their doors and dwelled in complete harmony within this rigid caste system of the deep south.

Joel Poinsett confided to Frederika that he saw no future in slavery. He reminded Bremer of a French gentilhomme, a man with the refinement of a Frenchman and the truthful candor of an American.

Upon return to Charleston, Frederika enjoyed waltzes and quadrilles, teas and evening entertainment's on the piazza. Her visit here made lasting friendships. She embarked upon a steamer for Havana and then made her way back to New York before voyaging home to Sweden. Her opinion of Charleston was exactly opposite from what Alcott, Emerson, and Whittier had led her to expect.

Jazz Age Screenwriter Mildred Cram Fancied Charleston

Maybe Mildred Cram was the inspiration for Nicole Diver, the sultry siren in Fitzgerald's Tender Is The Night, maybe she wasn't. The fictional Nicole emanated from the whiskey-fogged mind of F. Scott Fitzgerald as he recounted some rollicking house-party he'd been on at the Hamptons. Mildred Cram, a New York party-girl turned Hollywood screenwriter, was known to be on everyone's short list for guaranteed social sizzle. That such a cosmopolitan charmer would find our southern city fascinating in 1916 is a testament to Charleston's romantic appeal.

Any old movie buff might remember her name from the credits. In the 1930s and '40s she was a hot commodity in Hollywood, working as a screenwriter alongside Fitzgerald, Faulkner, Huxley, Wodehouse, and numerous others cashing in on the celluloid sensation. She was one of director Irving Thalman's script "hacks" specializing in dreamy dialogue for pampered stage hams like Gregory Peck and Joan Crawford. Thalberg had such a genius for making money that Fitzgerald made him the infamous character Monroe Stahr in The Last Tycoon. Thalman gave Cram her big break as a serious writer. But her first book was a travel story that features Charleston.

Mildred Cram was a Barnard College girl, and all that that implies. When a girl attends one of the colleges known as "the seven sisters," Radcliffe, Mount Holyoke, Smith, Vasser, Bryn Mawr, then it's a given that she'll be a classmate of future novelists, choreographers, and magazine editors, not to mention the darlings of the stage and opera.

How'd a brainy New York socialite discover our coastal southern city? Henry Grady is partly responsible. He's the Atlanta magnate who championed the "New South" image with his advertisements in national newspapers. When Grady died, *The Atlanta Constitution* kept up the mantra. "Keep your eye on the South" ran the legend across full page ads that showed high rise hotels, banks, and business towers emerging from the cities that Sherman had laid waste.

Southern Railway offered a package of seaport towns, hotel accommodation, and Pullman car comfort from Baltimore to Miami and New Orleans in 1916. Mildred Cram and her brother Allan, also a sport, decided on a whim to explore their forgotten southern roots.

Allan Cram dabbled in water colors enough to show his work in fashionable shows in places such as Concord, Newport, and Saratoga. He brought along his easel and palette, while his published sister packed her journal in her expensive matching luggage.

Bidding goodbye to friends at Penn Station, Mildred and Allan may as well have been departing for China rather than Charleston. The clickety-clack of the rails lulled Mildred Cram into a romantic expectation of what awaited her in the faraway land of Spanish moss, live oaks, and decaying mansions.

Though America had not yet entered the war in Europe, war talk was on the minds of everyone, everyone that is, but this harbinger of the flapper age, Mildred Cram. Reading her account of the southern tour leaves us with the feeling that Mildred is sipping sloe gin in the club car staring passively as the shanties of tenant farmers fade into the tobacco fields.

Yet there's something compelling in Mildred Cram's narrative, Old Seaport Towns of The South (Dodd, Mead, & Co., 1917). It's history the way Zelda Fitzgerald would have told it!

Rolling into Wilmington, Mildred and Allan are as giddy as teens on spring break. He, with sketch pad and she with note pad, track through this river town in search of the famed Spanish moss that's never before seen in her world travels. "I had expected to see Spanish moss swinging like witches hair from the branches, but there was none," Mildrid pines.

Wilmington was in a funk economically as its fertilizer imports from

Germany were interrupted by the Great War. In disappointment they trudged back to the Orton Hotel and read up on how the white man had caused the extinction practically of all the Catawba nation.

Disappointed with their two day sojourn in Wilmington, these world-savvy siblings board the train for the much-awaited journey to the capital of the Old South, Charleston. "The country between Wilmington and Charleston was inconceivably desolate and forlorn . . . an endless procession of dried tobacco fields, withered rows of shabby cotton, dirty villages, mud, swamps, and land."

If Wilmington disappointed, Charleston delighted our affluent visitors from the Big Apple. They rolled into the train station on John Street sometime after dark and were met by a carriage with a dark-skinned driver. It was the romantic entry that Scarlet O'Hara would have envied. Devoid of the neon street signs that tarted up New York, nothing but blue moonlight penetrated the palmetto fronds to dance on cobbled streets.

Narrow streets cloaked with antiquity one doesn't see in New York, but the city of Sienna was the way Mildred felt about Charleston. We're an ecumenical city from the beginning she notes, and that has given us an open-mindedness that eluded New England.

The tangy salt air pervaded her Charleston Hotel rooms on Meeting Street. She stayed down a hall from where Thackery had stayed when he was in town four decades previously. West Indian recipes and West Indian architecture made the turtle soup and Madeira wine linger in the minds of all who came here.

At St. Michael's she had a private tour by the church sextant. Mildred was hypnotized by his low-country accent and by the fact that the present organist was the sixth-generation descendant of the man who originally installed it. But Mildred Cram was astonished to see the sextant stand with his back blocking the door until she made a contribution to the building's upkeep.

The forlorn statue of William Pitt in the center of Broad and Meeting Streets already had been the object of automobile indiscretions, and the John

Rutledge house was looking stately, but in need of a facelift. She suspects that the elegance of old Charleston is concealed from the visitor's eye.

Cram paid homage to our city in a zany way that only the jazz age would foster, but her sojourns in Savannah, Jacksonville, Miami, Mobile, and New Orleans blur their adjectives when compared to our genteel city. Mildred Cram made it to Hollywood and wrote numerous novels, some becoming movies, such as "Forever" starring Gregory Peck. She knew Fitzgerald in his Hollywood years, and she knew Faulkner and Wodehouse well. To think that she knew our town and savored it's southern flavor above the rest of the seaports is a mark of her superior tastes.

South Carolinian J. Marion Sims Father of Obstetrical Medicine

Everywhere Marion Sims went, cities and institutions wanted to become a part of his legacy. After all, he was the most influential medical doctor of the Victorian Age. Consultant to Queen Victoria and Napoleon III's Empress Eugenie, attending physician to Alexandra, Consort of Czar Nicholas II, there has never been a doctor so sought after by celebrities as was James Marion Sims of Heath Springs, South Carolina.

With a reputation spanning two continents, we would assume that the good doctor likely earned diplomas from elite universities that prepared him to be a medical pioneer. In Sims' case, nothing could be farther from the truth. Sims didn't grow up in poverty, but he was born in a log cabin in a part of the state that was considered buckskin Scots-Irish frontier in 1813.

The man who has a statue honoring him in Central Park, a couple of medical instruments named for him, and at least two major hospitals founded by him spent his youth working in his father's tavern.

Sims' cabin was just three miles from Hanging Rock battlefield, one of the bloodiest encounters fought by Thomas Sumter, the Gamecock. Close by was the home of James Ingram, the farmer who hosted President Washington on an overnight visit during his Grand Tour of the South in 1791.

Marion Sims attended South Carolina College from 1829 till 1832. Carolina had fewer than one hundred students at the time, and students were known for their rebellions against authority. It's doubtful that he distinguished himself in earning his degree.

The announcement that he planned to become a doctor nearly broke Sims' father's heart. "To think that my son should be going around from house to house through this country, with a box of pills in one hand and a squirt in the other, to ameliorate human suffering, is a thought I never supposed I should have to contemplate."

A respected surgeon and friend of the family in nearby Lancaster was Churchill Jones, and young Sims went to observe   that doctor in hopes of becoming a medical practitioner himself. But Doctor Jones had taken to whiskey, and Sims got the impression that about all Jones was doing was passing out laudanum. He was disturbed at an apparent lack of interest in diagnosis, or effective treatment of the chronic diseases in the area. Before two years of this loose apprenticeship passed, Marion Sims came to Charleston to enroll in the newly established medical college.

In November, 1833, Sims arrived in Charleston, and he recorded his thoughts years later in his autobiography, "I was afraid to be a man; I was afraid to assume its responsibilities and thought that I did not have sense enough to go out into the rough world, making a living as other men had to do."

The way he tells it, Sims flunked out of medical school here. He says he was poorly prepared for the rigorous study required. He lasted just a semester.

Someone suggested that he try his luck in Philadelphia at the Jefferson College of Medicine.

Jefferson Medical School was not even ten years old and had an indigent care infirmary as a practical learning center for the students. One of Philadelphia's leading physicians, Doctor George McClellan, was the head of faculty. Under McClellan tutelage, Sims' fascination with surgery took flight. The instructional approach in Philadelphia was hands-on, whereas Charleston was more lecture-oriented.

In two years Marion Sims departed Philadelphia with all the formal medical training that he was to acquire. John Sims, father of Marion, was a strong influence in this 22-year-old doctor returning to Lancaster. A converted store on main street became Sims' surgery. But, as legend has it, Doctor Sims' first two patients quickly succumbed to their illnesses, and the community turned against him.

There may be more to the story of Sims leaving Lancaster than loss of confidence in his medical ability. He'd had picked up some libertine ideas while in Philadelphia. Sims had a common-law wife, a child out of wedlock, and some of his religious thinking didn't square with the locals. The doctor migrated westward as did so many Carolinians of that day.

From 1835 to 1853, Marion Sims practiced general medicine in the outskirts of Montgomery. One of his first patients was a poor pregnant woman who'd developed severe complications from falling off a horse. Sims alleviated her distress with some unorthodox measures. Intrigued with female ailments that were thought untreatable, Sims developed new instruments fashioned from kitchenware and practiced on suffering slave women.

Three slave women in particular, Anarcha, Lucy, and Betsy endured dozens of indelicate examinations and experiments, but each received relief from distress. Critics today accuse him of not using anesthesia on the slave women, but Sims says anesthesia was not readily available, and that he gave the women laudanum.

He pioneered forceps for delivery with one of the many children he sired with his common-law wife. He also developed silver sutures in female surgery.

Sims left Alabama in 1853 for New York and became one of the leading surgeons there. He argued with the chief surgeons about technique, so he formed his own hospital specializing just in women's' medical issues. Women's Hospital of New York secured Sims' reputation.

In 1862, Marion Sims went abroad in the midst of the Civil War, perhaps to avoid southern criticism.

In Paris he became attending physician to Napoleon III's beloved Eugenie. Sims remained in Europe and lectured at the finest medical schools, including the Universities of Leyden, Oxford, Cambridge, Trinity, and Edinburgh. There the great doctors, including Pasteur, crowded around him and took note of his new methods and cures. He became an instant celebrity wherever he went despite his cockiness and self-promotion.

In December of 1871, Sims was caught up in the outbreak of the Franco-Prussian War, and he volunteered for duty as a surgeon in the terrible battle at Sedan where Napoleon III was captured.

Returning to New York, Sims founded another hospital that took only cancer patients, the first of its kind. That hospital has evolved into Sloan-Kettering Treatment Center. He was president of the AMA and founded the American Gynaecoligal Society. He's buried in New York and his son Harry M. Sims continued the medical tradition begun by his father.

Browsing Through Charleston's First Newspapers of 275 Years Ago

You'd think that someone would have called our attention to the fact that this is the 275th anniversary of newspapers in Charleston. Of course, Boston, New York, and Philadelphia predate us in this highbrow endeavor, but few other cities in North America can lay an earlier claim to such criterion of the cultured life. Be thankful for microfilm though, for there's just one complete set of the earliest periodical, the South Carolina Gazette. Dateline Charles Towne, January 8, 1732, is volume one, issue one.

How did Charleston function as a bustling colonial seaport for 62 years without a paper, one ponders. There was a town crier who hailed the time and important news from the steps of the Exchange. You could pay a boy a farthing to run down to Broad Street and bring back the latest news. Surely there were periodic broadsheets announcing imported merchandise, slave auctions, or warnings of spreading epidemics, but trying to find reference of such notices is illusive.

Our earliest ancestors pored over months old newspapers brought in on trading vessels. These rag papers ended up in coffee houses and taverns such as the one still standing on the corner of Exchange and East Bay Streets.

It was Thomas Whitmarsh who first published a periodic, paper here. He announced in the winter of 1731 that it was his intention to do so, and his first paper was on the street January 8, 1732, with all the latest news from around the colonies and around the world. The establishment of the South Carolina Gazette remains one of the finest moments of our cultural history. Twenty months later, poor Thomas succumbed to one of the many diseases, probably yellow fever, that rampaged the early colony. He'd just put out edition number 86. Whitmarsh's bones rest in the church yard of St. Philip's.

Six months went by with no newspaper, and since the early paper had considerable gossip and innuendo, it's evident that such organ was sincerely missed. Louis Timothee, a recent Huguenot immigrant, stepped forward to assume the challenge.

Soon Louis anglicized his name to Lewis Timothy, and South carolina's first newspaper dynasty was established.

Thomas Whitmarsh's first newspaper column in January, 1732, established his purpose for the venture and identified his investment partners, Thomas Powell, Edward Hughes, and Peter Timothy. The paper's office was listed as lower Church Street. Of note is the statement that the paper intended to be loyal to the crown and the church. Opinions and editorials were penned under pseudonyms such as Agricola, Brutus, cicero, etc., but were thinly veiled disguises for Timothy and his faction.

The very first news article published in this region 275 years ago was a piece about the Ukraine and depredations made by Russians against the Turks. Surely no one in Charles Towne could have cared a fig about the Turks or the Russians, but it must have been seen as a triumph to possess intelligence from such a far away region. No source is cited, but it probably was old news reprinted from a recently arrived London paper.

This foreign news was followed by report of a terrible tropical storm that devastated St. Barts. The residents were going about their daily routines on July 24, 1732, in as calm a day as ever, when suddenly the weather turned violent, and two hours later, the island's ports and villages were demolished with heavy loss of life. Though the story was five months old, the news must have sent a chill across these coastal residents as to their own vulnerability, not only to the Indians, French, Spanish, and pirates who preyed upon them, but as well to strange natural disasters unheard of in Europe. Indeed, the suddenness of epidemic and violent weather lend an air of cataclysm that contemporary Charlestonians are fortunate not to share.

The foreign news in each weekly edition in the early 1730s seems apportioned between what has transpired with "His Catholick Majestie," the Archduke of a Austria, and the intrigues of "His Britannic Majestie," the King of England. One issue notes how an aide to the court in vienna was found shot to death in The Hague. A cabal conspiring against the Catholick Emperor is suspected.

Another news article describes how a Prussian courtier challenged a Berliner to a duel, the challenged gentleman dropped his sword, and as he knelt to retrieve it, the Prussian courtier decapitated him with one swift slash, right there on the streets of Berlin!

Public interest in the bizarre and the sordidness of humanity has long been a staple of the newspaper industry, as this early two-column news item illustrates. In the second newspaper published by Whitmarsh, he tells of a peasant near Paris who became infuriated at the laziness of his teenage son, whereby the father struck the poor boy so hard that he killed him. Realizing the terrible result of his sudden anger, the father hurled himself into the nearby well, breaking his neck in the process. The wife with her infant daughter rushed to the sound of the commotion and, as they peered into the well, a nosy hog nudged them both into the well. The hog slipped into the well and crushed to death the mother and infant. Thus, in an instant, an entire family ceased to exist. How many pints of ale were consumed over the retelling of that story along the Bay Street is anybody's guess.

The second ever newspaper published in Charles Town has for its lead story the merits of the wild plant, cannabis. Under the pen name, Agricola, Whitmarsh writes that the Colony will be wise in searching out new agricultural exports, and he recommends cannabis for treatment of venereal disease, jaundice, and as an ingredient in gunpowder. Agricola admonishes that "the strong smell can affect the head while "drinking a concoction made from boiling the seeds can make one stupid." Our ancestors were an inquisitive lot.

In the second issue, a sixteen-year-old girl who signs her letter "Martia" chides the editor for his use of male pronouns, and remarks that she has "more than a pretty face," and implies that she and her fair counterparts constitute part of Charleston's reading public. She says what we've all felt from time to tim, that the editor should frequent some other tavern for his news stories than the one he obviously patronizes!

Richard Furman and the High Hills of Santee Dissenters

The puckish upstate deacon declares that "you can't throw a kiss across a crowded room without striking an unintended Baptist." This is a dissenter state, and the reason why the Baptists have remained the predominant affiliation is the enduring evangelical zeal of that old patriot preacher, Richard Furman.

" Boy Evangelist' was Furman's earliest nickname, 'that Dam-ed Rebel" was Cornwallis' scourge, but upon his death, Charlestonians eulogized him as the state's most beloved preacher. Veterans of the revolution wept over the loss of their comrade whose oratory had proved more powerful for the cause of freedom than a regiment of armed men.

When the Reverend Doctor Furman thundered "I lift my eyes unto the hills," it wasn't the hills of Galilee that flooded his thoughts. Furman saw the High Hills of the Santee, those magnificent hardwood hills, 450 feet in elevation that cluster between the Wateree and the Lynches Rivers. These hills were incubating religious and political dissent long before the 'Liberty Boys" railed beneath Charleston's famous Liberty Tree.

High Hills folks formed a nucleus of independent thinkers that included surnames such as Furman, Richardson, Sumter, Waties, Anderson, Hemphill, Rembert, and Haynesworth. The Furmans had emigrated from downstate New York, refugees from the Esopus Wars that burned out the lower Hudson Valley sometime after 1755, the year Richard was born.

Today, Esopus is a high-priced real estate market, and gazing out on the river, one sees Saudi tankers approach the turning basin where they take on river water ballast to make their return to the Arabian Sea. In 1755, the whole region was aflame in the French and Indian War, and the

Esopus area, a corruption of the word, "Aesops," was particularly dangerous. The Furmans packed out as war refugees, abandoning all but a few pieces of furniture and plenty of books, some in Greek and Latin.

They weren't the only family in a state of flux, for this is the same time period that Longfellow records in his epic poem, "Evangeline," where the British forces uprooted French Acadians in Nova Scotia and dispersed them from South Carolina to Louisiana. It was Furman fortune to land in the Wateree region, a land that must have been Canaan to these refugees.

Young Furman was home schooled, and he was conversant in Greek by age 12. Ruddy and handsome, he was pius in a wicked backwoods land. Rhode Island (Baptist) College, later renamed Brown University, awarded Furman an honorary doctorate, as did South Carolina College. The frontier lad delivered the orations of Cicero to the long-leaf pines that whispered their approval through the High Hills of the Santee.

This old Claremont section of Camden District was a wicked breeding ground for malcontents, men living under aliases, and "lewd, lascivious women." Cock-fighting, dice, dirty-dancing, and cards trumped the catechism instruction by traveling parson, Charles Woodmason. For the Godly remnant, there was a small Anglican congregation called The Church of The Holy Communion, and the Furman family were pew-holders. But, itinerant preacher, Joe Reese, champion of the evangelical dissenters, was the one man responsible for pulling young Richard Furman away from the Anglican Confession.

These independent-minded Baptists disdained the hierarchy of bishops and kings, and snarled to low-country dandies, "No knee shall bow to King or Bishop, but to God Almighty alone." Some paraphrased that old infidel, Voltaire , "Man won't be free until the last king has been strangled with the entrails of the last bishop."

Under tutelage of evangelist, Joe Reese, a new preacher was winning souls with fervent preaching and praying around Stateburg in the High Hills. Furman was just 18, but his manly demeanor, his booming voice, and athletic, muscular Christianity began a great awakening from the Wateree to the fork of the Lynches. Country crackers and red-clay aristocrats alike came to hear the boy preacher who disdained vestments, pius creeds, and ritualistic worship.

Reese, Furman, and the well-known dissenter, Edward Tennent called the 1776 controversial gathering known as the Continental Association to solicit churchmen to sign a petition demanding an end to forced subsidization of the Anglican Church in South Carolina.

These old Cromwellians were descended from Scottish covenantors who'd signed an oath never to ally with the Anglican order of worship. They'd signed in blood and later revealed their pledge with a red kerchief about their necks, thus prompting King Charles I to refer to them as those "infernal red necks." Josiah Freeman, James Rembert, Huberd Rees, Matt Singleton, and General Sumter were the earliest signers of this new religious freedom movement.

The boy preacher, nineteen-year-old Richard Furman, pastor of High Hills Baptist Church near Stateburg, was an intimate of General Sumter, the partisan militia commander. Soon, the dynamic, Bible -thumping boy soon became a rifle-bearing reverend, one of the first in the High Hills to enlist in the patriot cause. Edward Tennent and Colonel Richardson prevailed upon the eloquent young man to join their upstate propaganda tour instead.

In this art of psychological warfare, Richard Furman was the Thomas Paine of the Carolina upstate, cajoling loyalist-leaning folk in small groups to switch, or sit idly by in the bitter civil war that was the revolution in the upstate.

Upon the war's end, Furman was the peacemaker, acting as a healer in the bitter divide and seeking redress of Tory grievances. He pastored his

church, published the Claremont Gazette, and helped organize the Claremont
Academy in Stateburg. Furman was a contributor of upstate news to the
Charleston Morning Post. Soon the growing Baptist congregation at
Charleston Baptist Church on Church Street, now First Baptist, called the
preacher from the High Hills. He delayed his answer, but felt compelled to
come to Charleston and lead the fastest growing church in the state.

Richard Furman was easily the most popular minister in the city; he was
the friend of that old Episcopalian statesman, Charles Cotesworth Pinckney,
and he was the speaker when the Society of the Cincinnati had its
celebrations. Furman's church increased by five fold with him as pastor,
and he helped charter new Baptist churches over the state. When the
revolution was at a dark ebb and Charleston had surrendered, it was those
fierce upstate dissenters who fought on under Sumter, Pickens, and Marion.
Those old veterans remembered Richard Furman as the moral authority of the
glorious patriot cause in Carolina.

The Incomparable John Rutledge, Father of Our State

The first time anyone in these parts ever heard the word "dictator" was
the spring of 1780 when the South Carolina Colonial Assembly delegated all
powers legislative, executive, and judicial to John Rutledge as our governor
during the darkest days of the revolution. The only power denied him was the
writ of execution unless by trial and jury. With the conclusion of this
emergency legislative session, probably held at the state house on the
corner of Meeting and Broad, John Rutledge was ferried across the Cooper

River to Rantowles Landing, and from there he disappeared on horseback into the wilds of the coastal plains drained by the Santee.

Charleston quickly buckled to the British on May 12, 1780, making for the gloomiest predicament imaginable for the local sons of liberty. General Lincoln's army and our local militia were no match for Clinton's, and had it not been for the pressure exerted upon them by heavily mortgaged Charleston merchants, the legislature would not have demanded that an entire Continental Corps be sacrificed in such a forlorn hope.

Dapper John Rutledge, with his courtly manners, elegant oratory, and piercing dark eyes ruled this state by executive fiat for twenty dreadful months when South Carolina's capital was just wherever Rutledge's saddlebags were secured for the evening. The "Demosthenes of the South," the State's most influential lawyer, this cosmopolitan, English-educated gentleman planter carried success or failure of the State's patriot cause squarely upon his shoulders.

Imagine Rutledge's plight as he fled the low-country that May evening headed for Peter Gaillard's plantation, The Rocks, near Eutaw Springs. His route was secured by a detachment of Marion's sharpshooters. Perhaps the British would burn Charleston; they burned Norfolk, and Charleston was more a hotbed of rebellion.

Embodied in the 41-year-old John Rutledge was the dream for a republican styled government, a state free of government-sponsored worship, but rather, all churches on an equal footing, and a policy of open commerce based upon the ideals of Adam Smith's laissez-faire principles. John Rutledge was one of those transition figures between the age of kings and government by congress and constitution.

What made this suave lawyer, so lacking in martial ability, the sole revolutionary partaker who could pull the State from the teeth of its conqueror and deliver her from internecine warfare?

It's true that Rutledge was a *deus ex machina*, the forceful dictator who saved his state and then resigned from power. These Rutledges, and there were eight of them, were descended from the Anglo-Irish, a part of the Cromwellian conquest of the emerald isle. For generations Rutledge men had been barristers or physicians in County Cavan. John Rutledge's father was an opportunist, or perhaps an Irish malcontent, but the immigrant Rutledge, an attorney, arrived in the port of Charleston sometime prior to December, 1731.

Andrew Rutledge, Senior, married a very wealthy widow, Sarah Boone Hext, and established himself as one of the several London-trained lawyers who applied the intricate body of English maritime law within a clumsy frame of Carolina statutes. Thus began the tradition of an unbroken succession of Broad Street attorneys with the surname of Rutledge that continues to this day.

Young John Rutledge was to the manor born in 1739; his Charleston education was the finest to be had here, Anglican priest John Andrews and classical scholar David Rhind. As a teenager, John read law with Charleston attorney, James Parsons, then the most prominent lawyer in Charles Town.

Unlike John Adams, Thomas Jefferson, and Patrick Henry who earned their legal credentials strictly in the colonies, sixteen-year-old John Rutledge traveled to the prestigious Middle Temple of the Inns of Court in London for the finest legal training that money could buy.

This privileged scion of Chehaw plantation, heir to Hext lands in Christ Church parish, and family mansions in Charleston, had money to burn as a youth in London's West End. He attended every new production of playwright David Garrick in Drury Lane.

Rutledge also frequented the Carolina Coffee House on Birchen Lane. Folks sailing to and from Charleston customarily stopped at this coffee house to drop off packages, letters, and news. Ship captains sold passage fare to Charleston from this shop, and it was a haven of revolutionary fervor long before 1776. Spies frequented the place, and English girls desperate to rendezvous with their colonial lovers made deals to secure passage. John ran a tab at the Carolina, and his fellow Charleston law student, Peter Manigault, had four times to allowance of Rutledge to spend there and elsewhere. Young lords and baronets in London were openly resentful of these Carolina spendthrifts.

Returning to Charleston in 1760, John Rutledge had the thrill of hearing a pilot boat hailing his ship has it approached the bar, and the pilot's first question was whether the new attorney John Rutledge was on board, because a certain lady desired him to represent her in a marital dispute! That was how he got his first case. Rutledge achieved a most favorable settlement in this publicized lawsuit, and his professional fee was the highest yet seen in the City! The Rutledges, father, son, and brother Edward, set up an elegant office in a brick building on Broad Street, opposite Orange Street. He soon became a member of the Commons, representing Christ Church parish. Soon, he was interim attorney general.

Maybe his marriage to Elizabeth Grimke was an arranged affair as were many of the elite family marriages, but this genteel lady whose prosperous husband owned a hundred-thousand acres as well as the fine mansion at 116 Broad Street, was the ideal prototype of South Carolina's first lady. She was destined to pay an enormous sacrifice in support of her husband's revolutionary politics.

John Rutledge was one of the Stamp Act delegates. His moderation prevented a repeat here of Boston's tea party antics. Of course, Rutledge coordinated the State's backwoods war, directing Sumter, Marion, Pickens, and others in a war against the tories. Then he called the Jacksonborough Assembly in 1782 to prepare for the eventual evacuation of the British. Postwar, Rutledge was a jurist extraordinaire; he served both as chief justice of the U.S. Supreme Court as well as the S.C. Supreme Court. John

Rutledge is the foremost of South Carolina's first family of law, and until John C. Calhoun, the greatest Carolinian.

Emma Jones was The Rebel Heroine Of Wentworth Street

For six months Charleston had been a conquered city, and for four months the Confederacy had been defunct. By August 1865, thousands of southerners had taken the oath of loyalty required even for such mundane things as receiving mail, transacting business at a bank, and moving freely about the state. Charleston was awash with union soldiers, carpetbaggers, and unemployed ex-confederates. Almost every home had become a boarding house, and many of the great mansions had became properties of the freedmens' bureau. Mrs. Jones' Rooms For Rent on the western end of Wentworth was where the city's blue-collar tradesmen rubbed shoulders with the occupying army and the legions of camp followers.

Court records tell us that Emma Jones was an Irish woman who immigrated to Charleston at age 16. Details of her private life are scanty, no husband or father is mentioned, but Emma had already survived the famine in Ireland and the civil war here. That she wouldn't survive the occupation of Charleston by these hated Yankees was a preposterous consideration for this plucky girl with an Irish brogue.

When a file of Union soldiers commanded by a corporal arrived shortly after 1 p.m. to arrest her, Emma Jones and a codefendant known only as Mrs. Byers, were petulantly awaiting their fate amidst a growing knot of by-standers thronging Wentworth Street. Some blue-jackted Union soldiers stood by accusingly, whereas a rabble of southern sympathizers gazed on menacingly.

The corporal barked a sharp command of "Halt! Face about." These were men of the 165th New York Infantry. They'd seen duty defending Washington, D.C., and most of them were mustering out in two weeks. This quelling public disturbances was the last obnoxious military duty any of them ever expected to do in conjunction with this detested war.

"What's the problem here?" quipped the corporal. A dozen or more off-duty soldiers of the 47th New York Volunteers, were, until recently, under Sheridan's command. "This woman has trampled on the flag of the United States in view of all on the street and has made a mockery of the symbol of United States authority!" Then a shrill Irish woman's voice could be heard, "Here's what I think of your flag," she said with a kick of her foot. The crowd was surly and the troops stood with rifles clutched awaiting orders. The two southern women, Jones and Byers, were hustled away to a Union officer to face charges of obstructing the peace and desecrating the flag. The bystanders were ordered to disperse. It was just another of the daily incidents in downtown Charleston during that miserable summer of 1865.

The Officer of the Day sent the women directly to jail to await trial on the charge of obstructing the peace in this martial law city. The jail was the old lock-up near Beaufain Street. In 1865, the jail was miserable beyond description, especially for two genteel women unaccustomed to the vulgarities of the street.

Even though a military tribunal would hear the case, the women were assigned local counsel. L. W. Spratt, Esq., was assigned the womens' case as defense counsel. Probably he was a Union man, as they came out of the woodwork down here once the hostilities ceased. In August, 1865, southern men who'd been too old to bear arms were taking the oath and going to work to support their families who'd never be accepted into citizenship again due to their military service in the Confederacy.

Spratt visited Jones in jail and found her utterly disconsolate, saying that she wished she were dead, that all had been a lark, that no harm was meant, etc. Byers said essentially the same thing, yet somehow, these spirited southern women seemed lacking in contrition. From New Orleans and Mobile to Charleston and Richmond, it was the same story, the southern men seemed subdued, but the rebel women refused to buckle to union rule. An example would be made of these two flag desecrators. The publicized trial had the makings of a spectacle, and an armed guard was called to patrol the streets.

The first witness called for the prosecution was Oscar van Tassel, a machinist and a boarder in Mrs. Jones' establishment. Under oath he testified to sitting at the dinner table on the August 15th, 1865, and hearing Mrs. Byers laughingly state to her niece that she'd received a present yesterday, a United States flag. The Byers woman then allegedly whipped out the flag and draped it over her niece's head and said she'd make a Yankee out of her. Somehow the flag landed on the floor, whereupon Mrs. Byers picked it up. The ladies in question, including Mrs. Jones, moved out of doors, onto Wentworth Street, and the flag again came out and was bandied about with Mrs. Jones slinging it to the street and trampling it, mocking it, and kicking it about, all in the presence of nearby off-duty Union soldiers.

Private Wagner, barely able to speak English in his heavy German accent, testified that he heard the commotion as he rounded King into Wentworth, and that he saw the throng gathering about the spectacle of the two boisterous women. He assisted the soldiers in restoring order.

As for Jones and Byers, they testified that it was a big misunderstanding, that the flag fell and was caught underfoot somehow, and that certainly no disrespect was meant to the icon of national unity.

Snickers up sleeves went around the court as southern sympathizers knew that these two women could play to the masses.

But the mood of the military judge changed dramatically as a Union officer, Captain Henry J. Inwood of the 165th New York Infantry, himself an attorney, rose to speak in defense of these two accused women. He stunned the court with his testimony that these women had been jailed without being served with a warrant, and that all rights attending to citizens had been violated by the United States government in this case. To prosecute further, he maintained, would shatter the good faith of the men and women who were seeking to get on with their lives in this reunited States. The good Yankee officer carried the day, yet the women were fined $100 for disorderly conduct, a fine equaling approximately $3000 today. The exciting story can be read in Tom Lowry's book, Confederate Heroines, LSU Press, 2006.

Oral Histories Speak of A Mount Pleasant Few Remember

Even the greatest historians of the ivory tower often fade in significance to those meticulous men and women who, note pad and recorder in hand, patiently coax octogenarians to reminisce. Perhaps it's because our students never cottoned to the rigor associated with economic or diplomatic history that we thrill to the social history of the ordinary people who leave us some recollections of a bygone era.

East Cooper residents are fortunate to have the writings of Betty Lee

Johnson, a former teacher who artfully sought out and wrote down dozens of
narratives of a cross-section of folks in our area, all of whom would be
well over a hundred years old now.

The Tiencken family is rooted as deeply in old Mount Pleasant as the
live oaks at Alhambra. Betty Lee Johnson interviewed Elise Tiencken Farmer
over twenty years ago. Many of us remember Elise's brother, Wilford
Tiencken, the courtly gentleman who retired from his government job in
Washington and returned to his beloved boyhood haunts. Wilford Tiencken was
one of the government executives who purchased land for the navy.

Having earned a law degree at at George Washington University to
supplement his Clemson engineering diploma, Tiencken was instrumental in
arranging the land deal and the blueprints for Bethesda Naval Hospital. He used
to tell of the ground-breaking ceremony there when President Roosevelt asked
him to move the cornerstone of the building back eleven feet. Though it cause no
end of trouble for engineers and architects, they redid everything just as FDR
asked, and to this day, no one knows why it was so important.

Elise Tiencken Farmer, Wilford's sister, recounted to the interviewer
that she was born in the old Tiencken family home at 216 Bennett Street.
That charming old house stayed in their family for well over a hundred
years. Compare that multi-generational connection with a dwelling to
today's Mount Pleasant.

Ninety years ago, Mount Pleasant children were bathed in the kitchen
before the cook stove. Electricity and oil furnaces began heating homes in
the 1930s. A Number 9 washtub filled with cold pump water and hot kettle
water was a luxurious experience, especially if the wood stove had been
stoked for the occasion.

Johnson records Tiencken as telling how each family had their own garden
to the rear of the big house. Of course, the village was not chock- full of
residences as we've turned it today. There were barns, a stable for the

cow, and many adolescents kept a goat to hitch to a cart. The goat proved
to be the finest disposal unit ever designed. There was no need of a
compactor, shredder, or garbage collector when "Mister Billy" was on the
premises. Chickens of every hue ran loose throughout the old village, and
one watched one's step through the oyster shell lanes that twisted around
more so than the city streets we cruise today.

About dusk the lamp lighter would make his rounds up Pitt Street and the
side streets singing a mournful song as he lit the few lamps that cast their
eerie flickers through the wee hours. The only one who could sing more
mournfully was the well-known chimney sweep who chipped the soot from
ancient chimneys that had breathed fire for our antebellum ancestors.

The Tienckens partnered with the Patjens in operating a sawmill over on
Factory Street. That street has been renamed Live Oak today, perhaps to
upgrade the neighborhood that once was the East Cooper Industrial Park where
everything from barrels to Confederate ironclads had been built on Shem
Creek.

The Patjens, Beckmans, and Tienckens had all served in the Confederate
army together, and all returned to this area that was destitute. These men
of hardy German stock wasted little time regaining their livelihoods. Many
Germans in this area immigrated following the collapse of the Frankfurt
convention in 1848, a political shambles that saw numerous German kingdoms
knuckle to the machinations of militaristic Prussia.

The Tienckens had a spring that bubbled forth wonderfully sweet water in
their yard on Bennett Street. Several springs and a few deep wells, like
the one that was on the corner of Morrison and Pitt, were noted for the
pleasant taste and curative effects of the water.

Tiencken recalls her mother making most of the clothing for the children
of her family, and she remembers how her mother stayed up til three in the
morning finishing an outfit, or mending one. Store bought clothes from

Charleston were special and not to be confused with everyday wear. Her
mother sewed the Confederate reunion flag for the Thomas Wagner Camp, a flag
that reputedly still exists.

The school house, the stores, and the post office were located in the
block of Pitt Street where the businesses are today. Tiencken says that
entertainment consisted of frequent plays at what we call the Darby
Building, but she knew it as the old Lutheran Seminary.

The worst hurricane that any old timer ever recalled certainly wasn't
Hazel or Hugo. It was the terrible cyclone of 1911, the one chronicled in
Francis Griswold's Sea Island Lady. Teddy Watts recollected how she'd seen
a tugboat power right across the middle of Sullivan's Island, so deep was
the tidal surge. It's estimated that at least 2000 folks perished on the
sea islands, their bodies washing out to sea. In this hurricane the refugees
who could get off of Sullivan's with the very short notice all came to the
Old Village.

One family that were refugees with the Tienckens after losing their
summer home was the Condon family of the department store fame.

Elise Tiencken was quite a tomboy as she grew up in this Tom Sawyer-like
village nearly a hundred years ago. She learned semaphore and sent funny
messages to the naval ships coming in and out of the harbor. Occasionally
she and her older chaperone would get invited for tea in the ship's
wardroom! How we would love to revisit that old Mount Pleasant just for a
day to savor its slower, more sincere style. Thanks to Betty Lee Johnson's
collection of oral histories in the library, we can get a glimpse.

128

Charleston Is Still A Sensuous City

Of the hundreds of essays that Professor George Rogers penned in his lifetime of teaching at USC, none is as interesting a look back as the chapter entitled "The Sensuous City," in his 1969 publication, Charleston In The Age Of The Pinckneys.

Rogers is the premier scholar among a revered listing of historians, including names such as McCrady, Wallace, Jones, to spend a lifetime devoted to South Carolina history. George Rogers was at the top of his class in 1943 at the College of Charleston. After the war, Rogers took a masters and a Ph.D. at the University of Chicago. From 1953 until his death in 1997, Rogers lectured and wrote on federal America and South Caroliniana. He's best known for his editing of the massive correspondence of Henry Laurens. But his little book, Charleston in the Age of The Pinckneys is often cited as his masterpiece. And the chapter on the sensuous city is the gem of that signal work.

It's obvious when reading Rogers' essays and books that he's read hundreds if not thousands of pages of personal correspondence, diaries, and old newspapers. No one can match him for detail and ability to capture the feeling of the times.

Eighteenth century Charles Town was "the fairest and most fruitful province belonging to Great Britain," notes the journal of Josiah Quincy, a colonial who traveled to Charleston quite often. Great Britain's new world colonial establishment reached from Barbados, St. Kitts, and St. Lucia northward to the province of Quebec. To the chagrin of the crown, the North American colonies had been financial disappointments, not matching anything like the returns from the sugar islands of the Caribbean. And the maintenance cost on the North American colonies was far higher, too. Charleston, the colorful port of

Carolina, was the great exception to this perplexing dilemma for Parliament.

The sights and smells of 18th century Charles Town impressed everyone who came here. Crossing the bar brought one into close proximity with Sullivan's Island. Before the palmetto log fort was built, the southwestern end of the island was a white sandy spit with dense underbrush. Two rough structures appeared to ship passengers, a pest house for unfortunate arrivals who'd contracted smallpox or yellow fever. Evidently, the back side of the island became a potter's burial field for diseased slaves and other immigrants. The other structure visible was a huge pyramid of logs for the signal bonfire that's alert the city if Spanish, French, or pirate ships approached.

Crossing the bar often took several days due to contrary winds and tides, but once into the harbor, the new arrivals are said to have exclaimed that our city was as breathtaking as Cadiz, or one of the Hanseatic ports on the Baltic. Dutch-gabled storefronts rose above three stout brick and log bastions. Enormous garrison-sized flags usually flew over the bastions, normally the cross of St. George flag, or the new Union flag waved from a pine staff. Fort Johnson, on your port side, frequently saluted incoming ships with a booming retort.

Only the deep-draft royal ships-of-the-line were too large to tie up at the quays, or bridges that served as berths in our colonial port. We'd refer to them as docks today, but they were curious affairs. Rogers states that running from north to south, present-day Market Street to South Adger's Wharf, the bridges extending out into the channel were Crokatt's, Rhett's, Middle, Elliot's, Motte's, Pinckney's, Lloyd's, and Brewton's. Most of these imposing triangular, wooden platforms had shops built on them where merchandise was received and marketed by colorfully dressed tradesmen. Stepping off the plank of a ship onto such a bustling exchange must certainly have been more exciting than entering O'Hare after a long, overnight flight.

Bay Street's west side was lined with three-story, gable-roofed stores with shopkeeper residences on the third floor. Pigs, chickens, goats, and dogs ran loose through the streets contesting the turkey buzzards for the offal discarded by the butchers and fish sellers. Proper folks were wheeled away in a carriage while the pedestrians wandered along the tabby-covered streets.

Bay Street was known to host pirate bazaars where excellent deals could be had on quality merchandise, no questions asked. Captain Morgan is said to have frequented early Charles Town with his booty-laden fleet. Tradd Street and Broad Street were the most trafficked inland thoroughfares, and each was more known for shops and offices than for private dwellings. Queen Street, named for Caroline of Anspach, was a center of taverns and inns. recent archaeological digs reveal that our ancestors drank far more ale and rum than they should have, and that they were forever smoking from those curved clay pipes.

Colorfully-dressed characters wandered the streets, and the newcomer's eye met with turbaned-African women balancing bundles on their heads while calico-jacketed seamen lounged on street corners looking for ways to spend shore leave. Scarlet-coated British naval officers came and went from the Exchange, and everyone knew that the most important man, next to the governor, was Captain George Anson, the commander of the Atlantic Squadron of His Majesty's Navy. Anson was easily the most famous naval officer of his day, and the most celebrated naval officer in British history since Drake. He'd circumnavigated the globe, fought dozens of sea battles with the Spanish, and was a noted card player. Anson's winning a sizable acreage of city land from Charleston gentlemen in a game of whist is perpetuated today in the name Ansonborough, one of the earliest suburbs.

Meeting House Street, the outer fringe of the little city, was home to two dissenter churches, the presbyterian and the congregational. These churches were barn-like at first, and lacked the grace and splendor of the stately St. Philip's, an Anglican foundation that Rogers cites was built with taxes imposed on the importation of rum, brandy, and slaves.

Clearly, no American city had the appeal to the senses of our Charleston, and no historian has captured the flavor of that early Charleston as has George Rogers in his Charleston in The Age of The Pinckneys.

Former Rhodesian Air Force Commander Loved Charleston

Raff Bentley never sought the limelight during the seventeen months that he lived here at the Ashley Marina aboard his Sparkman and Stephens yacht, Shamwari. It was thirty years ago this month that the tall, aristocratic Rhodesian and his young wife, Jennifer, sailed into Charleston harbor. If the press had gotten wind of this colorful expatriate sojourning here, they'd have done a spread in the newspaper.

For Raff, it was an unexpected stopover. A Walterboro physician had befriended Bentley in the Caribbean and had recommended that he seek medical care here for his aching arthritis. What was to have been a months's stay evolved into 17 months for these vagabonds. Raff's beloved Rhodesia, from which he was a self-imposed exile, was immersed in a terrible civil war. When he departed, it was to Majorca that they sailed, to house sit for a friend. To the few here who became his confidantes, Raff Bentley became one of those unforgettable romantic characters that authors such as Hemingway, or Robert Ruark chiseled from the harsh realities of human existence.

There were clues that this visitor was somebody extraordinary. That Sparkman and Stephens sloop-rigged yacht was custom designed to the specifications of a man used to ocean sailing. The British accent with a distinctive Rhodesian lilt was a treat to the ears in this city well-known for distinctive accents. He wore open-necked sport shirts, khakis, and sandals, and the few times he donned his blazer and tie, he cut quite a figure in Charleston restaurants with his pretty wife.

For the few who became regulars for happy hour on the fantail of Shamwari, the life-story of Raff Bentley was meted out over Ashley River sunsets and tumblers of Raff's favorite scotch whiskey. The man did not bubble with conversation, but in the quiet, English understated manner, he related his story matter-of-factly, and with just a little prying by the curious, the details of this legendary World War II RAF pilot came to light.

Bentley traveled with an Irish passport, though he claimed Rhodesian citizenship. It's a peculiar story that entails quite a bit of tangled colonial history unfamiliar to most Americans. Raff's father, while a Dublin teenager, was sent by his parents out to Rhodesia in the late 1899 to search for a brother gone missing in service to Cecil Rhodes. In the search he got caught up in the Boer War, fought the Boers across the transvaal. Somehow, while trying to locate the missing brother, he befriended a Boer girl who soon became his wife and future mother of Raff Bentley.

Rhodesia was a wild and murderous place in the early 1900s, and the senior Bentley was in a saloon somewhere north of Cape Town when a fight broke out with several men shot and one stabbed. One of the dying men passed a bloodstained, pencil-drawn map to Bentley and begged him to take it to Cecil Rhodes. Bentley fulfilled the request and personally delivered the blood- stained paper to Rhodes. It turned out to be the location of one of Rhodesia's largest tin ore deposits.

Bentley was rewarded with a lucrative management position in the Rhodes conglomerate. By the 1930s, there was a small Rhodesian town named Bentley and the family lived as feudal barons and loyal British subjects.

Young Alfred Mulock Bentley (Raff) was born on New Year's Day, 1916. His boyhood could have made for a scene in Isak Dinesen's Out of Africa. He went to Plumtree School in Bulawayo, and some of his chums were known to have killed their first lion by their 16th birthday.

While he was at Plumtree, the rumblings of another European war reached even distant Africa. Air Officer Swain came from London to recruit British colonial lads for Royal Air Force College, Cranwell, the air force academy of Britain. Raff Bentley was far and away the top candidate, but colonial lads were being recruited from Canada, New Zealand, and Australia, as well. Cranwell was known to be fiercely competitive and a brutally tough military school. The colonial chaps quite held their own there.

The photo album he carried showed a lanky fellow in Air Officer kit on the back row of the graduating Cranwell Class of 1936. He was assigned to 43 Squadron, RAF, "the Flying Cocks." When Britain entered the war in 1939, Bentley was a squadron commander of Vickers Wellesley bombers in Nairobi.

Raff Bentley's obituary in the Daily Telegraph (London, October 16, 1999), states that, " he moved as a flight commander of a bomber squadron based at Heliopolis in Egypt.. In 1940 he was raiding an Italian target in Libya when his aircraft was hit. Although an antiaircraft shell burst in the cockpit and killed his navigator, Bentley, who was seriously wounded, managed to land his aircraft safely ." Bentley told of the decapitation of his navigator by a German antiaircraft shell. Raff could see the tracer rounds of a German Messerschmidt's machine guns tearing into his wing. With his aircraft on fire and his canopy hinges jammed, he kicked the canopy open and tumbled out, hoping that his parachute was not ripped in his exit.

Bentley's Cranwell Class of 1936 was almost wiped out in the Battle of Britain. Raff, himself, flew in every theater of the war and almost every aircraft that the British had in their inventory, including the famed Spitfire with its powerful Merlin engine, and the Hawker Hurricane.

Following the war, the much decorated flyer returned to Rhodesia and maintained his air career in the Rhodesian Air Force, becoming Air-Vice Marshall in the mid-1960s. He owned a commuter airline agency as well as a crop-dusting business. While serving as Air Attaché at the Rhodesian Embassy in Washington, Raff read the cable from Ian Smith's government announcing the end of Rhodesia's colonial relationship with Britain. Ever loyal to his sovereign, Bentley chose to abandon his wealth in the land of his birth and become an exile.

While in Charleston, Air-Vice Marshall Bentley was a guest in October, 1977, at The Citadel's dress parade honoring the visiting Prince of Wales. Another British citizen locked eyes with Bentley in front of the Daniel Library that morning - Air Marshall Swain, the gentleman who'd recruited Bentley to Cranwell from Plumtree in Rhodesia. It was a classic understated Englishman's greeting, "Raff Bentley, I presume."

Harold Smith, Eyewitness To History, Retired To Charleston

No one but "Mrs. Ellen," his wife of fifty years, referred to Harold Smith by his first name. This proper Bostonian was always addressed as "Colonel," a rank he earned as the fifth man selected from the Army in 1947 to form the new "Blue Suit" Air Force. Few who sped past the Ashley House on Lockwood Boulevard in the 1970s ever looked up to the 5th floor balcony at the distinguished old gentleman who'd been an eyewitness to so much history.

Harold was deemed essential to the creation of an Air Force separate from the Army because of his managerial skills and his number-crunching ability. He was a tax-lawyer by training and a whiz at accounting. This was the man who took Rose Fitzgerald to his prom at Boston Latin School. And he was best man in the wedding of Howard Johnson, who became the restaurant and motel mogul.

The Colonel and "Mrs. Ellen" retired to Charleston in the mid-1970s when failing health no longer permitted him to do things like climbing up to repair the roof of Dunrovin, his wife's family home a few miles above Orangeburg.

Smith met and married the pretty Ellen Culler of Orangeburg when the IRS sent him as a special tax agent to check on compliance of some South Carolina hot shots who were suspected of fudging on filing tax returns. Smith, by then a tax attorney with degrees from Boston College and Boston University, was stationed in Columbia. When this sharp attorney with the Boston-Irish accent entered your office and asked to see you by name, it was the beginning of a bad day in Dixie.

Smith's well-to-do Orangeburg in-laws didn't know what to make of their new son-in-law with his up-north accent, Catholic religion, and his penchant for sipping whiskey on Sunday evening. But his wit and his World War I service was enough to make this Massachusetts Yankee in King Cotton's court a hit in the heart of the Bible Belt.

While growing up in Boston's "Irish-lace" district rather than the shanty-Irish side, Smith had many privileges in his youth. Boston Latin School is perhaps America's oldest and most elite preparatory school. He got to serve as an altar boy, crucifier, and choir member in the Cathedral of the Church of The Holy Cross when His Eminence William Henry Cardinal O'Connell was there, and briefly when O'Connell's successor, Cardinal Cushing came in 1921.

Being bat boy for the 1911 Red Sox was Smith's greatest thrill in a lifetime of memorable experiences. This was the era of Casey Hagerman on the mound with Bill Carrigan catching. The dugout was dubbed "County Cork." The Red Sox won 78 of 162 games and Smith retained a tattered photo showing him as a skinny lad in a red Sox uniform.

Of course if you're well-connected to be bat boy for the Red Sox and to attend Boston Latin, then you have to squire around a pretty girl. Smith did manage one date, his prom, with John F. "Honey Fitz" Fitzgerald's daughter, Rose Elizabeth. Honey Fitz was Mayor of Boston. Two years later Rose began a stormy seven year courtship with Joseph Patrick Kennedy, a fellow who did not stand well in the esteem of Harold Smith. But the Colonel, a lifelong republican, did go to hear Ted Kennedy when he made a speech at the Riviera Theater on King Street in 1979.

It was tradition for the men in Smith's family to serve in the military. This tradition dated back to the Civil War, a subject that he said received one paragraph's mention when he was at Boston Latin. The Ancient and Honorable Artillery Company of Massachusetts was the unit that commissioned this young lawyer as a second lieutenant in 1915. "The Ancients" were established in 1637 and had seen service in Indian wars, the Revolution, the War of 1812, and the Civil War. Four of its members became president of the United States and eight received the Medal of Honor. If war began, the Ancient and Honorable Artillery would be among the first called to active duty.

Lieutenant Smith went to France with Pershing's American Expeditionary Force. After being among the first Americans to see action, Smith was sent home with selected others to be interviewed by President Wilson. Secretary of War Newton Baker wanted articulate spokesmen in uniform to hype the sale of war bonds. Handsome Harold was one of a handful to become poster boy for the war bonds.

With the War's end came Harold's stint with the Boston DA's office and the celebrated trial of the alleged murderers and anarchists, Sacco and Vanzetti. Then came employment with the IRS and his subsequent relocation to South Carolina. Thanks to iced tea, broad verandahs, and Ellen Culler, Harold Smith became an adopted southerner in every way. It was with reluctance that he left the State for Army active duty in 1942.

For much of the second world war, Smith was in the War Department working with Henry L. Stimson, FDR's Secretary of War. He was a number cruncher and planner. He became the essential Army staff man, often moving in and out of the White House with quiet certainty.

In 1942, on a Saturday morning after Pearl Harbor, Major James Doolittle stuck his head into Smith's office and told him that the President had just selected Doolittle to lead a top-secret mission. Along with the mission came the instant promotion to lieutenant-colonel. Harold Smith walked down to the cloak room and quietly removed the lieutenant-colonel silver oak leaves from another officer's coat and brought them back to pin on Doolittle. Fortunately, Smith had a flask of whiskey in his desk for the impromptu sendoff of Jimmy Doolittle to recruit his famous aviators for the raid on Tokyo.

It was General John Cannon who contacted Smith about fulfilling the National Security Act of 1947 and its task of establishing the Air Force as an independent branch. His new military ID number was 000005. The picture among the dozens of autographed ones in his study that commanded your gaze was the one of Smith dining on golden plates with Chiang-Kai-shek at his palace in Taipei, Taiwan. Knowing the Colonel was having your own eyewitness to the history of the first half of the 20th century!

Remembering La Brasca's On Upper King Street

Nobody's complaining that fair Charleston has become another Kinsale, the Irish coastal town known internationally for its culinary excellence. Actually, we're delighted that gourmands travel here just to dine in the two-dozen establishments famous for featuring meals costing more than a day laborer can earn in minimum wage. Fifty years ago, the most talked-about restaurant here was a modestly-priced place frequented by everyone from Citadel cadets to the barristers of Broad Street. Effie La Brasca's Italian restaurant prospered on upper

King near County Hall for thirty years and served the finest Italian and Chinese dishes to a diverse clientele.

Back in the '50s and '60s Charleston had swell eateries that were pricey, but now they blur into sameness. Was it Charleston that had the Harbor House and Savannah that had the Pirate's House, or vice versa? There's no such confusing the place so many referred to as Mama La Brasca's, however. The aroma of the tempting spaghetti sauce was discernible as soon as you exited your car at the northwest corner of Cleveland and King Streets.

On any given day at La Brasca's you'd enter and be seated at your table only to spot two tables over Congressman Mendel Rivers and his wife, Margaret, or the legendary Sam Stoney, or perhaps, General and Mrs. Mark Clark, or his aide and driver, retired Sergeant Major Ed Sojourner. Of course, the place was always filled with cadets, the faculty of the various colleges, and the ordinary locals that characterize the soul of old Charleston.

For more than thirty years the little Italian diner prospered on upper King. Sometimes County Hall nearby hosted the most celebrated rock and roll bands of the era for wild Citadel parties. Bands such as Mitch Ryder And The Detroit Wheels, Little Anthony And The Imperials, Doug Clark and his hot dance band all ordered pizza and Chinese take-outs from the popular restaurant across the street!

Who was that dear, soft-spoken lady who oversaw the kitchen, the two dining rooms, and the cash register simultaneously? Most Charlestonians just assumed that Effie La Brasca was an Italian immigrant who arrived following the war. Well, thanks to Mary Zwingmann Scott who compiled La Brasca's life story for a private printing by the R. L. Bryan Company in 1971, we can share the fascinating story of this entrepreneur of Syrian descent. Effie La Brasca arrived in Charleston with very little and built a small empire based upon her recipes and her reputation for good value at a fair price. But, as Mary Z. Scott notes, it was Effie's initiative, hard work, and venturesome spirit that brought her renown.

Born to Benjamin and Rosa Basha, immigrants from Duma, Syria, Effie and her teenaged mother were deserted by her father shortly after her birth in 1899 in St. John's, Nova Scotia. Seeking a better life in the new world, Ben Basha got work as a nightclub singer. Fidelity was not his strong suit and he left his young wife and child for a freer life in Canada. Thus began the trials of Effie La Brasca that would mold her into the compassionate person we cherish.

Scott's compilation of Effie La Brasca's life story could be the stuff of a television mini-series. Her mother soon married a wonderful man named Sam Demetree, a Syrian. Effie thought that Sam was her real father right up until the time of her mother's death from ovarian cancer nine years later.

Circumstances never allowed for Effie to attend school, even for one day. She was a self-taught reader and never owned a doll, or any other kind of toy. Effie's stepfather was a traveling salesman and they ended up in Charleston since there was a sizable Syrian community here in the depression years. He opened a grocery shop on upper King Street near the intersection with Cannon and for years was known as the 'banana man."

George La Brasca, Effie's beau, was a sailor stationed on-board the "Donna Bollo," and he visited the store often in the afternoons for a coke and a dozen bananas. Effie Basha Demetree was a striking teen with a pretty face and figure, and more than a bit of devil-may-care in her attitude. Her courtship with the Wisconsin sailor brought her much rebuke and a hint of scandal, but marry him she would!

La Brasca was a native of Sicily, and like Effie, a Roman Catholic. Father Murphy refused married them in St. Patrick's on St. Phillip's Street because the banns had not been published, and because her father would not consent. But a protestant minister performed the rite so that they could honeymoon in Miami and get a priest there to do the nuptials again.

Times were hard during the depression, and at least once Effie and George were penniless. Their apartment was four doors north of Aimar's Drug Store on upper King, and about all the food that they had was a big bowl of spaghetti brought to them by Mr. Sarvarese who owned Savarese's Italian restaurant in that neighborhood.

After a few months of unemployment left them unable to pay the rent, Effie and George were evicted. Johnny Jervey contacted them and led them to an apartment at 22 Warren Street near Condon's Department Store. Jervey gave them $25 to cover the first month's rent. Soon, George La Brasca got a job with the Carpenter's Union and Effie worked with Read Brothers. Still, a lack of income tempted them to make bootleg whiskey for added income. She wasn't proud of it, and they were arrested for bootlegging, along with other Charlestonians.

After a few years of struggling, the La Brasca's moved to 50 Warren Street, a more spacious abode. A frequent guest at their family table was Mitch Robinson, father of noted local attorney, Klyde Robinson. He loved Effie's spaghetti with meat sauce, and in 1948, he encouraged her to open her own restaurant. Robinson even loaned her $10,000 and helped her to find a good location, an Orvin property at 975 King. Effie was so successful that she repaid her loan in seven months time! Robinson would not accept any interest on that loan. As a rule, Effie La Brasca never allowed a day to go by that she did not commit some act of philanthropy herself.

Copper Mogul, Philanthropist, Harry Guggenheim Loved Daniel Island

"Let me tell you about the very rich. They are different from you and me." So says Fitzgerald in his 1926 short story, "The Rich Boy." Hemingway's rejoinder in his story "The Snows of Kilimanjaro," 'Yes, they have more money." South Carolina is a low-income state, but the big money men have long had a passion for our live oaks, tidal marshes for duck blinds and our pine woods for deer stands. Multimillionaires Morrow v. Frelinghuysen, Bernard Baruch, and Henry R. Luce each owned working plantations or great hunting preserves on the Cooper River. But the Daddy Warbucks of the big money men ever to break a sweat under a sultry Carolina sun was Harry Frank Guggenheim!

Guggenheim owned Cainhoy Plantation, though he spelled it Cain Hoy, for nearly 30 years until his death in 1970. He purchased most of Daniel Island a half-century ago for use as a cattle farm. This was where he could pitch fodder off the back of a truck, sip iced-tea on his front porch, and draw a bead on a buck from his deer stand in the pines.

A grandson of 19th century, Swiss Jewish immigrants, this internationally-known philanthropist is remembered for his land investments, thoroughbred breeding, and corporate ventures. In his 70 years, he'd win a Pulitzer prize, endow Robert Goddard, the man who became the father of the space program, and establish more charitable foundations than any previous American philanthropist. But Harry Guggenheim was not without his detractors. Some critics maintain that his family exploited their copper monopoly during the two world wars.

But for a fellow born into great wealth as Harry was, you'd hardly know that was the case unless you followed him home. Harry's father pulled him out of Yale after a year and put him to work as an apprentice in their copper mines in Mexico. Daniel Guggenheim, Harry's father, was no celebrated student himself, but he valued practical learning, especially metallurgical knowledge.

By 1900, Daniel Guggenheim's family controlled the world's largest copper mine, and one of the world's largest silver mining operations. These holdings were centered in the Andes range and in the southwestern United States.

Harry was nearing age 20 when it was determined that he should study under the most renowned metallurgical scientists in the world, the masters of

142

Pembroke College's School of Natural Science at Cambridge University. Harry's year at the Sheffield School of Yale had prepared this rugged man whose calloused hands and experienced mind could could still work out calculus equations. In 1913 the professors who'd schooled the Empire's greatest metal-mining minds were pleased to award this scion of wealth his B.A. and M.A. in Metallurgy. His classmates moved on to exploit the Congo basin as Harry returned to build his vision for wealth as a humanitarian force.

Years before Harry was old enough to quarry copper from the family's open-pit mines, his father, Daniel, bought the Utah Copper and Silver Company. Daniel partnered with J.P. Morgan and Jacob Schiff in 1912 to mine the Kennecott Creek deposits in Alaska. Harry's father then acquired controlling interest in the Chile Copper Company. These pioneers of modern mining procedures would be labeled as environmental despots today, but standards for limiting erosion and water contamination were then nonexistent.

By World War I, the industrial and military uses for copper were on the rise. The war in Europe forced the price of copper sky high, and the Guggenheim family catapulted into wealth previously unknown in the Western world. They branched into nitrates for making explosives. Wilson's government threatened to nationalize the copper mines if Daniel Guggenheim didn't reduce the market price. But in the end, the allies never lacked for copper in their detonators as did the Germans.

Instead of profiteering in the family business during the Great War, the 28-year-old Harry purchased a Curtiss Flying Boat, learned how to pilot the craft, and obtained permission to start up a naval aviation unit in Manhasset, New York. He served on submarine patrol duty in Europe and returned home a decorated Lieutenant Commander. Even as an older man, Harry Guggenheim insisted on active duty with the U.S. Navy in Europe. Not many of America's mega-millionaires were as insistent about doing military service as was Harry.

All of the Guggenheim mining interests from Chile to Utah, and Alaska were consolidated into the Kennecott Company. The family fended off a hostile takeover from the Rockefellers. Ironically, when the Guggenheims sold out of Kennecott completely, it was Standard Oil of Ohio, a Rockefeller concern, that bought them out.

All of his life, Harry Guggenheim had to defend his father's business reputation from scurrilous attacks on his ethics. In the early days of the 20th century, Daniel Guggenheim had employed hundreds of Italian immigrants in his silver and copper mines in Utah and Arizona. When thousands of Greeks flooded Ellis Island, Daniel worked a deal with Leonidas Skliris, an unscrupulous labor boss. When the Greeks grew demanding about wages and conditions, Guggenheim tried to break them with cheap Japanese immigrants arriving in California. Later in his life, Harry funded studies in the furtherance of the living wage idea.

By the end of World War II, Harry Guggenheim was known internationally. It'd been his family, among a select few other Jewish entrepreneurs, that Hitler had frothed at the mouth about as wartime profiteers in World War I. But Harry, like others in his family, settled into a directorship role in the mining industry and began to devote more time to philanthropy.

Both Daniel and Harry Guggenheim became a commanding presence in pioneering aviation. Together, they contributed $2.6 billion to Robert Goddard and his jet and rocket propulsion lab. The Guggenheim Foundation is considered by many to be the leading patron, more so than the U.S. government, of rocket science. Charles Lindbergh, a close friend of Harry's, was a collaborator in this endeavor.

Maybe it was his Cain Hoy thoroughbred stable, a horse breeding and training facility in Columbia and Kissimmee, Florida, that gave Harry his greatest relaxation. Named for his low country plantation on the Wando, the stable produced Dark Star, the Kentucky Derby winner of 1953. Perhaps it was Daniel Island, that quiet place where he could get lost along dirt paths connecting his pastures. Harry Frank Guggenheim cherished his low country connection.

Micah Jenkins Was Lee's Youngest General

When Stonewall Jackson received a mortal wound to his left shoulder in the Battle of the Wilderness, Robert E. Lee lost his right-hand man. A less well-known casualty in the same friendly-fire debacle was the death of low-country native, Micah Jenkins, the boy-general of the Confederacy. Exactly 144 years ago this month, on May 2, 1863, the Confederacy was reeling from the tragic loss of Jackson, its hardest hitting commander.

But Charleston was also mourning a native son, a Citadel first-honor graduate who had shunned the path of wealth open to him in his family's sea island cotton plantation. In Micah Jenkins' brief life he graduated first-honor graduate of The Citadel at age 19, founded his own successful military prep school, married the beautiful daughter of a former governor, and was cited for gallantry by Confederate Generals Lee, D. H. Hill, Longstreet, and Jackson.

The Jenkins were Edisto Island planters whose fortune rose with the exportation of long-staple cotton. Micah Jenkins could easily have chosen a life of the gentleman planter, complete with verandah, panama hat, and mint julep. Rather, his romantic nature, fed by the novels of Sir Walter Scott, led him to start his own military academy where chivalry, honor, and military bearing united with Euclid and Milton.

Scores of teenaged cadets reported to Jenkins' Kings Mountain Military School, an upstate preparatory school for The Citadel. The crossroads community near the North Carolina border was still known as Yorkville.

Back then, fewer than one in 500 boys attended college or university, and those in South Carolina that did matriculate experienced a much different regimen than did their 20th century counterparts. Micah Jenkins was first-honor graduate at The Citadel in 1854 when the 12-year-old campus was composed of just two buildings on Marion Square.

A 15-year-old stripling of a boy, Micah arrived in November 1850 at city wharf on a plantation barge from Edisto Island. The trip up would have taken the better part of a day if the winds and tides cooperated. The Planters Hotel, now the Dock Street Theater, would have been the likely venue for the overnight before reporting to The South Carolina Military College.

The school term ran from November to November to accommodate the agricultural calendar. Jenkins would have been presented by his father, Cap'n John Jenkins, to their cotton factor and banker. These friends of the family were accustomed to governing prominent Citadel cadets through the intricacies of the Charleston social calendar.

Micah Jenkins' class of 1854 had just 13 graduates, and he was number one in academics and in military bearing. One year earlier, the entire Citadel class of 1853 had been expelled for insubordination. The cadets had had the same curriculum as West Point cadets, and some of their instructors were West Point graduates. But they had not the large corps with which to hone their parade ground command skills. Citadel cadets of the early years rarely drilled a unit larger than two platoons.

Family arranged marriages were the order of the day among cadet graduates, but his family and the watchful Charleston friends had little to do with Micah falling desperately in love with General D. F. Jamison's 18 year-old daughter, Caroline. Jamison was an Orangeburg planter, militia general, and former governor. As a legislator, Jamison was instrumental, along with J.P. Richardson, in establishing The Citadel. Jamison continued to serve in the state senate and controlled the state's military budget. Jenkins' wedding was one of the state's most elegant affairs in 1855.

The young couple settled into a hectic life as commandant of the newly-formed Kings Mountain Military School. The school in Yorkville had an enrollment greater than that of The Citadel, and Jenkins sent for Asbury Coward, his classmate, and Evander Law, two classes behind him at The Citadel, to come assist in the teaching duties.

These halcyon years were interrupted in 1859 by news of the secession crisis, and Jenkins responded to his father-in-law's request to form an infantry company of York county volunteers. He became captain of the Jasper Guards, 5th South Carolina Volunteers. Hopes by 1861 were that the crisis over disunion would be resolved in time for spring planting season.

By Manassas on July 21, 1861, 26-year-old Colonel Micah Jenkins commanded a regiment in Longstreet's division. He saw men fall all around him; some were his former King's Mountain students. At Seven Pines on June 1, 1861, it was Jenkins' gallant charge that shattered the 16th Michigan Wolverine regiment and saved the day for the Confederates. Jenkins presented the Michigan regiment's colors to South Carolina Governor Pickens.

Ordered to silence the Union artillery at Frazier's farm, Jenkins had two horses shot from under him and personally sustained three wounds in leading his men across a wide span of meadow to capture Union 12-pounders that were spewing grape shot upon the Confederate right flank.

He became Brigadier General Micah Jenkins in June, 1862, and was celebrated at age 27 as the youngest general in the Army of Northern Virginia. He wrote his wife, Caroline, then pregnant with their fourth child, that he blushed at the praise that commanders such as Hill and Longstreet heaped upon him and his men.

Micah Jenkins led from the front, a dangerous practice that gained the South an enormous advantage over the Union in the early stages, but such southern valor made many southern widows. Stonewall Jackson asked Micah Jenkins to ride with him in the evening of May 2, 1863, to reconnoiter the enemy position during a lull in the fighting in the Battle of the Wilderness. Jenkins' brigade was to spearhead the predawn attack and Stonewall wanted to get close-up intelligence on the best route of advance.

They made their close-in reconnaissance and were returning, a party of eight mounted officers, each in their plain dress fighting attire. A staff officer reached down to pick up a discarded Union flag and then all hell broke loose. Those red, white, and blue colors were spotted by Billy Mahone's regiment of Virginians and four saddles were emptied in the nighttime volley. Stonewall received his death wound and Micah Jenkins took a Minie ball to the forehead. His last words were a faint, gurgled exhortation for his brigade to press on!

Book On Captain Magwood A Must Read For Summer

Mention Bull's Island and we think of a paradise unspoiled by development. Mention the name Magwood and most East Cooperites think of Shem Creek and the seafood processing shed and the shrimp boats that plied coastal waters for more than a hundred years. Allude to Bull's Island and Magwood together and you have the newest "must read" summer book, "Bull's Island Memories By Robert Elliott Magwood."

This is a book that has been years in the making. There were setbacks for editor John Magwood, Sr., that date all the way to Hurricane Hugo. But setting down the stories of his late father, Captain Robert Magwood, is more than a son's tribute. These low country stories, and there are fifty of them, recall a coastal existence so foreign to us moderns that the subject, Cap'n Robert, emerges as a genuine folk legend.

Born 1899 in the old family home on a bluff of big Bull's Island, Robert may have been one of the last Americans to live a Tom Sawyer existence, according to his son, John. With 1500 acres of barrier island cotton fields, tangled wilderness, and bone yard beach, it was as remote as any paradise island ever could be. Magwood's stories have that salt marsh and pinewood savor about them that Archibald Rutledge captured years ago in "Home By The River." The pencil sketches illustrating young Robert's exploits on Bull's Island nearly a hundred years ago, such as Robert encountering the rum runners, or his killing a huge boar with just a hatchet, add a romantic touch to this memoir just released.

What boy could have had a more historic domain all to himself. Bull's Island was first noted by John Cabot who named the area Cape Romain, though he called it Cape Roman. Walter Raleigh probably used the island as well. Magwood's history of Bull's Island tells of how the native Seewee Indians called the place Onisecaw, and the first settlers came ashore there for fresh water. The native girls wore moss shawls and brought them a curious kind of flat cornbread. Then the warriors insisted on taking the white men piggyback overland to meet the Seewee chief. Whether William Bull ever owned the island, or not, is up to conjecture, but he had a deer skin warehouse there for his trade with the natives.

With such legends as Blackbeard's pirate treasure possibly buried there and the ghosts of shipwrecked souls wandering the desolate beach, no boy in America had a more fascinating playground.

Robert Magwood's uncle purchased Addison's Shipyard on Shem Creek in 1895 and then sold part of the land to Edward O. Hall, master shipbuilder. Later the land became part of the Darby boat yard, and more recently, a gated community of luxury homes as the nature of the creek has been altered. Robert Magwood kept a packing operation and his shrimp boats Susie Magwood and the Josephine docked there. Hence, the Magwood name has become synonymous with the local seafood industry here.

As a young man, Robert attended Porter Military Academy on Ashley and Bee Streets. In the 1920s the young cadets could choose either naval or army training at Porter, and Magwood naturally chose the seagoing service. Charleston Mayor Stoney wanted Porter to become a preparatory school for the naval academy and he offered the West Point Rice Mill on Chisolm Street as an inducement, but that grandiose plan never panned out.

Back in the 1920s rowing was one of the most popular of school sports. Magwood helped start the Porter Military rowing club. These plantation boys were used to rowing long boats up and down the Ashley River, so all they needed was some astute coaching.

Porter Military Academy had an athletic reputation of prowess dating back to the 1870s when sports teams were first beginning to be formed across the state. Porter had already whipped Carolina, The Citadel, and the College of Charleston in baseball and football. In rowing, these strapping farm boys also made their mark against some national competition.

One of the best rowing clubs in the country was, you guessed it, the United States Navy team. With efforts of local officials and the navy base, it was arranged for the navy rowing team to come to Charleston in the glorious month of May, 1920, to take on all challengers. Robert Magwood drilled the Porter crew daily. He knew that they had strength and a fast shell, but his oarsmen lacked the finesse of the elite east coast squads.

Magwood, serving as coach and coxswain, had his team sand their shell with fine sandpaper until the hull was as slick as glass. He asked the mess hall cook to melt bee's wax and have it delivered to the dock right before the big race. As the navy team, professionals all, went through their warm-ups, it was obvious to most that the locals were outclassed.

Quietly and confidently, Magwood had his crew mates flip the rowing shell upside down as the mess hall delivery truck pulled up to the dock. Quickly the boys applied coat after coat of bee's wax varnish to the bottom. No rules said that this was illegal. In the water, the Porter shell glided like a swan to the starting mark. But experienced Navy was too experienced to be embarrassed by upstarts. Their skill honed by numerous victories showed at the starting gun.

The course, marked out off East Battery, was a lengthy one and Navy was leading at the first mark. But here came the Porter boys with long strokes and oars bending to the fast cadence of coxswain Magwood. They closed with the navy boat and a duel ensued. The crowd on the Battery went wild. Porter pulled by Navy and never looked back as they rowed with herculean effort. Magwood's margin in his wax-slickened hull was over a hundred yards on his much vaunted competition. It was Porter Military's greatest victory!

Read this story and many others like it in "Bull's Island Memories by Robert Elliott Magwood," on sale at Pitt Street Pharmacy, The Wreck restaurant, Royall Hardware, Coastal Expeditions, Fifth Season, and SeeWee Restaurant.

Elliott Williams of Darlington Was A Mighty Man

"People sleep peaceably in their beds at night only because rough men stand ready to do violence on their behalf." George Orwell didn't know Chief Petty Officer J. Elliott Williams, USN, but he had men like Williams in mind when he formed that hypothesis. As long as there are threats to America's vital interests, there will be a need for rough men to stand ready to do violence in defense of freedom.

Elliott Williams of Darlington was Boatswain's, or Bos'n, Mate First Class Williams when he led a counter attack of swift boats against a greatly superior force of Viet Cong on the Mekong Delta, October 31, 1966. For leadership.

heroism, and devotion to duty far exceeding mission expectations, Williams was presented the Congressional Medal of Honor in May, 1968. When he retired after 20 years of military service, he was the most decorated enlisted man ever to serve in the United States Navy.

Born in the Depression in Fort Mill, Williams' spent his boyhood in Darlington. He was 11 when Pearl Harbor was attacked and Darlington, small southern town that it was, produced more than its share of war heroes. Lieutenant Commander Weldon Lee Hamilton received two Navy Crosses for heroism. Stewart L. Hamilton of Darlington received a Navy Cross, also. These hometown heroes' exploits were well-known to Williams and all South Carolinians.

Amidst talk of the Cold War, the Truman Doctrine, and Stalin behaving badly over Berlin, sixteen-year-old Elliott Williams had to have his mother's approval to enlist in the Navy upon graduation from St. John's High School. He could have had no way of knowing that 20 years later, he'd retire to his pension with the nation's highest military awards for valor including the Navy Cross, two Silver Stars, a Legion of Merit, three Purple Hearts, and three Bronze Stars to go along with his Medal of Honor!

Seaman Williams had been in his country's service exactly three years when Kim Il-Sung's North Korean troops surprised Syngman Rhee's South Koreans with a massive, predawn attack. Employing a full arsenal of Soviet-made weaponry, including the much-vaunted T-34 Tank and the new Yak turbojet fighter planes, the North Koreans sent their detested southern counterparts reeling in retreat. The American part of the fight soon became MacArthur's and Truman's nightmare, but Elliott Williams got the opportunity he had dreamed of. He'd be a part of an elite naval commando force that'd make raids into North Korea using small assault boats launched from warships in the Yellow Sea and the Sea of Japan.

Williams was a fierce-looking sailor possessing a bulldog countenance. He was a fellow no one would tangle with when sailors had shore leave. At 5'8" and

and a solid 210 pound frame, he could have been a linebacker in college football. Going on commando raids into Korea with a k-bar knife and M-1 carbine was more fun than shooting squirrels out of pine trees. At the Medal of Honor ceremony in 1968, Lyndon Johnson leaned over to the brawny sailor and drawled, "Williams, where'd you get that neck?"

Williams had married his sweetheart, sailed most of the seven seas, decorated for bravery, and was about ready to retire from the service when Vietnam escalated into a full-blown conflict. He'd had a full career and had achieved respectable rank and could have ducked this nasty jungle war. But with his usual insistence to be where the action was, Elliott volunteered for river patrol boat operations then being devised for the Mekong Delta.

Characteristically, he assured his superiors that he felt that he had the necessary experience for riverine warfare, and that he could lead young sailors into harm's way. Combatting an insurgency such as the one we faced in South Vietnam required that America train a legion of these Orwellian rough men prepared to do violence. Williams, a bos'n mate first class by 1966, was entrusted with the command of two river patrol boats on the Mekong. Normally, a bos'n mate commanded one boat, but even Rear Admiral Morton O'Toole was aware of Williams' prowess in combat.

A local retired sailor who served with Williams in Vietnam recalls that these PBR's, river patrol boats, were pound-for-pound the deadliest fighting machines on earth with their 50 caliber machine guns, grenade launchers, and M-60 machine guns. But their chief asset was their water-jet propulsion engines that moved these craft at blazing speeds in quite shallow waters. Their mission was to support special operations by the SEAL and Army Special Forces teams and to intercept Viet Cong insurgents posing as fishermen in sampans.

On the fateful day in October, 1966, when Elliott Williams' two river patrol boats were ambushed on a very narrow part of the Mekong estuary, the United States Navy needed a mighty man in command, not some fellow looking for a line on his resume.

Commanding PBR-105, the river boat he skippered as well as one other boat in his section, Williams noted two suspicious sampans ahead near a bend. They opened fire and Williams eradicated one of them with vengeance, yet the other sampan fled up a narrow rice canal.

In a flash of gunfire it became obvious that Williams had been led into a terrible deathtrap situation. Machine gun fire and rocket-launched grenades flew at the two small boats from three directions. The prudent thing was to utilize the swiftboat's speed and skedaddle. But Williams' fighting blood was up, and some of his men were already blooded. He called in Huey air support, but it didn't arrive in time.

Bos'n Williams not only returned fire, he ordered both boats full speed ahead with all guns blazing. The battle raged in shallow, bloody water with narrow bends and a jungle-protected enemy. Some sources say that Elliott defeated as many as a thousand Viet Cong that day. He refused movie and book rights on his amazing story, saying that Hollywood would probably get it all wrong.

Williams was a modest fellow, a good husband and daddy. His second career was as a United States Marshall. The great man died in In 2004, the Navy commissioned a new guided-missile destroyer DDG-95 named the USS James E. Williams. Williams' Patrol Boat PBR-105 is a legend in Navy circles, and a tour of the Patriot's Point Medal of Honor Museum will convince you that George Orwell was precise in his assumption.

England's Harebrained Schemes For Settling America

While we celebrate the 400th anniversary of the English founding, or floundering, at Jamestown, it's timely to note that even Queen Elizabeth I, maybe the wisest old bird ever to perch on the throne, had to make do with worthless intelligence and comical courtiers. Sage Queen Bess and her spy master, Francis Walsingham, tried to steer England between fantasy and fortune. Our mind's eye sees actress Judy Dench portraying Queen Elizabeth, suffering oafish buffoons such as Humfrey Gilbert, Davy Ingrams, George Peckham, and a host of rapscallions as they schemed for riches and fame.

In hindsight we can blanket those early English adventurers in glory, even laud them with encomiums for enduring hardships untold. But we favored sons of their doleful progeny can, with back glances, jab a little fun at their shortsightedness.

One of the most comical characters in Elizabethan England was a roustabout named Davy Ingrams. Surely his descendants must have ended up over here as snake-oil salesmen. No one has verified Ingrams' tall tales, but it was due to widespread accounts of his ship wreck survival and trek across uncharted North America in 1567-'69 that set prominent Englishmen to investing in get-rich schemes in the New World.

Ingrams was a sailor on-board one of Sir John Hawkins' trader-raider ships that lurked in the west African Atlantic hoping for opportunity to plunder Portuguese or Spanish slave ships. One particularly opportunistic Atlantic voyage turned sour for Hawkins when his captured Spanish vessels filled with African slaves were retaken by Spanish naval vessels somewhere near the Bay of Campeche. Ingrams was one of Hawkins' sailors that disappeared in this Caribbean fighting in 1568.

Somehow, whether it happened the way he told it, or not, Davy Ingrams footed it up the Mexican coastline, around the gulf coast of modern-day America, and made a cut-through using native trails till he exited on the northeastern coastline. There he was able to signal a French vessel. Ingrams and two other survivors made it to Le Harve. The story is too preposterous to be anything but true, and there's no other explanation for his turning up in England.

Ingrams became quite a celebrity in his day, and he made enough gold by repeating his story to rich men exclusively that he never had to do more than stay upright on a bar stool the rest of his existence. Ingrams' stories grew more fanciful with each new audience of subscribers. His biggest fish-on-the-line was Humfrey Gilbert, a bankrupt son of a wealthy papa with ties to the crown.

Meanwhile, during the 12 to 20 month trek that Ingrams made across the savage wilderness of Central and North America, Sir John Hawkins was desperately trying to locate his missing men. Perhaps Hawkins feared what tales these missing men might spread if the wrong people got them to talk. Hawkins fell in with Spanish officials and got caught up in the Ridolfi plot to assassinate Queen Elizabeth in favor of Mary, Queen of Scots. Now it appears that Hawkins was actually playing both sides of the gambit while cruising the Caribbean in 1569, for he, like a good double-agent, revealed the plot's seamy details to his sovereign, Elizabeth.

But, back to Ingrams, he'd already made it to Plymouth by way of Le Harve, and Gilbert was using Ingrams as publicity chairman for the greatest real estate swindle ever seen on either side of the Atlantic!

Since there was no one to refute the Ingrams story, and no mention was ever given to the whereabouts of the other two survivors, Ingrams concocted tales of vast riches in the interior of what was then Spanish America. Gilbert plied Davy with ale and his tongue wagged of fabulous wealth amongst the native tribes. He told stories of natives wearing suits of gold, and how some of the tribes were cannibals who desired nothing better than to dine upon the white meat of Europeans!

Gilbert, arch swindler of all land developers, promptly summoned young aristocrats to his Red Crosse Street London address. Sir Humfrey sat at his desk with quill and parchment and confidently sold over 8 million acres of land that he did not even know existed. His clients were members of parliament, earls and

barons. Young and old, gullible and some supposedly wise, they secured shares in
Gilbert's New World Land Scheme of 1580.

Gilbert's swashbuckling half-brother, Walter Ralegh, that's the spelling he
preferred, was still undecided about pursuing a career as a privateer or setting up
as a merchant. With the embellished tales of Davy Ingrams fresh on his mind,
the scent of easy gold fired his loins more than did the red-haired beauties of
Devon! He cast lots with Gilbert.

Historian Giles Milton recounts how one wealthy investor, Sir George
Peckham, bubbling with do-good intentions, planned to robe his share of New
World native inhabitants in "redde, blewe, yellow, or greene cassocks and a cappe
of such like." Another bragged of how he'd win favor by giving all he met glass
beads, looking glass mirrors, and trinkets. Such naive assumptions seem to plague
the best intentions of global planners from Walsingham to Wilson to Wolfowitz.

Sir Humfrey Gilbert bankrolled hundreds of thousands of pounds sterling
from his wild land speculations that would make the Yahoo land deal look
reasonable in the 19th century.
Gilbert told his rich investors that America best be settled first by roughnecks,
cutthroats, and other incorrigibles then locked away in London prisons. The
Crown hastily assented, so did the investors, and giddy Gilbert was off on voyage
number one.

Arriving somewhere off Nova Scotia, he assumed he was in our mid-
Atlantic coastline, Gilbert was chagrinned to find a harbor chock full of French
trading ships, a couple of other English ships, and pirates galore! Hard-charger
Gilbert sent word that all flags must dip to his conquering English crew. Then
Gilbert promptly ran his ship fast aground, to the guffaws of all assembled.

Humfrey Gilbert was lost at sea a few years later, to the discomfiture of his
trusting investors. In later years the Old Bailey threw out the land claims and
deeds of these greedy swains who'd bet all on the wild tales of Davy Ingrams and
the confidence scheme of Humfrey Gilbert. Seems that the more things change,

the more they remain the same!

Remembering The Noble Nine who Gave All On 6-18

From Saint Cloud to St. Louis they came here, from Boston to San Antonio, to stand for the noble nine firemen who fell June 18 in the inferno on Savannah Highway. Who among us would have had the courage to rush into that flaming structure heedless of personal safety? The words of General Patton come to mind, "It is foolish and wrong to mourn the men who died. Rather we should thank God that such men lived. "

At Denver International Airport the television monitor blared with CNN chatter when suddenly the announcer interrupted with breaking news out of Charleston. Within seconds a throng gathered and watched as the dreadful story unfolded. There was a report of nine firemen who'd sacrificed all on concern that someone might still be inside the sofa super store. For, unlike deaths in other tragedies and disasters, the death of a firemen poignantly illustrates the verse of John 15:13, "Greater love has no man than this, that he lay down his life for his friends. "

In a free society there's but a thin line between order and chaos, and history has shown that the scourge of fire has been more often the cause of Charleston's chaos than the "hell and high water" of storm, earthquake, or war. The Halsey map of Charleston graphically illustrates the burn areas of numerous widespread fires that have ravaged Charleston since the late 17th century. The old Phoenix Fire map reveals us as the earliest city to develop fire insurance protection.

East Cooper residents still recall enormous conflagrations where firemen from many stations responded with everything they had. In the 1970s the Blue Hawaii restaurant, where Alex's is today, became a raging inferno. Coleman Boulevard was blocked by fire engines crisscrossed in every angle tryi ng to put water on a hopeless situation.

Then who can forget the Trawler Restaurant fire, and years later, R.B.'s ? The smoke from the blaze of R.B.'s was spotted by aircraft a hundred miles off. Fearless firemen battled from boats in Shem Creek as well as from ladder trucks that perched them a hundred feet in the air on Shem Creek Bridge.

In the 1970s, a lovely old frame home at 640 Pitt went up in flames. With sorrow we recall that February night in the 1980s when 615 Pitt, an antebellum waterfront home, erupted into an uncontrollable inferno. Firefighters from Hanahan, Goose Creek, and Awendaw responded when the Old Causeway caught fire some years back. Sweat-soaked firemen waded into the marsh at low-tide to drag hoses into position. Remember the terrible night that Senator Hollings' beach home and that of Kyle Petty caught fire and the stiff beach breeze turned both homes into combustible matchsticks.

The fireman is a lot like the so-called "dog-face" soldier. No one knows his name or deeds until he is called upon for the ultimate sacrifice. Captain Mike Benke, Fireman James "Earl" Allen Drayton, Engineer Brad Baity, Fireman Brandon Thompson, Assistant Engineer Michael French, Captain Louis Mulkey, fireman Melvin Champaign, Engineer Mark Kelsey, now join the glory of the 343 immortals of the NYFD who perished on 9-11 as they went up those crumbling stairs of the twin towers.

Just yesterday NYFD fireman Daniel Pujdak fell four floors to his death while battling a blaze in Brooklyn. Daniel, I'm sure, was met at the Pearly Gates by our brave fellows from Monday night and a host of NYFD angels. The Emerald Pipe and Drum Society will have to perform another "Amazing Grace" for one of their own upon return of their 15 hour bus ride home from Charleston.

By my tally, 1,985 firemen have been killed in line of duty between 1990 and 2005. These men and women respond in the race of time, and often imperil themselves to rescue a pet trapped in a smoke-filled room.

The Mount Pleasant Fire Department web site notes Town Administrator Mac Burdette saying recently that we expect to add 25 to 30 new fire fighting positions. Council member and Fire Committee Chair Thomasena Stokes-Marshall "I cannot think of a more professional fire department than the one we have here in Mount Pleasant. Our fire staff is always looking at innovative ways to serve citizens ... ."

Who are our town's fire defenders? They never seek publicity, but here are Mount Pleasant's finest: Fire Chief Herb Williams; Assistant Chief Robert Wagenbrenner; Battalion Chief Bud Thames; Battalion Chief Scott Taylor; Battalion Chief Ron Alexander; Battalion Chief James Johnston; Battalion Chief Leon Lantagne; Fire Marshal Alton Tyler; Deputy Fire Marshal Terry Mueller; Deputy Fire Marshal Bianca Sancic; Training Officer John Whetsell; and Medical Training Officer Robert Wronski. Like Charleston's Chief Rusty Thomas, these men are always on duty.

Pass any fire station and the men are polishing the engines and double-checking the gear. If they aren't doing that, then they are giving safety inspections to businesses, fire prevention talks to schools, and walking the streets handing out smoke alarms. Mayor Riley, always at his best when things are at their worst, made eloquent testimony to their sacrifice, and Governor Sanford put the tragic event in an eternal perspective, and what a invocation and benediction by Reverends Dewey and Gallant.

Our Mount Pleasant fire stations each possess their own personalities. Fire Station 1 on McCants is led by Captain Mark Karst; Fire Station 2 on Egypt Road by Captain William R. Pace; and Fire Station 3 on 7th Avenue by Captain Steven Drozd. Out on Six Mile Road, Fire Station 4 is headed by Captain Clement Vanderhorst, and on Dune West Boulevard, Fire Station 5 is led by Captain Michael Allen. Make an opportunity to thank these courageous first-responders.

Before you finish this column, they will be putting everything on the line for our community once again. Never take them and their service for granted.

History books tell us that widespread fires ravaged Charleston in 1740, 1778, 1838, and 1861. The Atlantic Wharf burned for days in the early 1950s. Cadets of the late 1960s will remember the laundry catching fire. And forest fires have consumed hundreds of acres. Brave firemen contested their destructiveness. One memory we will retain to our graves, however, is the interrupting television report of "fireman down" on 6-18 at Savannah Highway South.

Zebulon Pike And The Great Western Conspiracy of 1807

Four graybeard historians reclined in the dining room of Corbett Hall, Colorado State University, recently and pondered a question that lingers on the mind of some westerners, namely, has Zebulon Pike, the explorer, gotten a free ride in the history books. Was he involved in the Wilkinson-Burr conspiracy to set up their own kingdom in the American southwest?

Apparently Pike was up to his eyeballs in a tangled web of international conspiracies and double-agent espionage. All that we remember today is a snowcapped Colorado peak that bears his name.

This mother of all conspiracy theories, played itself out in our federal court system 200 years ago this week. Aaron Burr's indictment for treason in June, 1807, remains the single greatest political shocker in our history.

Burr, Benedict Arnold, and James Wilkinson had been officers on the failed 1775 Quebec campaign in the Revolutionary War. Something ominous transpired then between these three men that was not in keeping with the ideals of the patriot cause. They began hatching a dark plan to make themselves imperial barons.

Zeb Pike's father was also on that disastrous Quebec expedition. Thirty years later, these men, plus Pike's son, were mentioned as conspirators in a scheme set up their own western kingdom. In 1807 James Wilkinson was our nation's senior military commander, and Vice President Burr was being sought in connection with the duel that killed Alexander Hamilton.

When "American West" referred to the lands from the Mississippi delta to the Ohio River, some frontiersmen's sense of opportunism overlay their feelings of patriotism. Just as the original colonies blasted Britain for failure to provide protection while at the same time restricting trade, so did many on the frontier think the same of our new federal government.

Burr and Wilkinson spawned a scheme to take advantage of the developing sectional rift, and young Lieutenant Zeb Pike became, unwittingly or not, their factotum.

When Joshua Chamberlain tersely stated, "Generals can do anything. There's nothing so much like a god on earth as a General on a battlefield," he did not have Wilkinson in mind, but the statement fits. Wilkinson was the protector of the West, and from his base at Fort Washington on the Ohio River, present-day Cincinnati, Wilkinson was governor-general of a vast domain. He garnered more respect there than did Congress.

The frontier was in constant danger from Indian uprisings, and Pike's father was a trusted staff officer in Wilkinson's western brigade. Young Zebulon was the brigade mascot, and naturally he looked up to the general wearing the gold braid.

There were numerous Indian wars in the Ohio Valley, but the Battle of the Wabash, or Little Turtle's defeat of St. Clair, was the one that left pioneers suspicious that the government wouldn't be capable of defending the territories. The combined nations of the Miami, the Shawnee, and the Delawares struck a regiment of regulars under the command of Arthur St. Clair in Ohio in November, 1791. The rout of St. Clair's forces on the Wabash is one of the U.S. Army's most ignominious moments. St. Clair and his men were sleeping off the aftereffects of a carousing night with the female camp-followers. The savagery of the dawn attack was unprecedented in the annals of American warfare. Little Turtle's warriors impaled their captives alive. Few soldiers escaped; none of the women did. Zebulon Pike's father was one of the fleet-footed survivors. Washington, D.C., sent no further aid.

Reorganizing at Fort Washington under General Wilkinson, the Army and the settlers felt like they were on their own at the edge of civilization. There was no higher authority than that of Wilkinson, and Wilkinson was the Pike family's ticket to success. Unknown to these hardy settlers, their governor-general was secretly in the pay of the Spanish government and betraying the red, white and blue!

Not only was Wilkinson involved in high treason, so was the vice president, Aaron Burr! For years since that ill-fated expedition against Quebec, Wilkinson, Burr, and others connived to establish themselves as Napoleon-styled, imperial barons over great dominions in the Spanish southwest.

General Wilkinson sought out young Lieutenant Zebulon Pike, the boy who'd idolized him at Fort Washington, and sent him on a perilous secret mission to scout the southern reaches of the Louisiana Purchase, just as Lewis and Clark were officially mapping the northwest territory. Pike allowed himself to be captured in Colorado by Spanish cavalry and taken to Santa Fe. What transpired between Pike and Spanish authorities has never been uncovered. It's suspected that Pike was furthering a conspiracy regarding his commander, General Wilkinson. He stayed captive only a brief while and was sent back to Wilkinson with fresh horses, provisions, and perhaps gold.

Wilkinson and Burr's grandiose scheme was in serious jeopardy when Jefferson and his confidante, Pierre Samuel du Pont de Nemours, maneuvered

Napoleon into selling America 530 million acres in the center of the continent, all for a bargain rate of 7 cents an acre! Napoleon's brother Joseph was on the throne of Spain, thus facilitating this bizarre land deal of France brokering Spanish land. Wilkinson became the mysterious "number 13" in a murky web of secret correspondence between Spanish officials in Mexico and his clandestine cohorts.

When Burr engaged in his famous duel with Alexander Hamilton and fled after mortally wounding the nation's first secretary of the treasury, the plot completely fell apart and Wilkinson tried to distance himself from Burr. Burr's daughter, Theodosia, was at the time, first lady of South Carolina, married to wealthy rice planter-turned politician, Joseph Alston. Charlestonian Thomas Pinckney had recently negotiated the Treaty of San Lorenzo to normalize relations between Spain and America during the upheaval of the French Wars of Revolution. Wilkinson was double-dealing with the Spanish, giving them false information about American plans, while passing along fraudulent communications to our Secretary of War, Henry Dearborn. Pike was Wilkinson's "Lewis and Clark."

The plotters were exposed and disgraced. Burr was tried in Richmond for treason, but poor prosecution saved him from conviction. Pike perhaps believed that by serving Wilkinson that he was indeed serving the United States, but there's no way knowing except by sifting through long-forgotten archives in Madrid. Zeb Pike died by concussion as a general in the War of 1812 leading American forces in a charge on British fortifications in York, Canada.

Remembering "Amazing Grace" Hopper, The Female Einstein

There was a time long past when men did not assume that women could master mathematics, physics, or astronomy, but by the mid-1930s, the faculty at Yale, males all, learned to accept it with grace, Grace Murray Hopper style. The woman who was the first to earn a Ph.D. in mathematics and physics from Yale (1935) was also the woman whose math skills ironed out naval gunfire coordinate issues in time for many of the epic battles of the Pacific.

A list of the 100 most influential women of all time compiled by researcher Deborah G. Felder, ranks Grace Murray Hopper as number 52 with Eleanor Roosevelt, Marie Curie, and Margaret Sanger as one, two, and three. The rest of us are content to know her as "the female Einstein" for her numerous mathematical and computer innovations.

Not many people from Charleston got to know Rear Admiral Grace Hopper, USN, during the 46 years that she served on active duty and in the naval reserve, but a local retired navy captain, my father, had the privilege to pick her up at her office at the Navy Yard and drive her across Washington, D.C., to speak at a Rotary luncheon twenty-five years ago. Admiral Hopper was quite a character, chain-smoking in her dress blues and fidgeting continuously with any gadget in sight.

Before introducing her, the president of Rotary told her that she could talk as long as she wanted, but that the members would leave promptly at 2 p.m. However, at 2:20 p.m. the tiny admiral who stood 5'6" and weighed 105 pounds was still speaking, and no one had stirred.

Grace Brewster Murray was a Brooklyn, New York, girl whose Jewish parents valued the education of their children more highly than leaving them an inheritance. She grew up playing kick-the-can with her brothers, and tinkering with every appliance in the household, a rather unladylike trait in the 1920s. Her father, a well-to-do insurance broker, suffered a financial reversal when blood circulation problems led to double amputation when Grace was in high-school. The family savings went to sending her to the finest girls' college in the land, Vassar.

The woman who pioneered the computer language COBAL and wrote software to pave the way for so many of the computer operations we take for granted today, forever endeared herself to us by flunking Latin in high school and having to sit out a year for Vassar admission. In fact, Vassar recommended that Grace enroll in a boarding school for an extra year of Latin. So Hartridge School in Plainfield, New Jersey, proudly lists Hopper as one of their own.

The Murrays knew that Grace was technically-minded when she preferred taking apart and reassembling alarm clocks to playing with dolls and tea sets. In later years the first thing anyone noticed when entering her office was the wall clock programmed to tell time counterclockwise. She kept her wacky-sense of genius alive as she deadpanned math and physics jokes that only an Oppenheimer could appreciate.

Vassar has more famous alums than New York has streetlights, yet the idea of a woman interested in electrical engineering, thermal physics, and Boolean mathematics intrigued even that progressive institution. When she graduated phi beta kappa in 1928 with a double major in math and physics, her college asked her stay on and become part of the faculty.

For all her geekiness, Grace Murray held a lifelong attraction for men. Whether they found her attractive, fascinating, or merely a curiosity is an enigma, but she married Vince Hopper, the man who headed NYU's famed English department for many years. Her Vassar sisterhood considered Vince a catch, and their marriage lasted 15 years.

There were women attending grad school at Yale in the 1930s, but Grace was the first to be listed in the ranks of exceptional Eli's. Her dissertation entitled "New Types of Irreducibility Criteria" insured her lasting employment in the groves of academe. Although her teaching legacy is in the Math department of Vassar, Hopper lectured across the United States, and the fact that she was a woman in a man's field, rarely was mentioned, for the fast-talking, fidgeting professor spellbound her audiences with "off the wall" approaches to mathematical conundrums.

When Japan bombed Pearl Harbor, Grace Hopper was 35 and a full professor at Vassar. She tried to enlist in the Navy but was told that she was too old and too thin. Undaunted by their chauvinist attitude, this married, diminutive female academic who desired only to serve her country prevailed upon the Navy to take her in active reserve status for the duration of the war. That was one of the best decisions the Navy ever made!

Once on active duty, the "Amazing Grace" Hopper turned her high-beam mind on refining the Mark I and Mark II calculating machine, a device facilitating naval gunfire accuracy. She was instrumental in ironing out wrinkles in getting big navy guns on target quickly while moving full speed in pitching seas, an advantage employed in Pacific battles. She soon patented her own device, the compiler, a similar mathematical computing device capable of doing complex logarithms. Some of the projects that Grace worked on are still classified, not so much for their content, but for fear of revealing the systematic thought-processes used in mastering solutions.

This math-wizard awed everyone with whom she worked, and though she talked nonstop and chain-smoked, Grace Hopper was always a down-to-earth woman given to staring deeply into one's eyes before she answered them. The computer languages FORTRAN and COBAL have her fingerprints, and the term "debugging" was coined by her with reference to pesky moths that made their way into the vacuum tubes of the early computers.

Hopper's standard attention step when giving speeches was to hand out a strand of fiber optic wire 11.75 inches long, the distance that light travels in a nanosecond, another of the terms she coined. She also handed out packets of pepper to illustrate pixoseconds. The U.S. Navy deemed Hopper's mind a national asset, and though she was a consultant to Sperry and Rand Corporations and a lecturer at Harvard, MIT, Princeton, and Cal-Tech, the Navy kept her on duty until her death in 1992 at age 85. Unlike Einstein, however, Grace Murray

Hopper was also an accomplished concert pianist!

Charlestonian Was Captain Kidd's Most Trusted Man

Call William Kidd a pirate, or call him a bounty hunter in service to the Crown, but the London Lords of the Admiralty called him a liar, and for crimes on the seas Kidd swung on a gallows at Wapping Dock on May 23, 1701. His gibbeted body swung in the wind for two years at the mouth of the Thames as a warning to would-be pirates. Kidd's legend is classic pirate lore, but what is less known is that Kidd's closest confederate was Charleston merchant, John Weir, once a seagoing adventurer who shared in Kidd's exploits, yet escaped censure and the noose.

The chronicle of Captain Kidd reenforces the suspicions that historians have regarding the nefarious role played by kings in clandestinely financing pirates, and then disavowing any association if the skullduggery is revealed. Elizabeth I, enriched herself through the exploits of well-known corsairs such as Drake, Raleigh, and Gilbert. Those sea rovers preyed upon Spanish shipping so successfully that Elizabeth's share of the loot subsidized the musicians and poets of the Elizabethan renaissance . . . Purcell, Byrd, Shakespeare, and Spenser." These sea dog's successful ventures brought them patriot status, even though some of their exploits were dark and dubious.

William of Orange, known as William III, had a similar notion a century later when he directed his coterie of supporters to finance a buccaneer to capture pirate galleys in the Indian Ocean. Kidd is an example of what happens to the "bag man" when the higher-ups fear exposure, and Weir, his Charlestonian sidekick, was an honest fellow who insisted that he signed on to Kidd's crew for prize money earned lawfully!

How did a respectable New York dry goods retailer such as William Kidd ever get himself busted on a piracy rap? And how did Charlestonian John Weir escape the notoriety of being an associate of Kidd?

Once a rover, always a rover, it appears, but Scottish born Kidd abandoned his commercial sailing for domestic bliss in New York with a pretty bride half his age. Prior to settling down, Merchant Sea Captain Kidd had performed service to New York upon occasion by chasing pirates away from the mouth of the Hudson, or catching the scurvy rascals that preyed upon English shipping on the Atlantic seaboard. For his services he got a share of the auctioned-off booty. It was legal, and Kidd had the reputation of a skillful bounty-hunter. But that was the 1680s and this was a decade and a half later, and piracy was all but eradicated except for a few swarthy cutthroats still operating in the Caribbean.

World-class piracy in 1700 had relocated to the Indian Ocean, and their lair of choice was Madagascar. From deep-water coves at Toliari, Nosy Be, or Tulear, bronze-skinned, tattooed renegades surprised, robbed, and tortured anyone afloat that ventured forth with fewer guns than they did. The British East India Company ships cruised convoy style through the Mozambique Channel to the Cape of Good Hope. Ships sailing alone had to cross their fingers that the blood-red flag denoting a pirate ship didn't close in on them from abeam. Pirates relished boarding merchant ships and terrifying their captives by executing them one by one and feeding the mangled corpses to the sharks. Kidd pledged to rid the seas of these vermin.

Kidd's New York backers, Cornelius Jacobs and Robert Livingston, were savvy traders who knew how to exploit the legal vagaries of cargo obtained under dubious circumstances. Tales were then circulating of enormous wealth being hoarded by salty thieves in the pirate citadels ringing Madagascar. The justification Jacobs and Cornelius used was the nuisance of these pirates occasionally preying along the North Atlantic trade routes.

All that Jacobs and Livingston needed was a daring sea captain who could walk the fine line of privateering without getting exposed as a pirate himself. They found their man in fellow merchant William Kidd.

To give a cloak of legality to Kidd's "pirate busting" operation, New York attorney general John Graham was prevailed upon to recommend Jacobs, Livington, and Kidd's scheme to London in hopes of getting a letter of marque granted. It all fell wonderfully into place as powerful Londoners and King William himself all coveted a share of the colossal profits that they expected Kidd to wrestle from the scum pirate princes.

Richard Coote, known as Lord Bellomont, had recently been appointed Governor of New England. Bellomont secured legal patents from his cronies in London that gave Kidd the right to plunder any ship afloat that appeared to be engaged in piracy. King William wanted a share because the potential for investor profits was enormous.

King William and aristocrats including the Earl of Shrewsbury, the Earl of Romney, Lord Somers, speaker of the House, and other Whig notables commissioned the galley *Adventure*, a 287-ton warship bearing 34 big guns, to be built at Deptford, exclusively for Kidd's privateering use. In 1700, it was the most powerful private warship ever built. As long as Kidd didn't embarrass his backers, everyone would have a whopping profit.

One of Kidd's first crew signees was John Weir of Charleston. Weir was a 40-year-old Charleston merchant and a devoted friend of Kidd from their drinking nights spent at Michael Hawdon's Tavern in New York. Much of Kidd's crew came from Hawdon's Tavern, including Robert Culliford, the shipmate who became Kidd's betrayer. Weir tried to warn Kidd of Culliford's intent to subvert the ship's mission to reckless piracy.

Upon Kidd's arrival at Madagascar, Culliford led a mutiny and gained command of the ship. Weir remained loyal to Kidd and continued to sail with

Kidd on another ship, but Culliford became the embodiment of evil piracy that Kidd eventually was charged with. One of Kidd's captures was questionable, and he killed one of his crew, but in a desperate move to avoid the taint of complicity, Kidd's London backers let him swing on the gallows rather than produce evidence they had that would free him. Weir bailed out of the venture in the Caribbean and made his way to Curacao, and back to Charleston. Kidd was apprehended by Lord Bellomont as he tried to reenter New York with some of his booty. Bellomont betrayed Kidd to score political favoritism with the Tories who were gaining ascendancy in Parliament. Meanwhile, Weir prospered as a merchant here.

Carolina Music With Maurice Williams And The Zodiacs

Fifty years ago this week, Maurice Williams released his recording entitled "Stay" as a Rhythm and Blues release, and it has remained the requested Beach Music oldie of all time. Blues singer, Jerry Butler, a.k.a. the Iceman, said, "If you don't know the words to this song, then you've got a hole in your soul."

Maurice Williams' "Stay" is the best-selling beach music hit of all time. The catchy words and tune have sold over ten million records. It's the theme song of the baby boomer cult movie, "Dirty Dancing," and its lyrics are tattooed in the recesses of everyone around here who came of age in the '60s. Lancaster natives, Maurice Williams and the Zodiacs, are still SC's official "ambassadors of soul music."

Like so many other young African-American recording artists, Maurice Williams grew up singing in his church choir. At age six he was plinking keys on an old upright piano in the living room of his home in Lancaster's mill section. By age 15, precocious Maurice already had a girlfriend, a churchgoing girl whose daddy was unusually strict about her staying out all night -- after all, this was 1955 in the rural south. He's never publicly mentioned her name, but one lonesome Carolina night up there in Lancaster, Maurice wrote a poem to this girl. "Why don't you stay / Just a little bit longer / Why don't you sta-a-a-y? / Your daddy won't mind, / And your mama won't mind, / If you have another dance, / Just one m-o-o-r-e t-i-i-m-e. / Oh, won't you stay / Just a little bit longer /." Williams' original words were "If you have another smoke," but the recording studio told him that he'd have to change it in order to play the song on the radio.

What's the name of Maurice's muse, the teenager who inspired pop lyrics rivaling Gershwin's "Summer time" as the the most famous music ever composed in South Carolina. According to pop music historians Bruce Eder and Stephen Erlewine, this same teen flame also inspired another of Maurice's hits, "Little Darlin'." "Little Darlin" was bumped out in August, 1957, by Elvis Pressley's sultry moaning about a "Heartbreak Hotel" and the thumping "Jailhouse Rock."

Williams' mother and sister played a rickety-old upright piano in their home, and before he was ten-years-old, precocious Maurice could plink out bars of several familiar tunes. "Blueberry Hill," and "On Top of Old Smokey" were blaring on AM radio sets across the South.

By his 15th birthday, he had his own band, The Royal Charms. Local boys, school chums, who'd heard Honky-Tonk coming out of nightclubs they weren't allowed to frequent, formed the band that would become Maurice Williams and the Zodiacs. Besides Maurice, there was Earl Gainey, Willie Jones, Norman Wade, and William Massey. Barely out of junior high, the music they knew best was old-fashioned gospel, but Rhythm and Blues also came on the radio, especially WBT out of Charlotte.

Be-Bop music, the term "doo-wop" is still a decade away in 1955, was not their ambition, for The Royal Charms really wanted to make their reputation in R and B. Their problem was that being so young, no one took them seriously. They performed their own arrangements of the Avalon Blues, Spike Driver Blues, Mississippi John Hurt's songs, Big Leg Blues, and a few pieces of their own composition. But, as minors, The Charms were unable to play the clubs that'd give them some recognition. From Lancaster to Pageland and Great Falls, Williams and his band did gigs in W.O.W. and American Legion Halls. Finally in the summer of '56, an envelope containing an uncopyrighted reel to reel recording of "Stay" and 'Little Darlin' dropped on the desk of Ernie Young of Excello Records in Nashville.

The Nashville producer thought he had adults back in Lancaster who were begging for an audition; little did he know how minor his clients would turn out to be. Williams and Earl Gainey went from store to store on Lancaster streets to solicit contributions for their bus trip to the Country Music Capitol. back then, Tommy Faile of Kershaw was cutting records in Nashville and wailing his twang on the Arthur Godfrey show. Could 5 black boys from upstate SC named Maurice, Earl, Willie, Norman, and "Sweet" William get something going on a shoestring budget in the music metropolis of Nashville?

Ernie Young liked what he heard, but he said that the Charms name would have to go. After a bewildering couple of days the boys decided to call themselves Maurice Williams and The Gladiolas. Then Ernie wanted more of a calypso island beat mixed into the rhythm, distinctly carrying the tune away from R and B.

The song, still not copyrighted, got a boost when Nashville stations asked the Gladiolas to drop a demo tape by for DJ's to rate. It was toe-tapping, sing-along music that was ideal for the slow-shuffling kind of dancing that appealed southerners flocking to the Myrtle Beach Pavilion. Young left the rights to "Stay" and "Little Darlin" with Maurice, and those two songs alone have earned him millions in royalties while he was still a teen. Both songs have been released by other artists.

A tour of western states in the late 1950s insured that Maurice and his band was no flash in a pan. They picked up Shane Gaston as a vocalist, and Shane's falsetto voice on "Stay" added an unforgettable dimension, especially when Shane made comical faces as he winced on the high notes.

Maurice was an honors student in high school and received a scholarship to Allen University, but he was booked solid on the university fraternity circuit. USC's Greene Street Greek row provided enough venues for Maurice Williams and The Zodiacs to make a comfortable living.

According to Williams, it was new group member, Bobby Gore, who saw a German automobile named the Zodiac and thought the group's name should be changed.

So up at O.D., Ocean Drive, at the famed Beach Club, when the purple lights were flashing and Maurice stepped to the microphone and yelled, 'It's Party Time!" and the guitars were driving home the rhythm, and Maurice's tenor voice bellowed "Ah, just a little bit longer," and Shane picked up with "Oh won't you stay," the entire world was put on hold. Maurice Williams and the Zodiacs are definitely here to Stay!

Discovery of S.S. Central America Overshadowed By Hugo

In 1989, the catch phrase "Meet me at Henry's" was a pat Charleston idiom for a lunch invitation to the city's oldest restaurant located on the corner of North Market and Anson Streets. For more than sixty years locals and visitors alike have been ducking into Henry's for libations, laughs, and rollicking good times. But most of us missed the jubilation that took place at Henry's on Wednesday,

174

August 9, 1989, when burly Bob Evans rose from his table of partying tourists and sauntered over to the beat-up piano against the rough brick wall.

Bob placed his beer glass down on a cardboard coaster and tapped on a few of the stained ivory keys. Soon a melody took shape and within seconds Bob was tearing into Scott Joplin's "Maple Leaf Rag." Suddenly all eyes were on him, Bob's panama hat bobbing up and down as he pounded the keys, and that ragtime piano beat had customers stamping time with their hands and their feet. That's when Tommy Thompson, Bob Doering, Don Hackman, Alan Scott, and eight other sun-bronzed sailors closed a circle around Bob's impromptu concert. What no one knew was that these seafaring hardies had just discovered the wreck of the *S.S. Central America*, the richest sunken treasure ship in history and that it lay just a hundred and sixty miles northeast of Charleston harbor.

There's a good reason that we don't know much about this story. Other than a press release that the *S.S. Central America* had been located and the salvage rights awarded to the Columbus-America Discovery Group, the subject matter was very much hush-hush. Even though the gold-laden vessel was a mile and a half beneath the surface, just the rumor of a lost treasure estimated to be worth a billion dollars was reason aplenty for Tommy Thompson and Bob Evans to be anxious.

Yet another reason why these begrizzled mariners were jubilant but weren't crowing like pirates about their newfound wealth was that a looming federal court battle over ownership gave them reason to keep their lips sealed. Unbeknownst to Thompson, just a few streets across Charleston, a former associate of his had finagled the highly secret coordinates of the wreck's location and was planning his own treasure salvage mission.

For three days and nights Thompson's high-tech salvage vessel, *Nicor Navigator*, stayed tied up at Union Street dock at the foot of Calhoun Street while its merry crew frolicked at local watering holes such as Henry's and East Bay Trading Company. Meanwhile, unbeknownst to the partiers, keeping surveillance over the docked *Nicor Navigator* was Thompson's shadowy rival who hoped to follow Thompson at a distance and plunder his secret find. Surely, there could have been no finer setting for a high-stakes maritime treasure thriller than this one unfolding in Charleston in the summer of '89!

Six weeks after their celebration in Charleston, Hurricane Hugo slammed into the port city dousing Henry's Bar and Restaurant knee-deep in sea water and throwing the rest of the region into months of cleanup and rebuilding. Hugo forced Tommy Thompson to shift his logistical base northward to Norfolk, and the amazing story of the *S.S. Central America* and its Titanic-sized treasure soon was eclipsed by another disaster, the great California earthquake.

In the early 1980s the U.S. Navy enlisted the aid of private engineers and oceanographers to develop sophisticated sonar for mapping the ocean bottom and searching for missing submarines. The mission was so top-secret that few outside the Navy's top brass ever knew of the research. Ohio State engineer Tommy Thompson was one of the bright young civilian minds employed in the development of extremely sophisticated search techniques. Not only did this team devise sensitive search sonar, they also pioneered search theory, using computers to factor in multiple oceanographic variables such as time lapse, current, temperature, and drift.

In 1985, a search team recovered many artifacts from the *Titanic* which went down in the north Atlantic 1912. This epic underwater archaeological coup gave Thompson his inspiration to go after the big one, the missing *S.S. Central America*, sunk in a hurricane off the Carolinas in 1857 on a voyage taking California gold to New York. Hundreds of divers had searched in vain in waters from Hilton Head to Cape Hatteras.

Thompson researched every archived bit of evidence he could find relating to the 272 foot, side-wheel steamer that'd ferried over a third of the gold mined in the great 1849 gold rush to investors and banks in New York. On that fateful Friday, September 11, 1857, somewhere off the South Carolina coast, a powerful hurricane estimated to be the force of Hugo and traveling the same path almost exactly 132 years earlier, swamped the sleek vessel sending 579 souls and three tons of gold to the depths of Davy Jones' locker.

The loss of the **S.S. Central America** became the greatest maritime disaster ever. The disappearance of that much gold helped bring on the international panic of 1857. Dozens of banks folded and numerous businesses went into bankruptcy. A minor footnote to all the sorrow was that John James Audubon's wayward son had entrusted to a friend sailing on the *Central America* a portfolio of exotic western birds that he'd painted in California.

Tommy Thompson's boat and its robotic underwater recovery vessel were well aware that Hugo was careening through the Caribbean, and they knew that their secret coordinates had been discovered by another set of treasure seekers intent upon plundering their claim. With boiling seas and howling gales, Tommy turned the *Nicor Navigator* toward Norfolk to wait out the storm.

Only three days after Hugo slammed Bull's Bay, Thompson's *Nicor Navigator* was back on top of Galaxy II, his code name for the secret location 160 miles northeast of here. Soon, Bob Doering, the camera operator, was calling Tommy into the darkened cabin where his sophisticated cameras were showing the ocean floor littered knee-deep in places with thousands upon thousands of gold coins and thick, shiny gold bars. Outside, the seas were pitching eight feet in the aftermath of Hugo. They were ready to deploy the underwater robot to recover the richest treasure ever taken from the sea. So, go easy on the rowdy tourists at the table next to yours; they may have just discovered treasure!

Woodrow Wilson's Youth Was Spent in Columbia

In the 19th century, most of our presidents had experienced some horrors of war first hand, either through Indian uprisings, skirmishes of the Revolution, violence associated with the Regulator movement, or the terrible War Between the States. However, Woodrow Wilson, or Tommy as he was then known, spent 15 years of his youth amidst the pathos and ruins of the heartland of the Confederacy. What Wilson experienced in Augusta and Columbia in the 1860s and 1870s became engraved so deeply into his consciousness that, as president, he sought to make America's entry into World War I part of his dream to make it "the war to end all wars."

No southern city encountered more vindictiveness on behalf of the victorious Federals than did Columbia. Between Sherman's bummers looting the city, then burning it, and the aftermath of ten years of carpetbagger rule, Columbia's citizens had every reason to despise both the destruction of war as well as the assault that it makes upon the moral fabric of society.

Years later, Woodrow Wilson still told stories of that war. His earliest memory was of standing on the front porch of the parsonage in Augusta and hearing a newsboy cry, "Lincoln's elected! There'll be war!" Then there was the steady tramp of soldiers marching to rail lines that'd take them to Virginia. Boys would run to the road shouting, "Joe, Joe, where's your mule?" On one occasion his father, Reverend Joe Wilson, cut Sunday preaching short and directed the women to report to the Arsenal because more gunpowder was urgently needed in Virginia. Joe Wilson had been a chemistry professor at Hampden-Sydney earlier, and his knowledge was invaluable in the munitions factory at Augusta.

What a strange war it was for Wilson, as it was for many Americans. His parents were descended from Scot and Scots-Irish immigrants who settled in Ohio. Neither had any interest in the cause of slavery. Two of Wilson's uncles were Union generals, yet his immediate family embraced the loyalties of their region. Reverend Wilson also served as chaplain to the battalion that guarded the Augusta Arsenal.

In 1865, young Wilson was eye-witness to the spectacle of Jefferson Davis and Alex Stephens in shackles as they were carted through the streets of Augusta by a heavily armed Union force taking them up north for trial.

Robert E. Lee passed through Augusta in 1870 and 14-year-old Tommy Wilson stood in the street cheering the grey-bearded general. Wilson remarked in later years that in all his experiences he'd never witnessed anyone with the near god-like aura of Lee. One of Tommy's friends broke through the crowd to present a rose to the aged commander. Lee stood up, bowed and begged to make the rose a present to his daughter who accompanied him, much to the crowd's delight. Wilson was every inch a southerner, yet his education and public service was spent almost entirely above the Mason-Dixon line.

At the trying age of 14, Tommy Wilson moved by rail with all of the family's household goods to the dismal, charred ruins of Columbia. Travelers in the antebellum South had often remarked that Columbia was the loveliest of southern state capitals. But Columbia burned the night that Sherman's army departed, and the shameful looting and vandalism of stragglers and deserters brought down that once-proud city.

What met the Wilson family as they took up residence in Columbia was a city half-deserted. Empty homes became havens for thieves or vagrants passing through. Almost everyone was unemployed. Martial law had been relaxed by 1870, but the locals still chafed under curt treatment from occupying federal troops. It seemed as though there were few whole men about, as many of the discharged confederates were amputees, or disabled from wounds. Reverend Joe Wilson had two jobs, one as professor of theology in the fledgling Columbia Theological Seminary, and the other as the pastor of the city's Presbyterian church. It was Mrs. Wilson's inheritance from her Ohio parents that allowed them to build the spacious home at 1705 Hampton Street.

The McMasters were next-door neighbors to the Wilsons, and the two families remained close for several generations after the Wilsons moved on to Wilmington for another pastorate. In fact, the Wilson and the McMasters families intermarried. And to make matters more interesting, Theodore Roosevelt's Savannah-born mother had relatives related to the McMasters. So, in the presidential election of 1912, Bull Moose candidate Teddy Roosevelt and Democratic candidate Wilson could each boast of one of those "kissing-cousin" distant kinships that can happen only in the South!

Removed from his boyhood pals in Augusta, Tommy Wilson became a loner, a brooding boy immersed in the adventure world of Frederick Marryat's and James Fenimore Cooper's fiction. The naval warfare stories of Britisher Marryat thrilled Wilson and led him to dream of a career at sea, captaining his own warship. This mid-19th century author, Marryat, with novels such as Mr. Midshipman Easy, The Phantom Ship, and The Naval Officer who inspired Forester, Patrick O'Brien, Melville, and even Joseph Conrad captivated Wilson in his impressionable age of 15.

Tommy wrote hundreds of pages of imaginary ship's logs detailing his own fantasy seagoing exploits, usually with himself as captain of a fleet serving to rid the Atlantic of scurvy-faced pirates. In later years one can see evidence of Wilson's passion and idealism as expressed in his utopian 14 point peace plan of 1919, part of which deals with freedom of the seas.

Oddly enough, this boy who'd graduated number 41 out of 121 in his class at Princeton, 1876, was not a very good student in his early years. Because of adolescent ailments Wilson was nine years old before he began school. Though he won debating awards at Virginia's law school and in his doctoral work at Johns Hopkins, Wilson never led his class.

Wilson was unusually shy around girls during his teen years in Columbia. As a gangly, awkward teenager with acne, he lacked self-confidence. Nor was he a good ball player. His mother was concerned at his fear of girls until one day in 1872 she glanced out the kitchen window to see him walking side-by-side with the pretty McMasters girl next door, both deep in conversation. He gained statue and fame, but Wilson's Columbia years at 1705 Hampton Street that he most often recalled.

Lieutenant "Cump" Sherman Was Popular Here In The 1840s

He'd be about as popular here as a water moccasin at a picnic, just ask any South Carolinian. William Tecumseh Sherman in 1865 slashed and burned a swath through the center of this state that smolders still in the memory of many natives. Ruthless, barbarian, uncouth -- these are the printable adjectives used to particularize our contempt for the man that tactician B. H. Liddel-Hart described as "the father of modern warfare." Be that as it may, the man that locals once affectionately called "Cump" was a *bona fide* sportsman and favorite of the social elites here in the 1840s when he was first lieutenant of the 3rd artillery company stationed at Fort Moultrie.

Some here corresponded with Sherman following the War, Anthony Toomer Porter and Mary Poyas Lucas, come to mind, but most Carolinians who'd befriended Tecumseh "Cump" Sherman rued the day they'd ever shown him a kindness.

Sherman, in later years, was as bitter over the war's estrangements as were the conquered southerners. In his eloquently written autobiography published in 1875, one of the most readable of the wartime memoirs, Sherman laments, "I am tired and sick of war. Its glory is all moonshine. It is only those who have neither fired a shot nor heard the shrieks and groans of the wounded who cry aloud for blood, for vengeance, for desolation. War is hell. I think I understand what military fame is; to be killed on the field of battle and have your name misspelled in the newspapers."

But in 1844-45, "Cump" Sherman was a sporting and sociable gadfly in this bucolic East Cooper stretch of sea pines and water oaks. Fresh from rounding up Seminoles in Florida who resisted exile westward on the "trail of tears," Sherman told wild tales to his Fort Moultrie messmates of Chief Coacoochee, nicknamed the "Wild Cat," and his band of warriors who terrorized the Indian River region of northeast Florida. He was critical of the government's decision of taking in Florida as a state of the union. He preferred leaving it to the Seminoles and whatever tribal remnants that desired to live in that tropical climate.

As an Ohioan, this 25-year-old West Point-trained lieutenant was frontier bred and much used to roughing it. Duty with the 3rd Artillery at Fort Moultrie was delightful "R and R" for officers and men rotating from duty on the Indian frontier. Well-heeled young officers were frequent guests in the homes of Charlestonians and the residents of Hilliardsville, as Mount Pleasant was then known. Deer drives, duck hunts, dove shoots, and frolics with the belles were all a part of an officer's social obligation.

Up on French Quarter Creek, a tributary of the east branch of the Cooper River, Bentham Poyas owned a fine country seat which he called Cedar Hill. Poyas' son, James, Jim to his friends, befriended "Cump" Sherman and several other officers at Moultrie who enjoyed a day's sport in the field.

Cedar Hill offered a home-away-from home for "Cump," and he whiled away many pleasant hours there bagging fowl and game amidst the self-sustaining, working plantation of these slave-holding Huguenot southerners who opened their heart and hearth to him. Just upstream was Cherry Hill, the plantation of Commodore Duncan Nathaniel Ingraham, a former officer on board the *Bon Homme Richard* commanded by John Paul Jones. Commodore Ingraham's son, also a naval officer, befriended Sherman during his California service in the 1850s.

On one of the many outings at Cedar Hill, "Cump" was on horseback rapidly pursuing hounds in chase of a buck then crashing through the underbrush. Suddenly a low-lying limb upended "Cump" and his horse, throwing the tall,

182

athletic lieutenant heavily upon the sandy soil. He hit hard against the ground with his shoulder striking his double-barreled shotgun in a bone-crushing fashion. Horse and dismounted rider struggled in the brush to right themselves, but Sherman's shoulder was dislocated and paining him so as to put him *hors de combat*. Jim Poyas yelled for "Cump" to close up and press on, and "Cump" manfully tried to remount. To the credit of his endurance and self-pride, "Cump" did continue to follow the chase, but he had to break-off and ride in early to allow his injury some tender treatment from Poyas' younger sister, Mary.

Almost exactly twenty years to the day, Major General William Tecumseh Sherman was rolling through Dixie on his famous "march to the sea," the brutal earth scorching maneuver that severed the Confederacy in two and broke its will to fight on. In February 1865, Sherman was preparing to march northeast from conquered Columbia when Mayor Goodwin called at his headquarters at the Duncan home at 1615 Gervais Street, now the site of the Clarion Town House Hotel. The city was not yet ablaze, but already Union stragglers were looting homes. Mayor Goodwin informed Sherman at his HQ that a refugee lady, a Mrs. Bennett Lucas, had sent word that she urgently desired General Sherman to call upon her at her home which stood on the outskirts of Columbia near the Charlotte rail depot.

Not knowing what to expect, General Sherman and several orderlies mounted and rode with Mayor Goodwin to the lady's home. Already a Union guard stood watch at the front steps. Upon his knocking, Mrs. Bennett Lucas introduced herself as the former Mary Poyas of Cedar Hill plantation and recalled to Tecumseh the winter of '45 when he'd dislocated his shoulder and she'd nursed him back to health. Instantly, he recalled instantly of her kindness and their friendship, and there amidst the scene of defeat and destruction, an oasis of tranquility existed because Mary Poyas had showed the book of watercolors that Sherman had given her 20 years prior with his tender inscription to her. "That's Uncle Billy's handwriting, sure 'nuff,' " exclaimed the sergeant as he halted his men from systematically looting the house. Sherman made a light joke about his men's rough ways towards the secessionists and then bade her adieu. He posted another guard on the house to secure it from further harm. Historians still believe that this is the same lady who legend has it sent Sherman a tender letter when he was ravaging Savannah, December 1864, begging the Union general not to destroy Charleston, as so many here feared that he planned to do. Thus, Sherman bypassed Charleston.

The Civil War's Most Complex Man Was Tecumseh Sherman

For more than 130 years we Carolinians have borne contempt for Tecumseh Sherman for tolerating, if not actually instituting, brutality against noncombatants in his infamous "march to the sea" in 1864 and 1865. Most of us either lost a relative fighting against his army or had an ancestor's homestead burned out by Sherman's "bummers." What is surprising, however, is that Tecumseh, "Cump" to his intimates, was a thoughtful, sensitive, highly-intelligent man who detested war as the greatest of all human ills.

The Shermans were originally Massachusetts people who received considerable land grants in the Ohio territory in the early days of the republic. Fate early on ordered Tecumseh's life, for just as things were looking up for the family, Charles Sherman, an attorney and Ohio supreme court justice, contracted cholera and died. The year was 1829, and Tecumseh was barely 9 years old as he was packed off as an orphan by his destitute mother to live with the nearby Ewing family.

From this summer of 1829 until his death at age 71, Tecumseh Sherman suffered lengthy bouts with melancholia. In 1861 Sherman became so obsessed with feelings of inadequacy and personal gloom that he had to relinquish his command temporarily and hide away to recuperate. It was Ulysses Grant, a man who'd been a plebe at West Point when "Cump" Sherman was a senior private there, who quickly assented to have Sherman in his western command.

Thomas Ewing was an Ohio politician in the 1830s who adopted Tecumseh but never officially took up the matter in the courts. That's an important matter because Sherman later married Ellen Ewing, and there were rumors that he'd married his stepsister! The two did grow up together, but their romance was perfectly legal, though unusual.

Ewing paid for Sherman to attend Lancaster Classical Academy, the finest school in Ohio. As a Whig politician, attorney Ewing managed to get elected to Congress and later to the U.S. Senate. While in Washington, Ewing made the decision for Tecumseh to attend the United States Military Academy at West Point. Out in Ohio few folks had ever heard of the relatively new military school. As Irish Catholics, the Ewings insisted that Tecumseh be baptized into the Roman Church. Sherman, however, remained unchurched and never discussed faith, even though one of his sons later became a Jesuit priest. At age 16, the strapping redheaded boy who loved mathematics was sent off to West Point on the Hudson.

By his own admission, he was a slipshod cadet. Spit shine and brass held no allure for him. Cump studied, and he was number 4 in his class of 43, but the superintendent moved him down to number 6 for excessive demerits. His Virginia-born classmate, Union General George Thomas, hence known as "the rock of Chickamauga," was his best friend.

Sherman was age 20 when he was commissioned as a second lieutenant in the Third Artillery and posted to Fort Pierce, Florida, where the last Seminole holdouts were being rounded up for removal. On several occasions the tall, powerfully built officer placed himself in harm's way rather than sending out a subaltern. Sherman never shied from the fray.

Sherman's stepfather and patron, Thomas Ewing, was made Secretary of the Treasury in William Henry Harrison's administration in 1841. Already Cump Sherman was imploring teenage Ellen Ewing to marry him. It took three years of courtship by letter and two trips back to Lancaster, Ohio, but by 1844, Cump received the letter saying "Yes!" while serving as a first lieutenant of artillery at Fort Moultrie.

Always the devoted sportsman, even though he admitted to shooting ducks on the ground before they were flushed to flight, something southern sportsmen wouldn't think of doing, Sherman accepted numerous invitations to hunt on Cooper River plantations. One family in particular, William and Caroline Carson of Dean Hall plantation, extended him hospitality. Dean Hall sits upon the west branch of the Cooper about 3 miles west of Cedar Hill plantation, another favorite retreat of Sherman while he was here in the 1840s. Caroline Carson was the daughter of James Louis Petigru, the ardent Unionist. When South Carolina seceded, Caroline, an even more devoted Unionist than her late father, wrote her friend General Sherman, begging him to capture wayward her son who'd enlisted with the Confederates and return him unhurt for a scolding! Cump Sherman promised Caroline that he'd do his best.

The Mexican War eluded this Ohioan; he was posted to California instead of experiencing the glories of Vera Cruz. Out west it was Sherman's metallurgical knowledge that confirmed beyond doubt that the yellow stuff at Sutter's Mill was really gold. He met Kit Carson, the famed scout and Indian fighter but wasn't impressed with this freckle-faced, skinny kid until he heard later of Carson's daring exploits.

On a trip back east in 1851, Lieutenant Sherman met with General Winfield Scott, and Scott lowered his voice and told him that a terrible civil war was coming between the North and the South, and for Sherman to prepare. This was a decade prior to the hostilities.

In the years prior to the Civil War, Sherman grew discouraged with the slowness of promotion and tendered his commission. First, he became a lawyer out in Kansas, and even though he never read much law, nor took a bar exam, he practiced the legal profession on the frontier. He also became a bank president in the fledgling town of San Francisco, but the Panic of 1857, caused in part by the sinking of the gold-laden *S.S. Central America*, caused his bank to fail. Just before the War, Louisiana citizens asked him to become commandant of the Louisiana Military School, the forerunner of LSU.

Even as Sherman was reducing Atlanta and planning his earth-scorching march to the sea, he kept up a tender correspondence with wife Ellen concerning the antics of their preschool children.

After the War, Sherman refused the post of secretary of war, and he refused to allow his name to be put into nomination for president. The weary old fighter became a board member for the Smithsonian, traveled extensively, visited his grandchildren, and wrote his memoirs. Two steadfast friends to the end were Confederate generals Johnston and Hood. Sherman died from pneumonia at age 71 while reading Dickens' new novel, *Great Expectations*.

The Naughty Lola Montez Danced The Fandango Here in 1850

Move over Jezebel and Salome, step aside Cleopatra and Lucrezia, there's another hoyden in the history books, the slinky siren, Lola Montez, whose string of lovers included princes, composers, bankers, and explorers. Lola danced and romanced her way across two continents, being blamed for a half dozen duels, one revolution and royal abdication, two homicides, and embezzlement. The Broadway "Whatever Lola Wants, Lola Gets" tune written for "Damn Yankees,"

was written for a stage vamp patterned after Lola Montez' raucous, rollicking
rags-to-riches-to-rags again life in the mid-19th century, and Thackery patterned
Becky Sharp in his *Vanity Fair* after her legend.

Eliza Gilbert, whose stage name became Lola Montez, was an Irish lass of
County Sligo. She and her widowed mother were reduced to poverty by the death
of her soldier father in India. Eliza's mother remarried another soldier and
pawned this unfortunate child off upon her husband's elderly parents. Unruly
Liza became an unholy terror to her step-grandparents who happened to be pious
Presbyterians. One account says that when she didn't get her way, she stomped,
screamed, and ran through the village streets wearing absolutely nothing.

At great expense the foster grandparents packed Liza off to boarding
school. The convent school had its hands full trying to rein in this rebellious
harridan, but she did learn how to demand her way in three languages!

Victorian society feigned prudery but fed lustfully upon the gossip of
eminent gentlemen becoming ensnared in an amour with saucy trollops. A
coquettish girl could live like a duchess if she charmed a philandering lord into
being her paramour. With this knowledge, Eliza ran off from boarding school
determined to become a dancer and an actress, both pursuits calculated to proclaim
her charms.

Returning to her native Ireland, hoping to make a go on the Dublin stage,
the precocious teen quickly lost track of her career goal and fell in love with a
handsome army lieutenant. When Liza's sham marriage hit the rocks, she sailed
for London vowing to live only for herself.

Just how she met such well-connected Londoners as Lord Malmsbury and
Lord Brougham is unclear, but with their financial backing, Liza made a new
start with her stage name of "Lola Montez." Lola boasted that she was the love
child of Lord Byron and a Spanish mistress.

Two accounts of her life say that her debut in 1840 on London's West End
was dreadful and that she was booed off the stage. Declaring that Londoners

didn't appreciate fine dancing, Lola Montez removed herself to the continent where the forerunners of such dance halls as the Moulin Rouge and the Lido were opening from Paris to Milan.

Not sophisticated enough to be a gentleman's consort, Lola took to the life of a courtesan. She slinked her way through the flamenco, the tango, the fandango, and the polka, but what her audiences remembered was her lasciviousness and her low-cut dress, not deft dance steps. Rich older men were pliable to her charms and Lola collected gullible goofs to pay her lavish upkeep.

Legend has it that she seduced Franz Liszt in a torrid but brief fling. To humiliate Liszt for spurning her, Lola burst into a room where he was performing and leapt upon a table dancing a daring tap dance and upsetting the plates. She was Alexander Dumas' girl about the time that he was writing the historical novels, *The Three Musketeers* (1844) and *The Count of Monte Cristo* (1845).

Lola's lovers squandered money on her and she obliged with stunning good looks, vivacious wit, and scandalous dancing in Parisian hotels, clubs, and parlors. Victor Hugo and Honore de Balzac fawned over her. Feminist George Sand was amused by Lola's wicked intrigues. Even the poet Alphonse de Lamartine composed verse about this sensational dance hall strumpet. On both sides of the English channel, Lola delighted in being labeled '*La Grande Horizontele*."

After a sizzling performance in St. Petersburg, Romanov Czar Nicholas I begged for a private audience with Lola in his study. He bestowed upon her a thousand rubles for her favors.

Ferdinand I, King of Galicia, offered Lola untold wealth plus a title if she'd become his mistress, but he was senile and Lola rejected his offer. She soon took up with Prince Ludwig I of Bavaria instead. Lola's recent lover had just been killed in a duel over her. She felt that she needed to settle down to a more stable lifestyle. Prince Ludwig doted on her and made her the Countess of Landsfeld in August 1845, when Lola was a savvy 27 year-old- jade.

Ludwig I, age 59, was so enamored with Lola that he brought her into his inner circle of advisors. Soon her evening pillow-talk was his morning diplomacy. Lola lashed out against the Jesuit arm of the church and made liberal allowances to the Bavarian populace that angered and frightened Austria's Prince Metternich. Metternich feared Lola's influence so much that he offered her a fortune to leave Munich. When senile Ludwig tried to crack down upon his Bavarian citizenry, the resulting riots led to the outbreak of the Revolution of 1848. When Lola lost her influence upon Ludwig, she burst into a council meeting screaming at Ludwig as she ripped off her blouse baring much more than her soul. Ludwig abdicated and she slipped away with the jewels.

Lola Montez took a steamer to New York and got herself an agent. She performed on Broadway and toured the east and south with performances of *Maratana* and *Charlotte Corday*. Luscious Lola tried singing, and her dance reviews in the U.S. won acclaim. On December 6, 1850, Lola performed "*Maratana*" on the Charleston stage along with her notorious "spider dance." The next two nights she performed "Charlotte Corday" and a reading from her book, *Lola in Bavaria*. Two weeks later, the acclaimed Jenny Lind, the angelic "Swedish Nightingale," sang at the same Meeting Street Playhouse where SCE&G is located today.

From here she traveled to Mobile and New Orleans, raking in thousands of dollars in each city. She took steamer passage to California and soon became the acclaimed "Queen of the California Gold Rush," performing bawdy musicals and coaxing fortunes from moonstruck men. Lola's untimely death at age 40 of pneumonia in New York in 1860 stunned the world.

Choctaws, Chickasaws, and Colonial Charleston's Indian Agents

Newspapers come, newspapers go as the cadence of bold print banners arrests our notice. Sometimes they enlighten, but most often they frighten and confuse us with their terseness and brevity. One headline stuns with a troubling report of lax border security. Another deflates us with reports of dirty deals in the awarding of government contracts. And all of this disturbing "news" is not today's newspaper, but rather the South Carolina Gazette of the 1747! The daily papers validate what Solomon said in Ecclesiastes, " Vanity of vanities; all is vanity. . . . One generation passeth away, and another generation *cometh: but the earth abideth for ever.*"

In August 1747 Charleston was sweltering under a heat wave and everyone who got away from the malaria-prone coast had already retreated inland. Across the Atlantic, Britain was mired in a war with France and Spain, and all three European powers manipulated Indian tribes over here to carry out vendettas. Cunning tribal chieftains proved that they were no slouches when it came to driving hard bargains for their military allegiance.

Charleston was the nerve center for Britain's lucrative Indian trade whereas Mobile, or Mauvila in French-Choctaw tongue, was the headquarters of French Indian commerce. The vast wilderness separating these two cities was all Choctaw and Chickasaw land. Prior to the white man the Choctaw and Chickasaw had been one great amalgam under the mighty Sioux nation. By 1747 the Chickasaw united with the warlike Creek that dominated upper Georgia and Tennessee.

The Choctaw allied with the French, and savvy traders such as Bienville, de Verbois, and Charlevoix, with the aid of Jesuit priests who spoke the native tongue, won the loyalty of these native people completely. Falsehood was not a part of the Choctaw-Chickasaw culture, but "cutting an advantageous deal" was very much a part of the European culture, so numerous misunderstandings arose.

The Charleston newspaper reported the occasional Indian massacre of whites. But, for two-hundred years Choctaw warriors retold tales of Chief Tuscaloosa who outwitted and defeated the Spaniard DeSoto and his murderous Spaniards. Though their weaponry was inferior, the tactics, stamina, and courage of the Indians was often more than a match for the colonial fighters. After the twin disasters of starvation and violent uprisings by the Indians at Jamestown, it became clear that the only way to survive as a colony was to curry the favor of the closest Indian nation.

The South Carolina Gazette tells about the most famous Indian agent of colonial times, James Adair, M.D., a London-trained physician with powerful connections at Whitehall and Westminster. Adair was straight out of the Renaissance mold that had produced Francis Drake and Walter Raleigh a century earlier. The explorer Adair went Drake and Raleigh one better: he immersed himself into the culture of what Rousseau called "the noble savage" and became one of the few white men to gain complete confidence with the tribes.

The Gazette records how Adair made Charleston's Church Street his headquarters and he ventured into the uncharted wilderness with mule-trains numbering 200 animals heavily laden with blankets woven in Bristol, beads and glass fired in Birmingham, and firearms manufactured in London. Two years later Adair would return from hundreds of miles away with the same beasts laden with deer and beaver pelts purchased by the yard from trusting Chickasaw hunters. Adair's yardstick was carefully cut to be about an inch more than a true English yard. Farther to the west, in what is now Alabama, French traders often carried much shorter yard sticks. Such simple ruses played to the advantage of the English over the French as long as James Adair remained agent-in-charge of Indian affairs.

However, sinister voices here whispered innuendo concerning Adair in the ear of Royal Governor James Glen while James Adair was away on his hugely profitable trade junkets to the Chickasaw nation in northern Georgia.

Though Adair had an exclusive patent to trade with the Chickasaw, and he had a dozen investors who were highly connected in London, already there was a mounting colonial fervor to disenfranchise London-backed Adair and place a local merchant, Charles McNaire, into that moneymaking sinecure so long held by

Adair. In his book, History of The American Indians (1775). Adair tells of the perfidy he suspected was occurring behind his back. This book also explores Adair's belief that the southern Indians were part of the lost tribes of Israel. It was a big seller in England but was overshadowed here by the war of 1776. Was Governor Glen receiving a kickback from his Charleston-based investors? Did the Carolina Assemby's double-crossing of Adair and his royal backers hasten the coming of the Revolution? Adair tells a different story from the headlines and reports of the South Carolina Gazette.

At the center of the political shenanigan was a renegade, Choctaw Chieftain Couechitto, nicknamed Red Shoes by Adair. Red Shoes was the son of Jean Baptiste Marshand and a Muskogee squaw named Sepoy. Often the Indians that were most dreaded by the settlers were half-breed men resentful of the way that the Europeans had taken advantage of their women. Indian traders took Indian wives as a token of respect for the tribe they traded with. Mixed-blood children suffered terribly when hostilities erupted. And several of the most murderous of the Indian leaders were mixed-blood sons of duplicitous colonial traders. Adair managed his affairs with decorum, but Charleston politics unseated him in 1747, and the rival trading house, McNaire's Sphinx Company, actually made the Indians on our border ally with the British on the eve of the Revolutionary War.

Red Shoes and Adair had a bond and were related by marriages to Indian princesses. The new franchise, McNaire and his "Sphinx Company," were inconsiderate of long-held Choctaw rituals to the detriment of colonial security.

Adair's mule-teams stretching a half mile in length trod a worn ancient path that preceded European settlement here. The path followed the broad path beginning at present-day King and Calhoun Streets and went through modern-day St. George, Bamberg, and Williston before crossing the Savannah River near Augusta. From there the trip could turn deadly as savages ruled the forests all the way to the Chickasaw capital in western Tennessee.

Whether it's commercial development, political double-dealing, or the ever-

present threats to port security, the themes in our newspapers have a reassuring
quality of *deja vu*.

Cold War Boomer Sub Surfaces At Patriot's Point

There's no better introduction to the Cold War than Tom Clancy's 1984
white knuckle novel *The Hunt For Red October (1984)*. That novel, published by
the Naval Institute Press, was so true to the mark concerning the super-secret
undersea war boat that at least one federal agent left the theater to call his office
about the film.

The Cold War is the oddest armed struggle ever waged in 5000 years of
recorded history. When Ronald Reagan said in 1981, 'Here's my strategy for the
Cold War; we win, they lose," the Gipper had an "ace in the hole," the U.S.
Navy's silent deterrent nuclear submarine force. Now, almost 20 years after the
end of the Cold War, America's only memorial to the cold warriors is the conning
tower and sail of SBN-644 Lewis and Clark surfacing in a sea of green grass off
Patriots Point Road in Mount Pleasant.

The Cold War officially began in August 1945 following America's
detonation of two atomic weapons in Japan and our rejection of Soviet oversight
in the Sea of Japan. The armory of this ideological struggle *extraordinaire*
included supersonic aircraft, sensitive listening radar, ICBM missile silos, high-
tech espionage, and the "ace," the stealthy nuclear submarines that old salts
called "Boomers."

The nuclear submarine is the most curious offensive weapon ever imagined.
In Clancy's novel and subsequent movie by the same name, the undersea ballet of

murky deception plays out between Uncle Sam and Crazy Ivan, maneuvering sleek black undersea tubes, each packing more destruction capability than all previous wars combined.

Our local Cold War relic, *The Lewis and Clark*, was commissioned in December 1965 on LBJ's watch, just six weeks after the jolting northeast power blackout that plunged New York and New England into total darkness. The blackout brought down the curtain for Barbra Streisand's "Funny Girl," but a week after *Lewis and Clark* was commissioned the James Bond movie thriller "*Thunderball*" premiers.

Had she been called, the L&C's nuclear reactors alone could have powered New York City and its environs with just a pier-side hookup. Her length was 425 feet, which means that if they set her down in Williams-Brice stadium, the bulbous nose would protrude a bit into the fairgrounds parking while the tail fin, or sail, would interrupt the Cock-a-boose club. She's a long, slender-waisted girl at just 33 feet on the beam. But, oh what a wallop she carried. The crew numbered 140 men. She originally was designed for Polaris missiles, something every Charlestonian knows was hush-hush for years up at Goose Creek. A decade later she became more lethal with the up-grade to the Poseidon missile.

If we do some simple math, each Ben Franklin class nuclear submarine, such as the L&C and her sisters, carried 16 submarine-launched-ballistic-missiles. When launched, the warhead did a star burst with ten independent warheads of 50-kiloton blast yield each moving with supersonic speed to a prefigured targets as far as 2400 nautical miles distance. Remember back to "Fatman" over Nagasaki in August 1945? Fatman possessed a 21 kiloton blast yield, so the L&C's ultra-destructive doomsday launch capability was 16 Poseidons, each with 10 independent, pre-targeted warheads with more than double the Nagasaki explosion power. Imagine sitting in Charleston harbor and slinging a watermelon over Seattle and that's a graphic image of what a nuclear-powered sub is able to do, substituting the business end of a fission for the tasty melon. America's strategic plan classified the L&C mission as one of eliminating airfields, communication networks, and naval facilities so that our strategic bombers could get through with the really big bombs.

How'd we ever get to the point where we and the Russians prowled about menacingly with such firepower on our hips? Mother Russia suffered 500 years of barbaric invasions prior to the 20th century, and her clumsy attempts at diplomacy frequently left her out-bluffed by all countries west of the Elbe. For a hundred years it appeared that Britain and America were steering Manchuria out of Russia's sphere as a source of everything from materials to labor and seaports. And that collectivist ideology of Leninism-Marxism couldn't compete with a vibrant market-driven western world.

Shortly after World War II, Harvard-scholar, George Kennan was in Russia as advisor to Averell Harriman, our ambassador in Moscow. Kennan sent Truman what's been labeled at the State Department as "the long telegram." Condensing the ten page telegram to one line, Kennan is telling Truman that dialogue, diplomacy, and trade negotiation will never work with the Soviets -- only the clear and overwhelming threat of total destruction could ever dissuade them. Less than a month after this, Truman used his bluntest language ever with Soviet Foreign Minister Molotov. Truman later likened his approach to Molotov and Stalin as "taking a two by four to the head of a mule."

The CNN web site on the Cold War cites statistics that may be accurate in saying that the US spent approximately $5.5 trillion dollars on armaments and logistics for this mammoth ideological 50-year snit. While it may appear that it was two sumo wrestlers straining over a dining room table engaging with interlocked pinkie-fingers, in reality, the real scenario could have gone apocalyptic numerous times. CNN's site states that if dollar bills in bundles of one inch high equaling $200 were stacked like brick upon brick, then what was spent just on nukes would be a stack that reached the moon and back. Put another way, an assessment of $21, 646 was made for every person in the United States.

Tom Clancy's *Hunt For Red October* has some scenarios taking place off the coast of Charleston, and for a reason. Moscow long targeted the Holy City as a home base of boomer

subs and as a warehouse for sub-launched ballistic missiles. We won, they didn't.

So, when driving on Patriots Point Road past that hulking black steel tower and tail-sail, all that remains of the once mighty SBN-644 *Lewis and Clark*, reflect on another of Ron Reagan's one-liners: "No arsenal, or no weapon in the arsenals of the world, is so formidable as the will and moral courage of free men and women." A double handful of submariners are retired in the Mount Pleasant area; give those courageous, hand-picked, highly-skilled men a high-five for freedom!

How The Locally-Built USS Tillman Helped Save The World

Fifty Ships That Saved The World: The Foundation of The Anglo-American Alliance is the title of Britain's parliamentary conservative member Philip Goodhart's book published by Doubleday & Company (1965), and as alluded to in its title, this is the closest thing to a thank-you note Americans received for $50 billion ($700 billion in today's currency) of World War II lend-lease aid. For Charlestonians a very interesting sidebar to Uncle Sam's awarding of billions of depression-era tax dollars in the 1940s to a desperate, unprepared Britain is the colossal ramp-up of the Charleston Navy Yard and the history-making ships that were built there.

Though the ship yard has been closed for a decade now and developers cloy for revitalization of that storied river bank, there was a time when freedom's arsenal was the business there. Three generations of Charleston naval ship yard workers knew those mammoth buildings as their workshop.

At the turn of the last century when Teddy Roosevelt was president, the secretary of the navy picked Port Royal as the most favorable site on the east coast for an enormous naval complex that would become headquarters for the sixth naval district. Port Royal harbor was deep an did not require constant dredging. However, Charleston politicos stole the project away from the Beaufort area, much to their chagrin. When constructed, the project was the largest outlay of federal spending in the nation. The payroll alone was the greatest stimulus for economic revitalization here since the area's collapse in the 1860s.

On a sizzling hot July 29, 1918, Miss Mary Tillman, granddaughter of U.S. Senator Ben Tillman, smashed a bottle of bubbly across the bow of DD-135, USS Tillman, a destroyer named for the senator who'd done so much to wrestle funds for the navy yard. This was the first ship built at our shipyard.

The USS Tillman was 51 weeks in the building stage from keel to launch. Her splash into the Cooper just 4 months before Armistice Day in 1918 signaled a bold new era in Charleston's maritime history.

The destroyer Tillman soon fell pawn to political cutbacks in postwar congressional budget battles. After only three years of service, DD-135 Tillman, 341 feet of flush-deck destroyer, was mothballed at the Philadelphia Navy Yard. The Tillman seemed destined for oblivion, but ship production at the shipyard continued.

The Charleston yard built the USS Twiggs and a half-dozen other sleek destroyers that saw minimal service in the '20s and '30s. Our yard developed its own subculture
and during prohibition, the bootleggers knew that businesses surrounding the navy base were prime candidates for blind-tiger operation. Teetotalers or not, our shipyard workers deserve the gratitude of the free world, though few sensed a danger in the 1930s.

It's doubtful that congress would have been awakened to the need for additional funding for our aging shipyards if German Admiral Raeder's massive expansions of the Bremen and Hamburg shipyards in the 1930s had not been observed by American newsmen William Shirer in Berlin and Ed Murrow in London. Europe's difficulties soon tested America's political and industrial resolve.

Britain's *annus horribilis*, 1940, became Charleston Navy Yard's *valde prosperitas*. FDR's "destroyers for bases" deal with Churchill took place on September 2, 1940, and several of the 50 American destroyers conveyed to Britain had been built at the Charleston navy yard.

Between 1939 and 1941 all oddsmakers in this country were saying Britain would fall to Germany. Washington power brokers demanded that our mothballed destroyers be traded to Britain in 1940 in return for the pledge that the British fleet would sail for American ports when Britain surrendered to Germany. Churchill retorted that his people's morale would collapse if such deal became known, so the 99 year lease for American use of British bases was hastily hammered out. The USS Tillman was renamed the HMS Wells, as the Brits were naming their destroyers after cathedral cities. The Charleston-built USS Twiggs became the HMS Leamington, a submarine hunter.

Hitler's u-boats corralled Britain with an "iron necklace" blockade. Though British naval inspectors said our "gift" ships were in much worse shape than they'd expected, they increased patrols and convoy escorts and reduced losses enough to give Britain breathing room.

Even though the $50 billion lend-lease agreement brought America out of the great depression, the idea of aiding Britain as we tried to avoid the hostilities was controversial in Congress. FDR first told the public about Lend-Lease in a radio address on the night of December 17, 1940, and Senator Alben Barkley and Representative John McCormack rammed it through a divided congress on January 10.

For Charleston's shipyard, the ramp-up in production meant Liberty Ships galore and a new lease on life! New neighborhoods were constructed to house the thousands of skilled workers who moved here. Byrnes Downs west of the Ashley and Ben Tillman homes outside the navy base were constructed for shipyard workers.

The USS Tillman, renamed HMS Wells, was rigged as a British destroyer at Hull and she immediately went on patrol in the English channel. On her 1st escort of a convoy, Wells struck out in a contest with a wily u-boat. She endured bombings by German land-based Heinkel bombers. The Twiggs, renamed Leamington, saw constant action in the savage north Atlantic naval war of 1940-'41. Both ships pounded German positions as the allies went ashore on D-Day in 1944. The HMS Wells was finally dismantled in 1945 at Troon, Scotland, not far from the Royal Troon Golf Club.

Sir Philip Goodhart, formerly the conservative member of parliament from Beckenham, Kent, writes in his book that "these old, top-heavy and rusty destroyers are, in the author's judgment, the fifty ships that saved the world." If Britain had collapsed to German occupation, Western civilization as we know it would have ceased forever.

On December 29, 2006, Britain made the last payment on her World War II lend-lease agreement. The check from the Royal Treasury was made out for 42.5 million pounds sterling ($83.5 million). The terms stated ten cents on the dollar, 2% interest over 61 years. On December 31, 2006, British Economic Secretary, Edward Balls, wrote the official thank-you to the United States for its aid in World War II, but Charleston's shipyard workers never received any thank-you other than their bi-weekly pay stub.

Why All The Fuss About Gerald And Sara Murphy?

The Murphys, Sara and Gerald, we see them everywhere we go these days. They're featured in the *New York Times*, splashed across *Vanity Fair*, and forever popping up in paparazzi shots on the internet. Suddenly it's as if the guardians of what passes for taste and refinement have rediscovered these reluctant icons of *la bonne vie*, these ex-pat American idlers who epitomize the bohemian "Lost Generation."

Even now a grand exhibition of Gerald and Sara Murphy's nonconformist lifestyle is being hosted by Williams College in Williamstown, Massachusetts. In 2008 the exhibit moves to New Haven where Gerald spent four years at Yale. Glossy magazines and society columnists are abuzz again as they were in the heyday of Jazz.

Gerald, the scion of Mark W. Cross and Company, 5th Avenue fortune, and Sarah, a legacy of the Cincinnati ink magnate, Frank Wiborg, never had to impress people with who they were. She was also the great niece of General Sherman. The Murphys' peers are as familiar to us as to them: Yale classmate Cole Porter, the novelist Fitzgerald and his zany wife Zelda, Pablo Picasso, Igor Stravinsky, Ernest Hemingway, John Dos Passos, Archibald MacLeish -- the list of their compatriots seems endless.

Gerald Murphy and Sara Sherman Wiborg Murphy never denied F. Scott Fitzgerald's claim that they were the inspiration for the characters Dick and Nicole Diver in Fitzgerald's, *Tender Is The Night* (1934). There's no way of estimating how often the Murphy's understated elegance has been imitated, or more likely, counterfeited, by pop culture mavens.

For her part, Sara was the older, bolder, more self-assured one of the handsome couple. Her beauty was not breathtaking, but she had *Town and*

Country good looks; in fact, her engagement picture graced the cover of *Town and Country* in 1915. Picasso temporarily abandoned his cubist style to paint Sara four times during their exile years in Paris and Antibes. Sara's many gentlemen admirers refused to avert their gaze from the Picasso canvas where she wore only a long, double strand of pearls. Fitzgerald was fascinated with the way Sara strolled along the Riviera so unaware of her beauty and the commotion that she caused among men. Her way of flipping the knotted strings of pearls so that they hung down her bare back became an affectation of the flirtatious Nicole Diver in Fitzgerald's *Tender is The Night*.

At age 17 Gerald Murphy was herded off to Yale by his traditionalist father. Gerald's father, Patrick Francis Murphy, a proper Bostonian-turned-New Yorker, bought the Mark W. Cross leather goods import house and turned it quickly into a multimillion dollar concern by 1910. "A woman with a Cross bag wishes to be seen by two people: the man she likes best, and the woman she likes least."

Patrick Murphy made money so effortlessly that he was able to ensconce himself in his mahogany office and read the works of Lord Macauley uninterrupted by his busy sales staff. "How many times must I tell people that I am not interested in making more money!," was a remark of Gerald's father, Patrick Murphy, to Gerald chums visiting from Yale. This was the man who introduced the wrist watch, the thermos, and numerous other luxury items that first sold here exclusively at Mark W. Cross Company. Definitely he desired the Ivy League for his sons.

Yale was not Gerald Murphy's ideal of a university. No, it wasn't his grubbing for grades, and it had nothing to do with being accepted by his classmates, for the gods had bestowed grace upon this favored son. Yale seemed a place where young men wore their ambition on their sleeve, and to Gerald Murphy, money and success were things assured. Gerald Murphy wore the mantle of European gentility and was a fish out of water among the strivers and speculators of 1920s America.

Cole Porter became a tag-along of Gerald's at Yale, and was tapped into the exclusive secret society Skull and Bones because Gerald whispered the name to fellow Bones man Archibald MacLeish. Years later, though, Gerald and Sara were adamant that no boy of theirs would be sent off to Yale. Regrettably, Gerald and Sara's sons died in their teens, one of tuberculosis and the other of meningitis.

It was the 18th Amendment that drove these New Yorkers into abandoning America for the left bank of the Seine in 1921. Prohibition never stopped anyone who wanted a drink over here, but the very idea that government would take on a parental role irked the Murphys. However, Gerald and Sara were repulsed by the cold formality of their parents and the enormous wealth that had removed from them any sense of human misery or discomfort.

Sara decorated their Paris apartment with a measured restraint, especially considering the purchasing power of the dollar versus the floundering French franc. But that was one of the endearing traits about the Murphys; everyone knew that they possessed wealth, but they managed to live in restrained elegance.

Sara's parties attracted the trendsetters. French painter Henri Leger was a fixture at these late night soirées; so was Igor Stravinsky, who often leapt a ballet *Pas de Chat* when summoned by Sara. Always, the coveted invitations to Gerald and Sara's impromptu dinner parties meant eclectic tastes and agreeable, witty companions who forever impressed Scott and Zelda Fitzgerald as the *nec plus ultra* of 20th century refinement.

One night when not enough cut flowers could be procured to fill a rented barge on the Seine for a late night dinner, Sara sent Gerald to buy hundreds of match car toys which she piled in pyramids of color on tables and in corners. Picasso was so fascinated by the profusion of tiny toys that it became his inspiration for two of his cubist themes. Cole Porter wrote some of his best music as spur-of-the-moment pieces for Sara.

Lest you think that these artistic idlers were poster children for Thorstein

Veblen's *Theory of Conspicuous Consumption* , the reality is that they lived
modestly for the millionaires of their day. Gerald gave away money to all who
beseeched him. Becoming weary of F. Scott's poor mouthing, he even paid for
Scotty Fitzgerald's education at Vassar. The Murphys memorial may well be the
repopularizing of their understated manner as opposed to our era of greed and
self-absorption.

The Oldest Political Faction Here Was the Barbados Party

Tracing the political process back to the first colonial cliques or factions
isn't easy. But it appears that the earliest political party south of Richmond and
the James River is the Carolina Barbados faction, known around here in the 1680s
disdainfully as "those Goose Creek men," or simply as "those 'badian baronets."

Local teacher, author, and former Goose Creek mayor Michael Heitzler has
recently published a history entitled <u>Goose Creek: A Definitive History; Vol. I.</u>
<u>Planters, Politicians, and Patriots</u> through the History Press of Charleston (2006).
Heitzler reaffirms what many of us have long suspected -- that Berkeley County
and the Goose Creek vicinity contain a fabulous treasure of forgotten colonial
legend and lore. This lore includes the rise of our first real political faction, the
Goose Creek Men.

Colonials arrived here already belonging to a political faction because of the
English Civil War. Royalists disputed with Roundheads over the nature of
government and the church. There were quite a few Cavaliers strolling the streets
here, but it is of note that our first governor, William Sayle of Albemarle Point,
was an old Puritan who'd fled London because of the restoration of the Stuarts.
Even so, the Lords Proprietors took pity on him and made him acting governor

until the arrival of Joseph West.

Predictably, colonial Charleston turned out just as politically divided as anywhere else where free men speak their minds. The politicking began in earnest here about 1675, about the time the settlers relocated from Old Town on the Ashley to White Point on the peninsula. That's when the big money Barbados men gained the ascendancy in the colonial assembly.

The Barbados Men were sugarcane planters of the West Indies, most of whom had fled England with the execution of Charles I in 1649. They were Cavaliers who wore their hair long to their shoulders, Stuart style, gentlemen to the manor born. Sir John Yeamans was the spokesman for this moneyed lot of 50 men who preferred to distance themselves from that mishmash of English, Dutch, and Irish profiteers, rogues, and gentlemen speculators drummed up by the London Proprietors. The proprietors were out to improve upon the low-budget Virginia model that had ruined so many of the Virginia Company. Unlike the Virginia experience, Carolina had a distinct Barbados connection. A string of bad hurricane years sent fifty fine English dandies fleeing Bridgetown, Barbados, for a fresh start on our coast.

Removing themselves a day's distance by boat up the Ittiwan River, later renamed Cooper, these High Church Anglicans preferred King over parliament and rum over ale and beer. They were not inclined to religious toleration to the extent that the Charles Town men allowed dissenters, Jews, and Catholics. At the root of the issue was the fact that these men had been at the center of Bridgetown, Barbados, and they jolly well planned to run things here. Their own Goose Creek barony by 1710 consisted of opulent country seats with romanticized names like Otranto, The Elms, The Oaks, and Mepkin. Their owners, men like John Yeamans and Maurice Matthews, were rowed up and down the river on barges fit for a pharaoh. Matthews also bought up much of the waterfront east of the Cooper. An oak-lined thoroughfare that he had constructed still bears a corruption of his name, Mathis Ferry Road.

Barbadian baron John Yeamans was a Bristol brewer who'd sold the family business so that he could get into the lucrative West Indies sugar trade. Yeamans made a profitable marriage with a very wealthy widow in Bridgetown. Rumors flew that he'd hastened her late husband's demise by slipping large doses of poison in the man's rum drinks. By the time Yeamans moved to Carolina, he was 65 years old and irascible. With nearly a million pounds of sugar sitting in warehouses around Barbados, Yeamans, was on paper at least, one of the wealthiest men on this continent. This old political kingpin would have happily lived out his remaining years in the West Indies had not a series of devastating hurricanes and at least one severe drought ruined the sugarcane harvests.

There was one other reason, though, that brought this tide of rich young Barbados Englishmen here. Lord Ashley Cooper's legal advisor was none other than John Locke, the most respected political thinker of the latter 17th century. Locke was a dreamer and he had a utopian notion that a new type of nobility based partly upon heredity and partly upon ambition would lead to a New England on this side of the Atlantic. Barbados was then the fiefdom of the Earl of Carlyle. The Earl got a cut of everything that these savvy sugar planters produced in Barbados. But, in Carolina under Locke's scheme, the wealthy landowners could become landgrave nobles and catapult their wealth exponentially through a scheme called quitrents. For a few years here, it worked just as Locke hoped that it would, and the Goose creek men completely dominated the scene in the local assembly on Broad Street.

Carolina lured these highborn, ambitious English ex-patriots with land and the fancy aristocratic title of landgrave. These scions of old-world gentry represented the conservative view of King, Church, and *noblesse-oblige*. Yeamans, Mazyck, Rutledge, Middleton, Daniel, Stanyarne, Howe, Matthews and Johnson were among the prominent 'badian Baronets. They arrived with a vast army of slaves accustomed to this climate and plantation work. The White Point peninsula men were just acquiring land, Africans, and a primitive knowledge of agriculture.

One of the big issues was whether to trade with the pirates. Captains such as Morgan, Bonnett, Rackham, Steed, and Teach frequented these waters and converted their loot into easy silver on the wharfs of Charles Town. Goose Creek men readily sold them victuals and rum. The White Point men wanted that trade to end, but the Goose Creek men saw it as a way to increase the circulation of silver and gold in the fledgling colony. Plus the pirates were a good ally against the Spanish in nearby Florida.

The Barbadian men of Goose Creek may have been arrogant and they may have ruthlessly dominated the colonial assembly for their own benefit, but the rabble and their betters of peninsula Charles Town did gain the upper hand by the eve of the Revolution.

Sally Baxter Hampton's Antebellum Romance Frozen in Time

Born in any other age than the antebellum, flirtatious Sally Baxter would have been one of the formidable four-hundred, *haut monde* of New York. Her father, a Wall Street merchant and warehouseman, was rich, and her mother was regal and aloof. The Baxter brownstone at 286 Second Avenue was a noted salon for New York's smart set.

As a seventeen-year-old, raven-haired beauty, Sally was turning the heads of young gallants and mellowed old married men alike. The buzz of the city was that Sally Baxter was Thackery's girl and that the famous Victorian novelist was infatuated with her. They whispered that he wrote her into his best-selling novels such as *Henry Esmond* and *The Newcomes*. Some gossips even ventured that William Thackery planned to divorce his insane wife and elope with this lithe beauty who was even younger than his own daughters!

Reading through Sally's letters, dashed off in teenage ardor, punctuated with dashes, we see her exclaiming joy, fervor, and sometimes fury as the prating of the scandal mongers swirls about her. That this New York *debutante* was soon after whisked off her dainty feet by ruggedly handsome Frank Hampton of the South Carolina's famed Hampton dynasty is the apotheosis of the Southern romances that forever captivate novelists and screenwriters.

William Makepeace Thackery was the Victorian novelist who gave literature its foremost *femme fatale* in *Vanity Fair* character Becky Sharp. Clever and pretty, Becky Sharp was forever a self-centered hoyden . But with Sally Baxter, Thackery had an ideal heroine "slender with dark wavy hair, dazzling white skin, bright red cheeks -- redder lips, large full mouth, bright dark eyes, with sweet voice but haughty and imperious at times."

In Sally's defense, she was hardly ever out of her parents' presence when Thackery visited them, and her letters to him were school girlish without innuendo other than sharing with him her innermost thoughts. Nonetheless, William Thackery broke off an amour in England for a tender alliance with this "pretty wild girl" that he wrote his mother about. Thackery's daughters destroyed the letters he wrote to them about Sally.

William M. Thackery, 20 years Sally Baxter's senior, allowed his fascination with this teen ingenue to roam. He went into a funk when Sally's engagement to Frank Hampton was announced in New York's society columns and begged off ill when invited to sit with the family at the wedding in Trinity Episcopal on Wall Street, December 12, 1855.

In any other era, Sally Baxter probably would never have met Frank Hampton. Their paths would never have crossed had not Sally's father brought her south to restore her health from a persistent cough that responded to no cure.

George Baxter doted on his daughter, and when Sally, age 16, succumbed to symptoms of consumption, father dropped everything for a health-restoring cruise to Charleston in the winter of 1854.

The original plan was for father and daughter to steam into Charleston and take rooms at the Mills House Hotel, travel by rail to Columbia for a few days, and then rest at a posh resort in Aiken before returning to New York via Savannah.

For once the charm of old Charleston didn't get much notice from these New York travelers. George Baxter carried letters of introduction from prominent New Yorkers for meeting the well-heeled in each city he visited, and one letter was addressed to James M. King, law partner and son-in-law to federal judge and prominent Unionist, James Louis Petigru.

Sally was entertained in Charleston by Susan Petigru King, whose home on the corner of Meeting and George Streets was a gathering spot for notables such as Caroline Gilmer, Sarah Pratt Willington, and Harriett Pinckney Holbrook. Susan King had just published a novel entitled *Busy Moments of an Idle Woman*, and privately in correspondence to Thackery Sally reveals that King is loud, vulgar, and that her novel is "very trashy." Sarah Willington and Sally Baxter became swell intimates in a week's time between teas at the Mills and dinner parties about town. That two northerners in 1854 could arrive here with nothing but letters of introduction and then be received in Charleston's finest homes evening after evening is a testimony to the genteel character of antebellum Charleston.

She and her father rolled into the train station of Columbia and were immediately taken to their hotel. Columbia in the 1850s was perhaps the most beautiful state capital in America, and many travel diaries attest to that assertion. Prewar Columbia was a recreation of John Winthrop's "shining city upon a hill" with the Congaree, Saluda, and Broad Rivers framing it, and with the bright dome of the new capitol, it was the epitome of Tocqueville's America, a brave new republic far removed from the troubles of Europe.

Sally's father had an introduction in Columbia to Doctor Francis Lieber, the famed lecturer at South Carolina College. Lieber was the great philosophy professor from the University of Berlin here on a mission to make South Carolina College the nation's greatest classical institution. It was through a dinner party at the Liebers that Sally first met the tall, broad-shouldered knight-errant Frank Hampton, and both New York belle and southern aristocrat - sportsman fell in love at first sight. Of course, what girl's heart wouldn't melt when the most eligible bachelor in the state sends over a beautiful basket of fresh strawberries complete with a handwritten note of admiration!

Sally Baxter became a Hampton, an adored new member of that patrician clan of Saxons who epitomized the old southern ideal of Hellenism. She became the mistress of Woodlands Plantation outside of Columbia when she was just 21. Though her illness worsened, Sally bore her husband four precious children before she passed away of tuberculosis in 1862. Her prince charming, Colonel Frank Hampton, was killed at the Civil War battle of Brandy Station exactly nine months later. Their love story is grander by far than Margaret Mitchell's fictional Scarlett and Rhett.

Reading Sally's letters is like listening to an enthusiastic young woman talking to her sister, friends, and parents. Ann Fripp Hampton of Summerville has collected, edited, and published these letters in a wonderful little book entitled *A Divided Heart: Letters of Sally Baxter Hampton, 1853 - 1862*. After five pages it'll soon become one of your favorite books!

What Were We Thinking A Hundred Years Ago

There wasn't even talk of bridging the Cooper one-hundred years ago for such engineering feats that have to factor in the curvature of the earth were financially out of the reach of our State's politicians. No matter, with ferry boats such as the Sappho, Lawrence, and Palmetto, and colorful ferry captains such as Shaine Baitry to banter with, visiting Mount Pleasant and the islands was as exotic as ferrying across to Cape Cod or Block Island was for new Englanders. Examining the pages of the *Charleston Evening Post* for the last week of September, 1907, one glimpses the unhurried pace of this genteel old southern city.

The Grace Bridge was a generation away from connecting Charleston to Mount Pleasant. A *Post and Courier* column a year ago by Wevonneda Minis celebrating the new Ravenel Bridge relates how Solomon Rosen used to take his family by ferry to the Mount Pleasant dock at Hibben Street for a week's stay on Sullivan's Island. Getting over there from their Montagu Street home required planning and took just about all day to execute. Arriving with that special wind-blown look of having crossed the bay was a routine affair for our forebears and they whiled away the time by reading the *News and Courier* or the decidedly more local *Evening Post*.

The *Evening Post* discarded on the ferryboat Palmetto at the end of the day, Wednesday, September 25, 1907, had some interesting headlines. One tells of "American Payroll The Envy of the World." So said Secretary of the Treasury George Cortelyou at the opening of a new department store in New York city. Charleston papers then contain more goings-on of New York and Chicago than we notice today. Ferry boat passengers whiled away the two hour harbor crossing read on September 25 of a New York garment worker plunging to his death from a skyscraper. Then there was a piece about Right Reverend Arthur Foley Winnington-Ingraham, Lord-Bishop of London, delivering an address at Trinity Episcopal on Wall Street before traveling on by rail to Richmond.

Rail news fascinated everyone in 1907, and the newspapers reported on rail mergers, rail crashes, and even a new rail crossing here at Market and East Bay. News of a head-on rail crash between two fast-moving trains near Cherbourg,

France, was the day's most horrific news.

On the financial pages, cotton futures and over-the-counter cotton mill stocks, over a hundred of them in South Carolina, warranted more space than do today's NYSE quotes. Of the listed New York Stock Exchange companies, the *Evening Post* singles out railroad companies as of most interest to local investors.

Civil rights makes front page news in 1907. A black attorney of Baltimore, W. Calvin Chase, denounces Teddy Roosevelt's administration saying "The time has come for the Negro to assert his power in politics . . ." as he demands the appointment of black men to federal positions. Chase was also editor of a newspaper called *The Bee*, a vanguard voice for racial equality.

The hurricanes of 1911 and 1912 were still years away and coastal planters were making money on long-staple cotton, and a few were still planting rice. To their alarm that September 25th, an *Evening Post* item told how Central American long-staple cotton rivals that produced in South Carolina, and at a fraction of the labor cost. The reporter told how the Central American cotton being grown in Colombia is of Egyptian quality. Colombians shipped directly to Hamburg, Harve, Liverpool, and Bristol. These words burned farmers whose grandfathers witnessed Britain switching to Nile-basin cotton during the War Between the States rather than intervening in the blockade here to obtain our crop!

We see that multiculturism wasn't high on the education agenda in 1907 as another headline informed that Wu Ting Fang arrived from China to insure that Chinese children received a proper education America. Coolies and children of laundry men, etc., were barred from attending public schools in California. Similarly, South Carolina failed to enact mandatory school attendance laws because child labor in textile mills kept costs down and stock quotes up. Charlestonians maligned upstate mill town children with the perjorative "lint heads."

Readers of the *Evening Post* ferrying across to the islands on the Sappho or the Palmetto didn't pause too long over national and international items, however.

This was the Republic of Charleston and Mount Pleasant and the barrier islands were the resorts of choice for the locals. Even the merchant advertisements had more appeal to us than did the national and international news reports.

Inside the September 25, 1907 paper a local story recounted how telephone wires will soon connect Charleston to Bowman and then Orangeburg beyond. Thursday, September 26, will be "German Day" in Charleston, the beginning of a week long Octoberfest. The grand day will kick off at the Schuetzenplatz near Marion Square with addresses in German and English by Herr Doctor C. J. Heximer of Frankfurt. Germans loved Charleston as a haven from Prussian militarism.

At the Atlantic Coastline Railroad office on John Street there is a special priced fare to Washington, D.C., roundtrip for $16.15. See W.E. Rennecker or J.S. Walpole, agents, or call them. The ACL phone number is 7. Imagine a one-digit phone number, but so few people had telephones then.

In 1907 there were no chain stores to swamp the local merchants. Puckhaber's Bakery at 464 King Street offered daily fresh hot dinner rolls that were "a luxury only when the skill of the baker has given that indescribable luscious flavor to his productions." Aimar Drug on upper King Street manufactured Pure Cod Liver Oil as well as ABC Head and Hair Cleaner. Lawrence M. Pinckney, with offices at 15 Lamboll Street, advertised expertise in real estate, stocks, bonds, insurance, and all other types of investments.

For fifty cents a month 1907's *Evening Post* delivered news plus society tattle otherwise missed while over at "the island." Without *The Evening Post* how would one have known of the VIP wedding between William Gilmore Simm's granddaughter, Charlotte Percival Rowe and H. Fullerton Buist, performed at the plantation home of the bride by St. Michael's rector, the Reverend Doctor John Kershaw. In 1907 area residents were still three generations away from having the *Moultrie News* for the lowdown and the Ravenel Bridge for a five-minute crossing!

213

Traveling Through Time In old Colleton County

Every Charlestonian knows that the sun rises somewhere beyond Breach Inlet, suspends itself lazily over Fort Sumter and after meandering over West Ashley it sets just west of the Ashepoo over in Colleton County. That's the Carolina West. It's a good thing that Horace Greeley was living in New York when he said "Go west, young man," for our fellows would have interpreted west to mean Walterboro!

Colleton County is an often overlooked treasure. Difficult though it is to believe, there are locals who've driven 400 miles to tour colonial Williamsburg, but they've not motored 40 miles to visit historic Walterboro! For the historically-minded there's no better source of old-time tales than Beulah Glover's *Narratives of Colleton County, The Land Lying Between the Edisto and the Combahee Rivers*, privately published, 1962.

Glover tells how Colleton County got its name from Sir John Colleton, a Cavalier who lost hundreds of thousands of pounds sterling in support of Charles I during the English Civil War. Upon Cromwell's revenge on royalists Colleton fled to Barbados with just his sword, plumed hat, and boots. For twenty years he dwelled in Bridgetown, or sometimes on a dinky, remote estate miles inland. Finally in 1660 Charles II restored Stuart rule to England and took it upon himself to reward the men who'd been faithful to his father, the beheaded Charles I. After all, what did it cost Charles II to give away land in the New World whose ownership was disputed with Spain?

Colleton was among the most swashbuckling of the Cavaliers. John Colleton, original founder of the Lords Proprietors' cartel, received an enormous tract of land lying west of the 1670 Albemarle settlement on the Ashley. Sir John figured his lucky star had risen and that this new bonanza would recoup the fortune he'd lost in siding with the Stuarts. Little did he realize how this uncharted New World wilderness would slip through his fingers.

John Colleton did recover his wealth in another way, however. Along with Charles II, Charles's younger brother James, John Locke, and other London insiders they formed the Royal African Company, one of the largest and most profitable West African Slave corporations. These savvy, unscrupulous aristocrats knew how to turn a buck out of a pound of flesh. Their Royal African Company agents branded each slave with a large "RAC" on the chest and shipped them off to a hellish captivity in either the Caribbean or, you guessed it, Charleston. It was obvious from the beginning that our forebears were cut from different cloth than that of the pious tall hat Puritans of Massachusetts.

Colleton was influenced by John Locke, legal counsel to Lord Ashley Cooper, to open up the Carolina western lands for settlement. Part of that land is known today as Colleton County. Locke saw Carolina's west as a dumping ground for swarms of dissenters fleeing persecution by the "high-church" Stuarts. John Locke was a freethinker, not much of a spiritually-minded man, and for this reason we see an emergence of what we call religious toleration creeping into western thought . Unity of church and state was a driving force in 17th century Europe, but Locke's willingness to embrace religious pluralism in this English province is a true bell-ringer moment in modern history.

Colleton's land began to fill with Presbyterians and Baptists. folks who were dissenters. These men and women were considered "beyond the pale" by staunch Anglican supporters of the restoration. Fortunately, Barbadian John Colleton was never that discriminating. He made his money from the sale of African slaves to the incoming settlers wealthy enough to afford them.

By the time of the American Revolution, these Colleton dissenters were the spine of Low Country resistance to Britain. When Charleston fell to Lord Rawdon in 1781, the west country of the Ashepoo, Combahee, and Edisto, now known as ACE Basin, became a military quagmire for British convoys and occupation forces.

Continuing on the romantic road through Old Colleton, Highway 17 South runs straight into Jacksonboro. Approaching this historic hamlet on the causeway we pass unaware the turnoff to Parker's Ferry, the old ambush site where Marion's swamp raiders, August 28, 1781, threw into havoc the 300 Hessians and loyalists of British Colonel de Borck. Marion, a feisty little Huguenot, verbally ripped into fellow patriot commanders Harden and Cooper for their failure to pursue and destroy what was left of the routed enemy. The Old Parker's Ferry Road today is much the same path that the colonial road followed.

Not far from Parker's Ferry over the black Edisto is the estate of Colonel Isaac Hayne, the patriot rice planter and upstate iron foundry investor. Hayne was run down on horseback by "Mad Archie" Campbell, a career British cavalry officer. Colonel Hayne was out on military reconnaissance and ducked in to check on his plantation when a British scouting party surprised him. With reckless disregard of his safety, Hayne and his splendid thoroughbred attempted a daring leap over a rice ditch. But he was quickly captured when his horse lost footing in the mud. When Lord Rawdon hanged Hayne as a traitorous example, Campbell remarked that he'd rather have shot the good man dead on the spot than to see him strung up like a petty thief.

Patriot Hayne is buried in the ruins of the old Hayne Hall near Jacksonboro. His execution led to a massive uprising of dissenters statewide who rallied under Marion, Sumter, Pickens and a dozen other partisans who finally drove the British out of our state. And if ever you're in London, detour to see Campbell's grave marker inside St. James Piccadilly; it's a fitting tribute to an honorable adversary of our forefathers' struggle for independence.

The Edistoah Indians called their river "Pon-Pon" and so did the early settlers. The alluvial soil could grow any crop in abundance, and fishermen for two centuries have known the secret of the west bank of the Edisto as waters that produce the tastiest large bream and shad.

English settlers who preferred the writings of John Bunyan to the *Book of Common Prayer* found this fertile west land of Colleton to be their New Canaan. Return next week for more exciting tales from Old Colleton's land and the interesting origins of Jacksonboro, Walterboro, and Round O.

Finding History On The Back Roads Of Old Colleton County

What a shame that Kenneth Grahame, creator of those lovable rodents in *Wind and the Willows*, didn't own a river house on a bend of the Edisto or the Ashepoo. Grahame's memorable line about messing around in boats might have been rendered "there is nothing, absolutely nothing half so much worth doing as messing about" the back roads of Colleton County! Certainly Ratty and Mole would have preferred that Toad Hall be nestled in a rice field off Ivanhoe Creek. For miles of unspoiled marsh vistas, acres of longleaf pines and water oaks, you must tour historic Colleton County.

The old-timers remember Colleton as the haunt of Carew Rice, the celebrated silhouette artist whose Low Country marsh scenes adorn the walls of fine homes across the South. In his heyday in the 1940s, '50s, and '60s, people from all over America traveled to visit this country boy artist whose medium was scissors and black paper. The Cavallaro Restaurant on Savannah Highway, now preserved as an auto dealership, had a beautiful private dining room named The Carew Rice room.

Meandering down Highway 17 South, the Savannah Highway, one passes unknowingly by Poco Sabo plantation, once the property of Meyer Robert Guggenheim where, local tradition has it, that the first Quarter Horse bred in

South Carolina was foaled in the stables of this 200 year-old estate.

Few today can recall the mysterious man with the accent who holed up for weeks in a guest cottage of Bonny Hall on the Combahee. In the late 1930s this antebellum rice plantation was a shooting preserve owned by the Doubleday family, and they welcomed Somerset Maugham to hide away here and write as he gazed upon endless miles of ruined rice fields cut by the lazy river.

Ghosts frequent the byroads forming the triangle of Jacksonboro, Garden's Corner, and Yemassee. In the early months of 1865 Sherman's army swept through here before angling north to Columbia. Eyewitnesses reported seeing as many as seven huge plumes of smoke on the horizon as grand old homes were torched with all their outbuildings and crops. Hardee's Confederate cavalry captured and hanged dozens of Sherman's bummers whose backpacks so burdened with stolen silver had caused them to straggle. Late night travelers have sworn that they've seen these grizzly beings dangling from oak limbs amongst trails of Spanish moss in the moonlight.

Colleton is the land of Duncan Clinch Heyward, whose classic book, Seed From Madagascar, colorfully tells the history of the Carolina rice culture up through the devastating hurricanes of 1911 and '12. Heyward was the last of the patricians who governed South Carolina as the squires once presided over the shires of England.

Shortly after the ferocious hurricanes battered the rice dams, the boll weevil clawed his way into our state. Old properties went on the market one by one, and a prominent Charlestonian became a pariah on Broad Street because he saw a market in luring industrial titans from the North to invest in sporting preserves in the Low Country. The Firestones came and bought shooting preserves, and so did the Kelvins. Thomas Edison loved to hunt down here as did Grover Cleveland. The locals were divided with some rejoicing over the preservation of these old estates and others resenting the rich nabobs from off. Perhaps no hunt club in America carried as much cachet as did Okatie, variously spelled Okeetee, or the

Marshall Field family's Chelsea Plantation and Pineland Hunt Club just across the line in Jasper County. The list of notables who've stomped mud off their boots near the deer shed of Okatie would make the Fortune 500 crowd blink.

Cherokee Plantation near Yemassee was once the hunting lodge of Robert Beverly Evans, the president of American Motors Corporation. In 1978 Evans personally renamed the downsized Jeep Wagoneer the Jeep Cherokee after his beloved Colleton County hunting lodge. Before Evans purchased it the place was known as the old Blake place, and before that simply as Board House Plantation.

The plantation overseers of these fine estates are highly esteemed citizens within the county social structure. Many a Broad Street lawyer, banker, or broker has added luster to his reputation by having a plantation overseer connection out in Colleton County! Today, thanks to the Lane family's efforts, much of this semitropical paradise has been preserved forever as the A-C-E Basin.

The part of Highway 17 South, that has recently been widened between Jacksonboro and Garden's Corner, once was as familiar as the palm of his hand to Colonel Robert E. Lee of the Army Corps of Engineers. There are fortifications in the woods along this road that Colonel Lee designed to protect the vital railroad link to Savannah in the earliest months of the hostilities. On the 30th of November 1864, Confederate forces won one of their last victories of the War at Honey Hill Plantation just off SC Highway 278 two miles outside of Grahamville. Confederate Major General Gustavus Smith and Beaufort native, Colonel Charles Colcock won a hard fought victory over Union General Hatch's Northerners. After the War, Gus Smith, a former West Point professor of engineering, became one of the pioneers of property and casualty insurance.

The county seat of Colleton County is the historic town of Walterboro, a former inland summer retreat for rice planters. It arose from a collection of taverns, inns, and shops on the Charleston-to-Augusta road. The Greek Revival courthouse in Walterboro (c.1821) on the corner of Hampton and Jeffries Streets was designed by Robert Mills and built by Jonathan Lucas. Beulah Glover's book

Narratives of Colleton County says that one source maintains that the old courthouse was actually built by Colonel William Thompson after a design made famous by Robert Mills. Robert Barnwell Rhett delivered the earliest clarion call for secession inside this courthouse in October 1828. Mount Pleasant secessionists argued that we have a prior claim to that dubious honor with a heated debate at the Ronkin Shell Tavern on Ferry Street, but no one yet has adequately documented date and participants.

Kenneth Grahame's Ratty and Mole never got to float down the Edisto or the Ashepoo, or motor with the top down along a back road leading to Pringle Bend, but we can do that and so much more any Saturday exploring old Colleton County.

How An Aussie From Down Under Discovered Forgotten History In Carolina

Ever wonder who those odd souls are who rummage around libraries searching for peculiar blue bindings with white lettering, the sturdy no-frills cover on a poor scholar's unpublished dissertation? No high-gloss paper jacket adorns these utilitarian tomes. No zingers by well-known writers extol these books' merits. There's just a businesslike description of a grad student's research. What about the researchers themselves who prowl about archives and dark stacks in cavernous reading rooms. The doctoral students are modern versions of Chaucer's poor student in Canterbury Tales of whom the host intones "Nor tell a tale that puts us all to sleep. Tell of adventures, have a merry say."

Just the notion of probing around a collection of unpublished dissertations adds to your charms a measure of Brahmin cachet. For those curious-minded history buffs who are venturesome enough to look beyond the slick volumes with arresting titles that vie for your attention at every library, dig around until you discover one of these plain-wrapper works. But be warned, even the first sip of a Chardonnay may not reward the taste buds, for that oak and smoke tang belongs to an acquired palate.

Such as search led to the discovery of Richard Waterhouse's 1973 unpublished dissertation entitled *South Carolina's Colonial Elite: A Study In The Social Structure And Political Culture Of a Southern Colony, 1670 - 1760.* What piques our interests are three small words on an inside page: Johns Hopkins dissertation.

At 318 pages the book has a good heft. Check out the bibliography. The best part of it all is that Waterhouse is an Aussie, a scholar from Down Under, and he sleuthed through our historical societies and archives unearthing hundreds of facts about colonial Carolina that many historians never imagined. But it's his research hypothesis that is so intriguing.

Richard Waterhouse received his doctorate in history from Johns Hopkins in 1973 and later served as chairman of the history department at the University of Sydney where he holds the position of professor today. I corresponded with Doctor Waterhouse recently about his research experiences here in South Carolina.

"First let me say that in revised form the dissertation became a book that was published by Garland, NY, in 1989. A revised and illustrated edition of the book was published by the History Press, Charleston, in 2005. I am much more fond of the second edition because the History Press did a splendid production job on it."

"When I arrived at Johns Hopkins from Australia in 1969 my intention was to write a Ph.D. dissertation on Puritan New England. But my Ph.D. supervisor, Jack P. Greene, held the view that too many students were working on New England and that the colonial South had been much neglected. He also told me that, in economic terms, the South was much more important in shaping the colonial and imperial economy.

"So I decided to write about colonial South Carolina. When I began I knew very little about colonial South Carolina or what it was like in the 1970s. In July 1971 I caught a bus to Columbia, found a room in a boarding house ($40 per month), and began to work in the State Archives. I worked from 9 a.m. to 9 p.m. on weekdays, from 9 to 5 on Saturdays and from 2 to 5 on Sundays".

The only breaks I took involved watching some USC football matches and sometimes fishing in the local rivers (I am a lifelong fishing fanatic). I didn't much like Columbia; most of the locals and that included the college students, had very little interest in an Australian who was a Ph.D. student at Hopkins. The graduate students at USC, especially those writing dissertations on colonial South Carolina, tended to regard me as a rival and were also a bit suspicious that I might steal their topics and material.

'I didn't get to Charleston until April 1972. I spent a month staying in a very cheap hotel (I shared a bathroom) and working mostly in the Historical Society and sometimes in the Library Society. I fell in love with Charleston. I loved the fact that you could walk everywhere, I loved the distinctive character of different streets, and I loved making trips out to the sea islands as well as up river to places like Middleton Place and Drayton Hall. I also learnt to fish off the sea wall, but not with much success. Most of my leisure hours were spent walking the streets and photographing pre-Revolutionary houses.

'After I graduated and took a teaching position at Sydney, I made two trips back to Charleston in 1976 and 1979 to collect material that was later included in the book. In the 1980s I began to research and write Australian history, and I now hold a chair in that field. But my knowledge of colonial American history, and of SC in particular, has helped shape my understanding of how the British experience in North America shaped the form which the British authorities gave to the Australian colonies.

'Finally I still make regular trips to the US to teach a comparative course in

222

US-Australian history at UNC Chapel Hill. I will be doing that again in November 2007. One day I would love to revisit Charleston. Along with San Francisco, it is my favourite US city.

'I note that you also asked about food and eccentric people I may have met. When I lived in Charleston I couldn't afford to eat in good restaurants although I did eat at a couple of well known seafood places. I found that I didn't much like the southern tendency to deep fry seafood. What I did learn to like was grits and sausage. In Australia I was accustomed to English style beef sausages and I found that I really liked the spicy breakfast sausages I could get in the Charleston cafeterias.

'I still like southern food, although most of the good southern restaurants I have now tried are in New Orleans and Durham, NC. I also forgot to mention that in my travels around the Lowcountry from Georgetown to Beaufort I usually hitched. For the most part those most willing to give me a ride were African-Americans driving pick-up trucks, and usually I got to ride in the back. It's all a bit unthinkable now.' " Cheers, Richard!

The Original 9-11 That Still Has Us Grieving 33 Years Later

Lest we forget, the alarming sound of those numbers 9 - 11 had a local resonance to them 27 years before everyone else associated these digits with the specter of global terror. In Charleston, Wednesday, September 11, 1974, dawned overcast and muggy as all eyes were on tv weather legend Charlie Hall imploring him to tell us if the tropical storm offshore was going to head our way. By noontime the storm no longer mattered, and for many nothing here would ever be the same again. By 8:45 a.m. stations interrupted programming with a special bulletin. What was to be a routine Eastern Airline quick hop to Charlotte went down in a fireball three miles short of its destination. The passenger jet's manifest reads like a Who's Who of Charleston, and the headline in Wednesday afternoon's *Evening Post* is the three inch apocalyptic type size reserved for something like the end of the world.

The month of September had gotten off to a grand start in 1974. The political climate was calming somewhat following Nixon's disgraceful departure. Gerry Ford's modesty and self-deprecating golf jokes got us to laughing again. There was continuing speculation that Ford might offer a blanket pardon to Nixon and perhaps even to Halderman and Erlichman. But the nightmare of Watergate was coming to an end.

Elsewhere the world seemed to be loosening up from the grip of war and oppression. Vietnam was just behind us and George Busbee had just defeated Lester Maddox in the Georgia Democratic gubernatorial primary. And up in Newport Ted Hood, as skipper of the 12-meter yacht *Courageous*, was cruising to convincing victories over the Australian yacht *Intrepid*. On the sports page, former Florida Heisman winner Steve Spurrier separated his shoulder in the Rams - 49ers game.

On Tuesday, September 10, Charlestonians saw local beauty Cheryl von Lehe, Miss South Carolina's picture wowing the judges in Atlantic City. That weekend she'd be crowned 1st Runner-up Miss America, but by that time our city and state would be in deep mourning for the tragedy that resulted from a routine short flight gone terribly wrong.

The radio and tv break-in was heart-stopping: "At just after 7:30 a.m. [September 11, 1974] Eastern Airlines Flight 212, McDonnell Douglas DC-9 crashed 3.3 miles short of runway 36 at Douglas Municipal Airport in Charlotte, North Carolina. Of the 82 persons aboard the aircraft, 11 and two crew members survived the accident. " Charleston changed forever in an instant. Though it took hours to confirm the dead, when the list was finally made public, it confirmed the rumors that were sweeping the city. Among the dead, the dean of MUSC, the admiral commanding the Sixth Naval District, two U.S. Navy nuclear submarine commanders, three executives with the *Post and Courier* newspapers, Walter Cronkite's CBS evening news editor, the local manager of WCIV television, a department chair at UNC, a member of the Newton Piggly-Wiggly family, and a score of beloved Charlestonians and Summerville natives. The Lowcountry was in shock and the story led the evening national news channels.

Dense fog overlay the Charlotte airport that morning and flight 212 was on a routine instrument approach. Cockpit recordings indicate the usual banter of politics, oil prices, etc., among the flight crew, and then the altitude warning alarm sounds.

Several explosions were heard before and after the crash which went down on the John McDowell dairy farm near York Road. Several dazed survivors staggered away. Barbara Cox of Charlotte told reporters that a badly burned man stumbled to her house asking for help. She gave him water and a blanket.

Columbia-based stewardess Colette Watson was the heroine of the tragedy. Frightened, dazed, and bruised, her training kept her focused and the 26-year-old helped many to get out of the burning aircraft. She and passenger Francis Mihalek pulled an unconscious copilot who suffered two broken legs through a hole near the cockpit.

"We were heading down in a normal descent, it seemed," said Mihalek when interviewed from his hospital bed. "All I could see was a real dense bank of fog. I thought I saw a tree go by the window and a fraction of a second later, I knew it was because we hit. I unbuckled my seat belt and realized fire was all around me because my hands were burning. I could hear the stewardess calling for help."

Guy Henderson and his brother-in-law missed the flight because the motel clerk forgot to give them the requested wake-up call. William Todd, an administrative aide to the Charleston County School District, also missed the early A.M. flight.

Rear Admiral Charles Cummings, USN, was killed in the crash. He had been Chief of the Sixth Naval District for just 13 days. He and two nuclear submarine skippers, also killed in the crash, were on their way to Washington, D.C. Hospital Corpsman, John A. Toohy, a survivor, had been released from the Naval Hospital as a patient to attend his father's funeral.

MUSC lost its Dean for Academic Affairs, James W. Colbert, Jr., M.D., age 54, as well as two of his sons, Paul and Peter. Doctor Colbert was a nationally-known physician who had previously been Assistant Dean at Yale Medical School as well as Dean of the St. Louis Medical School. Younger son, Stephen Colbert, a nationally-known television personality, was not on the ill-fated flight.

All of Charleston mourned the loss of such fine citizens taken from us in the bloom of life. The family of Dr. and Mrs. F.M. Ball lost their son, David. Harold Newton of the Piggly-Wiggly Newton family died. E.J. Thornhill, III., another prominent name, was also among the dead.

Suddenly we had no interest in the antics of Evel Knievel or whether the State should fund a second medical school. Within the week President Ford pardoned former President Nixon from any charges that might arise in the future connected with Watergate, but Charleston was otherwise occupied in mourning its losses of Eastern Flight 212. The Lowcountry will never forget the tragedy of 9-11-'74.

Revising Our Opinion On Carolina's Colonial Elites

When colonial history's your passion and excellence is your obsession, there's a likelihood that the coordinates of your quest will eventually place you in the office of Professor Jack P. Greene at Johns Hopkins University. You don't know of Jack Greene the historian? Check out the 7 pages of his books on Amazon.com; he's a legend among historians. Greene's the foremost among the wise men of American Colonialism, the Revolution, and whatever it is that's called "post colonial theory."

No coincidence that Richard Waterhouse, currently Professor of History, University of Sydney, discovered Greene's ivoried corner of Academe in the early 1970s. Australian "mates" share the same peculiar fascination with colonial matters as do the "Yanks." There's a common suspicion that Mother England isn't as fond of our ancestors as we are!

Waterhouse could have expected that Professor Greene would pack him off in the direction of picturesque New England villages in search of puritanical double-standards, or other as yet undiscovered measures of colonial intolerance.

But far was it from the inquisitive mind of Jack Greene of Johns Hopkins to send this Aussie lad, 4th generation son of the bush, sleuthing to sniffy Connecticut or nasal New York. No! Greene packed Waterhouse off to the American version of the Aussie bush, that would be, you guessed it, old Carolina.

Since then Waterhouse has published his dissertation under the title *A New World Gentry: The Making of a Merchant and Planter Class in South Carolina, 1670-1770 (The History Press, 1989).* Normally unpublished dissertations collect dust on library shelves. It's rare that one breaks into the popular presses for the general readership, but Waterhouse's insightful look at our emerging culture caught the eye of more than one publisher.

Besides being an entertaining read, this welcomed addition to Carolina lore examines our earliest years and sheds new light on the evolution of a unique slavocracy that back then had no intention of becoming a democracy.

The scope of this man's research transcends the range of our 19th and early 20th century historians whose point-of-view was decidedly provincial.

Flip through his bibliography and you'll discover the fruit of the vast Johns

Hopkins stacks. In addition, he's shaken down the Rhodes House Annex of the Bodleian Library at Oxford, and numerous other archives in Barbados and Bermuda. Locally, Richard cased the Charleston Library Society and the S.C. Historical Society's manuscripts in the Fireproof Building. Tales of Richard's sojourn here in Charleston are as fascinating to us natives as are his additions to the scholarship on our ancestors' schemes and shenanigans.

What really was the motivation of the well-to-do Barbados gentry, to uproot from an established, moneymaking situation and move over to a wild and primitive Carolina? How did Carolina's early settlement dispose it to an oligarchy whereas Pennsylvania's settlements and New Hampshire's did not?

Though Waterhouse does not embrace the differences between Carolina and other colonies, his study leads to these speculations. What was unique about Carolina's early years that made slavery an even greater necessity than in Virginia? The answer lies partly in the quixotic personalities and peculiar ambitions of the earliest power elites. Add into this happen chance human mix the sometimes radical ideals of London colonial advisor John Locke, and you get close to discovering Jack Greene's genius in sending his advisee Waterhouse probing into this this locale named for that enemy of virginity, the "bounder from Britain," King Charles II.

In the aftermath of Charles's boisterous restoration every faction of English society nervously weighed expectations with their concerns for whether the new cartels would aide or hinder the colonials' accumulation of wealth. In Barbados there was jubilation among these old Cavaliers that "Good Time Charlie was back in London town."

However, economic and political life wasn't simple or easy for the expatriate gentry; England's diplomatic alignments shifted and soon she was at war with the protestant Dutch, and befriending the Catholic French. Charles's marriage to Katherine of Braganza, a Catholic Portuguese princess, sent groans of agony amongst the protestants, and it created new fears of Spanish aggression throughout the Caribbean.

In Barbados this shifting tide of alliances coincided with the sharp drop in sugar prices on European markets. Also a new Parliamentary Staples Act (1663) requiring all goods shipped to English colonies from anywhere in Europe to be reshipped into English ports and reshipped in English ships, an economic inconvenience to Barbados. Cromwell himself, had done less to injure royalist opponents than this Crown government was doing to advance the loyalists!

Shifting alliances, declining sugar prices, and weather phenomena, drought and hurricane, made the run-up to 1670 a losing proposition for the high rollers of Barbados. Compounding confusion to the economic equation of restoration politics, Jamaica came on stream as the rival sugar producer. The Barbadian advantage was neutralized and and powerful men such as Sir John Yeamans and his Carib confederates looked for a new venue to exploit. A handful of savvy Dutch traders here were ready to break the mercantilist bonds that underlay the colony's very existence!

Waterhouse maintains that the likeliest candidates to depart Bridgetown, Barbados, for Charles Town were the grandsons of the original Barbados. Several sailed to Virginia and some moved to other Caribbean islands, but the big money Barbadian hustlers to a man all came to the new port of Charles Town.

Ship records were reviewed of who came in here between 1670 and 1680, and he concludes that of 683 persons arriving, 177 had Barbados origins, 25 came from assorted islands such as Antigua, Nevis, etc., 9 emigrated from American colonies to the north, and 129 arrived directly from English ports. The balance was a *hoi poloi* of indentured servants, traders, thieves, and transients.

The Royal Africa Company directors, James, Duke of York (later King James II), the Duke of Albemarle, John Locke, and others made it possible to flood the new colony with fresh slaves direct from Africa. The profit hungry settlers could combine cheap land with affordable slaves. The big men of fortune from Barbados were already leveraged with land and slaves upon arrival.

What the Australian professor Richard Waterhouse does is to rethink the colony's first hundred years with respect to the evolution of economic, social, and political power elites, and his work is now the gold standard of colonial scholarship for South Carolina.

Celebrating The Revival Of America's Historic Grand Hotels

Along with high-speed internet, click-of-the-mouse travel arrangements, and wide-open, cruise-control motor ways we celebrate life's good fortune these days in the fast lane. Chain motels vie for our favor by pledging that we won't lack in consumer delights if we check in there for the night. Each motel room is interchangeable with the previous one and indistinguishable from the succeeding ones.

There was a time when we loaded the family up in the Packard and motored along scenic two-lane roads through woodlands, townships, and two-horse farms. Less hurried sojourners sought refuge for the evening in a stately hotel where quiet elegance was the order. Whatever became of those refined establishments of a nobler era?

With careful planning and few extra dollars it's still possible to experience these delightful throwbacks to yesteryear, the grand hotels that are an anomaly in our frenzied world. It's possible still to savor the lifestyle of generations past and to sample the refinements of a halcyon bygone era.

Quite a few cities still possess at least one old hotel that keeps up the appearance of gentility, that secure "aura of old money," the rich leather, polished mahogany, beveled mirrors, and cut glass chandeliers. From the gentlemen's bar wafts the aroma of burl tobacco with low-laughter and hushed conversation amidst leather-bound volumes adorning breakfront cabinets. Life lived along these lines is of another dimension but certainly worth our time in experiencing, even if just for a night or two.

The grandest old dame of hostelry is the meticulously restored Willard Hotel located at 1401 Pennsylvania Avenue, Washington, D.C.. Recently, it has been restored to its 1901 facade and luxurious interior. In 1860 Abe Lincoln checked into the Willard for ten days of festivities prior to his inauguration. His room charge, dining room, and tab came to more than $800, or $16,000 by our standards, and Abe couldn't pay it all when he checked out. He had to work out an arrangement with the front desk. Maybe that's what was clouding his judgment when Charleston was hoping for some reconciliation over the Fort Sumter occupation!

In the 1870s President Ulysses S. Grant preferred to have his afternoon whiskey and cigar in the Willard lobby just a short walk from the White House. Whether Grant was personally corrupt, or not, is difficult to gauge, but his henchmen who accompanied the old general quietly pocketed envelopes of appreciation from patronage seekers. The term "lobbyist" originated in the Willard's elegant mahogany, brass, and leather lobby.

For history-minded travelers there's a plus in staying in these old hotels that have such a storied past. The old saying "if these walls could talk" is certainly true for the magnificent Drake Hotel in Chicago. The Drake was the Midwest's answer to New York's Waldorf. Built with the unlimited fortunes of new industrial might, the Drake became a rendezvous for Edgar Lee Masters, the prominent attorney and author of *Spoon River Anthology*. Masters was much the ladies man and used the Drake for his assignations.

William Jennings Bryan frequented The Drake Hotel, as did Marshall Field. In 1968 The Drake was under siege by antiwar protesters who wanted to storm Hubert Humphrey's room. The Illinois National Guard stationed phalanxes of troops in front and rear as the media broadcast the chaos to the world. Today, the Drake is as grand as ever, and you can dine at a table opposite the Swifts or the Armours.

If your itinerary takes your through Richmond, by all means check into the newly refurbished Jefferson Hotel in the center of historic Richmond. The Richmond aristoi point out that the Jefferson represents that understated southern elegance that makes it the South's leading historic hotel. The Renaissance Revival architecture accented by marble columns and Tiffany stained glass once hosted the fabulous 1895 engagement party of Charles Dana Gibson and Irene Langhorne. She became the celebrated "Gibson Girl," the darling of artists and photographers. Thomas Jefferson is about the only great American never to stay at The Jefferson Hotel! He was 100 years too early for the great inn that bears his name. Frank Sinatra loved it, so did Elvis, Cindy Crawford, Tom Wolfe, and Anthony Hopkins.

Closer to home is the Windsor Hotel in Americus, Georgia. It's a most imposing Victorian five-story brick edifice complete with castle-like turrets. It's imposing staircase in the lobby inspired guest Margaret Mitchell to incorporate a similar scene in her novel *Gone With The Wind*. The Windsor was a stopover for opera stars and vaudeville performers. Today, you're more likely to see Jimmy and Rosalyn Carter and a secret service agent having lunch.

If ever in Aiken for the horse season, it's imperative that you stop in at the historic Hotel Aiken. This charming luxurious inn once played host to the Duke of Windsor. It was also the immediate refuge of FDR's paramour Lucy Mercer Rutherford when that great man died rather unexpectedly at Warm Springs in April 1945. Since then the Hotel Aiken's gentlemen's bar has entertained more high-goal polo players than anywhere east of Texas and south of Saratoga.

But if travel is not in your immediate future, you can simply stroll down Meeting Street to the historic Mills House Hotel. Sure it was reconstructed in the 1970s on the site of the original Mills, and an extra story has been added, but so many interior aspects have been preserved that you can still get a sense of the grandeur of this splendid 19th century edifice. That wrought-iron balcony that you see above you at the entrance is the one that Robert E. Lee stood on as he watched the Great Fire of Charleston in 1861.

It's difficult to imagine April 1860 when the national Democratic convention adjourned after failing to nominate a candidate among the four contenders. The convention itself was headquartered at South Carolina Institute Hall, but the delegates were lodging at either the Mills, the Charleston Hotel, or the Planter's Inn. Beauregard was known to frequent the Mills House as did the staff of President Jefferson Davis during his visit here in 1863.

Whether it's the Mills House of Charleston or the Roosevelt in New Orleans, the Desoto in Savannah, or the Belmont Inn of Abbeville you're bound to be intrigued by the fascinating tales you hear at America's historic hotels.

College Football in 1909 Was Far Different Than It Is Now

Rutledge Avenue north of Calhoun Street was mostly rural in 1909. Hampton Park had a few buildings left over from the West Indian Exhibition, and the Enston Village for the poor was nearby. A year or two earlier Citadel cadets had chalked off a gridiron football field along this dusty road. There were no stadium seats or lights, and few women spectators attended. Football ranked with boxing for leaving participants bloody and unconscious. Few ladies ventured near the boisterous contest where men with pocket flasks and cigars wagered bets on which set of roughnecks could pound the others. With horse racing on the wane in South Carolina, college football established itself forever in that raucous sporting season of 1909.

Sports news appeared below the fold on the Entertainment page of *The Evening Post*. The Entertainment page was for theater goers and they could find play reviews such as the one appearing in early October entitled "*A Gentleman From Mississippi*" then playing at the Academy of Music. Mark Twain was still churning out books, and reviews of his works were common fare with local sports news right below it. In November of 1909 the Entertainment page featured Mark Twain's daughter's marriage to a Russian baron. On the same page sports enthusiasts were fascinated by pro-baseball titan, Ty Cobb, the ten-thousand dollar man of Detroit Tiger fame.

Football was so new then that the reporters had to be given weekly instruction on the finer points of the game. The ball was described as a pigskin leather oval inflated to 70 pounds per square inch. The pigskin inflated bladder was supposed to be resilient enough to cushion the runner against hard falls. Refs sought to stifle college yells as taunts incited violence on the field and amongst the spectators. The addition of cheerleaders years later was an attempt to channel the crowds' taunts into a more sportsmanlike banter.

A ball carrier could dash open and then go down on one knee while shouting "Down," and the referees were supposed to honor that call, disallowing bone-crushing late hits. However, the crowd booed a runner who didn't brave the savage open-field tackles that left a dozen players dead in the 1909 college season.

The College of Charleston opened the local football season with a match against Porter Military Academy at Porter's parade ground at Bee and Ashley Avenue. On an October Saturday afternoon The College blanked the Porter boys 51-0. Names standing out for The College were Ligon, Riley, Stoney, McManus, Hollings, and Lesesne. Porter cadets who played both offense and defense were Seabrook, Magwood, Hart, and Jeter. A half mile away at Hampton Park, Citadel cadets wrangled with Marine Officer Candidates of Parris Island.

Running hard from the fullback position, Passallaigue scored late in the second half to give the cadets a 6-0 lead. But those hard-nosed Marines dominated the second half to win convincingly 16-6. Bulldog stalwarts on defense for 1909 were Cogswell, Rogers, and Duckett.

These football teams numbered approximately 15 players each. Students manned wheelbarrows to carry away the carnage from the wide-open play. There was as yet no passing the ball, but the no-notice drop kick and the quick kick were vicious offensive weapons. Injured players were piled bloody, unconscious, with arms-a-kimbo into the wheelbarrow. On the sidelines older men puffed away on cigars.

In 1909 there were no "football scholarships" for recruiting outsized players with the speed of a white-tail buck. A boy signed onto his college's football roster and played his heart out for the dear old blue and white, or orange and purple. The press didn't report on every off-field utterance and antic of these players who pioneered modern football. No mention, either, is made of ticket sales or attendance. No statistics measured and compared the two teams' performance.

The Medical College formed a football club in 1909 and scrimmaged The College and The Citadel. There was another baseball / football club in town and they called themselves West End. If they had a connection with the dairy of that name it is not stated in the *Evening Post*, but West End was a formidable force in city sports. Porter Military Academy played a college schedule, and, though 1909 was not a good season for them, they did have seasons where they defeated USC and The Citadel.

In late October the University of Georgia rolled into town to play The Citadel. No mention is made of either team having a bull dog nickname or mascot. But the newspaper described the Georgia team as heavy and unable to run against the feisty Citadel defense led by bone-crushing open field tackling of Duckett and "Gawdge" Rogers.

Citadel did not post its starting lineup until a few minutes before the game. In a rockem-sockem contest that was waged mostly around midfield, the cadets held Georgia to a 9-9 tie. This story was one of the first to break above the fold to the treasured space where theater and book reviews dominated on the Entertainment page. Cogswell, Duckett, and Passalaigue enjoyed a day or two of local fame, but football had arrived in the Low Country with that one mismatched contest being fought to a tie by the local boys. Carolina went over to Atlanta to play the engineering students at Georgia Tech and got trounced 53-6.

Local athletes usually stayed around to play at either The College or The Citadel, and those players without college ambition signed on with a club team which competed with the colleges. Rudolph Siegling, however, was a well-known local lad who was captain of the Princeton eleven. And one of the Hanckel boys was co-captain of the Clemson team.

The final game of the season was in early November and it was the City Championship between The Citadel and The College of Charleston. The game was played at Hampton Park on a crisp autumn afternoon. Citadel ran over The College 30-0. Holding down key positions for The College were von Kolnitz, Hollings, and McManus. The All-South championship was won by Sewanee beating LSU. After our local game the spectators rode over to the fair grounds to see Buffalo Bill Cody and his Wild West Show with real war-painted Indians! Can any such glorious afternoon ever be recreated in Charleston?

Seeing 1817 Charleston Through The Eyes Of Eben Kellogg

None said it better than Rab Burns, "ploughman poet of Auld Lang Syne" with his immortal phrase, "O wad some power the giftie gie us To see oursel's as ithers see us! It wad frae monie a blunder free us . . . ." Few, if any, take kindly to criticism no matter how constructively rendered. The icy retort is doubled, too, if the antagonist is "from up north." But there's a time and a place for words plainspoken, for democracy has made us protective and proud as well as prosperous. Plain words are what a New Englander recorded when he visited here and he spoke candidly, not to us, but in a journal intended only for a friend back home. The 1817 diary of Ebenezer Kellogg may be the most candid observation of our area ever penned by an outsider.

Kellogg was a Yale-educated theology professor at Williams College in Massachusetts. His doctor advised the 27-year-old to travel south, as far as Mobile or Havana, to cure the chronic consumption fatigue that plagued him. Kellogg's New York physician, a lung specialist by the name of Burritt, advised against stopping in Carolina, urging rather sailing on to the West Indies. When the transport grounded on a shoal near Bull Island, this New England professor hauled his trunk over the rail and hitched a ride on a fishing boat heading in. Kellogg crossed the Charleston bar on the afternoon of November 26, 1817, precisely 190 years ago.

Just what did this Connecticut-born Yankee record in his journal during his three-week rest in Charleston? As with any historical writing, perspective needs to be considered. Kellogg was a fourth-generation New Englander of English Puritan descent. His ancestors were among the second wave advancing into Plymouth Bay Colony. This young visitor was a stern Calvinist from a section of the country that was antiwar and anti-Calhoun in the 1812 hostilities. The journal that Kellogg kept was a travelog for his Williams College colleague, Professor Chester Dewey. Lastly, this visitor from the North had never laid eyes on anyone who was not a free man until he stepped out on Market Street and East Bay that 1817 November afternoon.

The Kellogg journal begins with feelings of relief at setting foot on land after a week of rough seas. He describes our barrier islands as sandy, windswept stretches with only here and there a shrub or a tree. He records that Charleston is

discernible by the ever-prevalent low-slung cloud of smoke that hovers over it.
Two light houses designate the harbor entrance, one on Sullivan's and the other
on James Island. But Kellogg probably meant the lighthouse on Morris Island.

Our adventurer took a night's lodging at the Franklin Hotel and then
checked into a run-of-the-mill boarding house on King Street. In those early days
of the republic, the one thing travelers never left home without was a wallet
containing letters of introduction. Of course, it was expected that the recipient
would receive you into their household and treat you as dear to them as the friend
who'd written the letter.

With Charleston being the 3rd most active commercial port there were
many close relationships between our people and New Yorkers, Philadelphians,
and Bostonians. Kellogg's sole letter was addressed to the Reverend Doctor Haran
Whitney Leland, a New England Calvinist summoned south to the pulpit of
Second Presbyterian. Kellogg's 1810 Yale classmate, Fredericke Grimke, an
attorney, was his lone acquaintance upon arrival.

Ebenezer Kellogg was as eager as any foreign visitor to walk our streets and
gaze upon our seawall and Barbadian architecture. Strolling about Charleston 190
years ago discloses that this 137- year-old city already possessed an air of
independence. The Revolution was nearly 40 years in the past and the War of
1812 had been resolved thirty months previously. Kellogg observed that
Charleston had a mean, dirty appearance compared with the cities of the North.
East Bay Street was lined with grocers, ships' chandlers, cotton warehouses, and
auction barns. The most appealing streets he noted here were Broad, Church,
Meeting, Tradd, and King. Nothing west of King was worth the notice as it was
mostly undeveloped and rough.

Kellogg was an astute observer of people and architecture and seemed
sincere in passing along to his friend an accurate picture of this proud, aristocratic
Charleston. He appears only mildly disdainful about the institution of slavery.
The style and material of construction in Charleston appeared inferior to New

York and Boston. Large, dull grey-brown bricks made the city appear dingy. Only a few buildings were painted or stuccoed. Charleston appeared decayed and partial to function over form or beauty. Kellogg makes no comment that the war of 1812 has just ended or that commerce nationwide has been crippled by the 1812 war plus the Napoleonic contention.

In Kellogg's opinion, Charleston's semblance was most like that of Albany, the capital of New York. Wooden houses here were seldom painted and brick ones possessed a facade like those seen in Holland, or in the Dutch part of New York City. However, every home here boasted an abundance of greenery and blooming vegetation.

Hardly any block in Charleston contained more than one dwelling. Most set amidst shops or outbuildings. A wealthy planter named Colonel Stevens befriended Kellogg and entertained him one evening. The Stevens house was described as two rooms per floor set 30 feet back from the street, completely concealed by citrus trees and camellias. Charleston homes were set back from the street's noise and dust and concealed by lush foliage. Kellogg had never seen an urban setting quite like this before.

Calling upon a Charlestonian at his home in 1817 was a peculiar affair according to our Northern diarist. A footman stationed near the street announced the visitor to a doorman serving inside the house. Once the guest entered a piazza and traversed a verandah to the grand entrance hall, another servant, the parlor butler, ushered him into a receiving room. This elaborate protocol insulated Charlestonians from unwanted interruptions.

The insistence upon privacy and the high brick walls separating the homes produced, in Kellogg's view, an insular demeanor amongst inhabitants here. But, for Ebenezer Kellogg's most candid observations about Charlestonians, look for next week's column here in the Moultrie News!

More Of What A New Englander Saw In Charleston In 1817

When Ebenezer Kellogg, a Williams College divinity professor, visited Charleston and Savannah over the winter of 1817 - 1818, he kept a detailed travel diary for his colleague and mentor, Chester Dewey. Dewey, an ancestor of philosopher John Dewey, never got to read the insightful 134-page travelogue because it disappeared with lost luggage in Georgia.

In the 1940s a history buff at a garage sale rummaged through a box of old letters and fished out this neatly bound gentleman's journal. Realizing that here was something of inestimable value to historians, the buyer turned the volume over to the University of Georgia. In 1948 Professor Sidney W. Martin edited Kellogg's writings and published excerpts in the *South Carolina Historical Quarterly*.

The value to us 60 years later, and 190 years after Kellogg's Charleston visit, is that we have a rare peek into antebellum Charleston, a detailed description of everything imaginable from an astute observer. Ebenezer Kellogg's trained eye gives us an opinion never intended for public view.

Kellogg, a twenty-something-year-old academic whose collateral descendants would make a name in the cereal business, kept accurate weather records for his friend, Chester Dewey, a scholar whom many credit as being one of the fathers of meteorology. In last week's column we examined how Kellogg viewed our city as dingy and constructed of poor materials and workmanship. He adds that the inhabitants were ill-prepared here for any chill in the temperature and that a great many thin-clad men and women suffered dreadfully from a dip in the temperature.

As he walked Charleston streets by day observing our citizens at work and leisure, Kellogg noted that homes here seldom had a carpet of grass adorning their yard. Kellogg says that it'd be impossible to keep a yard fresh. But he does give Charleston credit for colorful shrubs and citrus trees.

Charleston streets are described as unpaved and cut through deeply with wagon ruts that hold water in the wet season. He does not note the profusion of oyster shells that other writers mention as being used here for surfacing streets. Charleston streets were unsightly, muddy, and impassable by foot due to horse-droppings. Every house had a carriage block for ladies to dismount gracefully from a carriage, and gentlemen were expected to scrape their boots prior to entering any building.

A curious aspect of Charleston gentlemen was that they preferred to drive their coach themselves with the servant sitting idly by them, rather than being chauffered as one would be in proper New England. Charleston gentlemen had affection and fascination for their horses and slaves. Kellogg notes several times that the servants appeared happy, well-treated, and often idle. Kellogg notes that Charleston was not as industrious as the New England area.

Charleston churches embraced slaves in their worship services, and some churches, notably the Methodists, involved the slaves actively in the worship. In other churches the slaves gathered either in the aisles or in the balcony. Kellogg saw one positive aspect here deriving from slavery in that Christianity spread widely into what had been a pagan culture. It's clear in this diary that abolition sentiments had not swept New England yet.

One of the highlights of Kellogg's visit here was the afternoon he spent with his Yale classmate, Fredericke Grimke, a local attorney. Both men had been in the Class of 1811 at Yale. Grimke took Kellogg to visit the Charleston Library Society, the oldest continuing subscription library in America, dating back to the 1740s. There, in the upstairs of a building on King Street, Kellogg examined the 9000 volumes of theology, history, geography, philosophy, literature, and music. Many volumes were imported from London, but the general impression Kellogg had of our wonderful library was that it was not neatly kept and that it was dusty.

A life-sized statue of Apollo was just a plaster copy and hadn't seen a dust rag in months!

The one building that Ebenezer Kellogg commented favorably upon was the Circular Congregational Church on Meeting Street. That building was subsequently destroyed in the fire of 1861. The Exchange Building was very ordinary, and St. Michael's, a Christopher Wren model, was out of proportion with windows too large for the height of the walls and the depth of the columns. He said it was as if various parts of Wren's blueprint had been thrown together and mismatched to ill-effect.

Our visiting commentator does not seem to have had many dinner invitations, but when he accepted dinner invitations, he was struck by the number of servants each household contained. Servants appeared often to be just standing idle, or sitting around. It was comical to Kellogg that at a dinner, the host gave a command to a nearby servant, who-in-turn, relayed the command to a more distant servant, who carried the request beyond the room.

Without so much as condemning the South with indolence and lassitude, Kellogg does imply that the institution of slavery is as ruinous for the master as it is for the slave. Servants sat in the chilly hallways of their masters' parlor and awaited a summons. Sometimes they sat there in the bitter cold for hours into the evening while the merry sound of laughter could be discerned from within closed-off rooms.

The two aspects of our southern culture that riveted Kellogg's attention as he toured Charleston and then Savannah was our attitude toward religion and our relationship with the Africans in our midst. He did not sense that our tastes were as cultivated as those of New Englanders. Our lumpy beds with gauzelike canopies draped over them remained a curiosity. He never got accustomed to the mosquito or the no-seeum that struck terror at night. Kellogg described us as being sickly, a condition which he attributes to dirt everywhere. But at least our streets were not as noisy as Boston's, for ours were not paved!

242

Provoking as these observations are to us who think of Charleston as Augustine's "shining city upon a hill," we can take some small comfort that Ebenezer Kellogg never intended that we should hear a word of this private commentary. However, as with 17th century Englishman Samuel Pepys' private journal, and the musings of many another a private-minded person, confidential thoughts often become public knowledge.

John Andrew Rice Came Out of The 18th Century

Maybe it was the sweet gum trees that shaded the back lots of rural southern homes. Perhaps it was the mica that lined the wall of the well from which drinking water was drawn. Those backwoods counties from Mississippi to Carolina were forgotten, off-road places, but, odd as it seems, more than a handful of America's first Rhodes Scholars ripened in just such a rustic environment.

Some readers might recall the roisterous, down-home intellectual from Yazoo, Mississippi, Willie Morris. Morris was the football-player with the southern drawl who won a coveted Rhodes Scholarship while attending the University of Texas in 1956. By age 33 he was the editor of Harper's Magazine and the toast of Manhattan.

Alums of the University of the South recall Doug Paschall, the Tennessee native, Sewanee footballer, who won a Rhodes in 1966. Paschall's popularity at Oxford reached so far that The Lamb and Flag pub stocked his favorite Tennessee bourbon just for him and his numerous converts! Academician and author, Paschall succumbed to cancer just a few years ago.

South Carolina's contribution to this galaxy of cerebral country-boy scholars is John Andrew Rice, of the Colleton County Rice clan. This son of a Methodist parson emerged as one of the foremost of bucolic bookmen whose Oxford scholarship and southern brogue brought national acclaim.   In a "Faulkneresque" South in the 1930s, John Andrew Rice was a "shrimp and grits" version of Chicago's pedagogy progressive, John Dewey.

Rice's Grandmother Smith, "Cotton Ed" Smith and that ilk, called the boy by his proper Christian name, John Andrew, as was common among stern-minded Methodists just before the turn of the last century. He was John Andrew, even to his boyhood chums at the Webb School in Tennessee and to his own students at his famed Black Mountain College.

Like later southern counterparts at Oxford, Rice was a frustrated genius wedged uncomfortably between two cultures, one boasting erudition and refinement and the other clinging to agrarian chivalry and the Walter Scott conceit. Growing up the son of a preacher who crowned his career as president of Columbia College, it was inevitable that John Andrew Rice would grow up bookish and precocious.

Sensing that Columbia was pointing young John Andrew to the University where Episcopalian attitudes prevailed a bit too similar to those of Charleston, Reverend Rice packed the lad off to Webb's Tennessee boarding school under the tutelage of the ex-Confederate-turned-classical-scholar, Sawny Webb.
Anyone who dares think that the old Confederates were all gray-whiskered holdovers from a Celtic past should read up on Sawny Webb. This brilliant, wizened-old war veteran was either a holdover of Hellenic learning of the vaunted classical academies of the antebellum South, or he was the forerunner of those "ham bone" scholars from Dixie who became the toast of Oxford from the the jazz age up to the turbulent '60s.

At Webb School in Bell Buckle, Tennessee, the boys were grounded in the classics, and they recited Homer in the Greek the way Hugh Swinton Legare,

George McDuffie, John C. Calhoun, James Petigru, Augustus Baldwin Longstreet, Jabez Lamar Curry and a host of early Carolina intellectuals had done in Carolina backwoods schools such as Bullock's Academy and Moses Waddel's famed Willington. However, at The Webb School, there was much more of the Socratic style of teaching where logic through the power of deduction was refined.

So thoroughly prepared for university was young John Andrew that his relatives eagerly awaited to see which direction the budding bookman would take. His choices were the University of South Carolina, then still a bastion of classical learning despite its fondness for sour mash and frolic. And there was Wofford, the Methodist stronghold in the upstate that catered to more sober-minded seekers of truth. The Citadel in Charleston was entirely out of the question. "That dude factory" as Ben Tillman referred to it, was allegedly a place where Episcopal planters sent their sons to meet other scions of wealth in the State's social hierarchy.

Perhaps it was the tinge of irreverence in Sawny Webb's and brother John Webb's pointed classroom questions, or maybe it was the early roots of Humanism that Rice read into those Greek recitations and Latin orations, but this star of the Webb school eschewed Carolina and Wofford, the one being too social, the other too evangelical. Rather, Rice chose Tulane University, then the nexus of the southern liberal intellectual tradition.

Unlike Willie Morris and Doug Paschall, two more recent southerners who were selected as Rhodes Scholars, John Andrew Rice was not a football player, nor was he one of those boisterous boys who partied late into the night, yet aced his class work the next morning. What Rice had in common with the extroverted scholars Morris and Paschall was the edgy demeanor. Rice used his Tulane and Oxford degrees along with his University of Chicago studies to mount a challenge to the disjointed curriculum of the American liberal arts education. Never able to stay at any college long enough to achieve tenure, Rice started his own college in the backwoods of North Carolina.

While at Oxford's Queens College, prewar World I, Rice befriended fellow American, Frank Aydelotte, the man who later became president of Swarthmore College. Aydelotte's reconfiguring of Swarthmore's curriculum into a Oxford-like learning environment influenced Rice. In Harper's magazine in 1937 Rice wrote, "That what you do with what you know is the important thing. To know is not enough."

John Andrew Rice is remembered as one of America's first Rhodes Scholars. His passion for education reform was not rewarded with results such as Aydelotte's transformation of Swarthmore, but John Andrew Rice left his legacy in his memoirs, *I Came Out Of The Eighteenth Century* (1942), one of the greatest autobiographies ever penned by a southerner. But his true legacy is the educational dialogue that he started in 1933 at his experimental Black Mountain College near Asheville. John Andrew Rice was a Carolinian whose roots in Rousseau and the Enlightenment inspired him with radical notions about democracy and education that we were too tame to aspire to in that era that begged for change.

Christmas In Charleston 57 Years Ago

If you were in town for Christmas 1950 here are some things that probably are still fresh on your mind. If you weren't in town, or weren't even born, then let this be a glimpse back to the golden age when we shopped locally, our grocer had a standing order weekly and delivered it, and everyone knew your name. Since there were no malls or shopping centers, two-way traffic on King Street was bumper to bumper. The shops from Society Street south to Wentworth overflowed with customers. One of the few chain stores, S. H. Kress located on King, smelled of fresh popcorn and passers by were rewarded with a free sample.

Newspaper headlines recall a time of transition as America found itself in a nasty Korean conflict that appeared headed for a nuclear showdown with Red China. But despite the angst of war, Charleston's local merchants flourished while tourism was but a small slice of the economy.

We were still a small city then and our biggest local news story of the 1950 Christmas season was that Westvaco promoted hometown boy Frank Thompson as its regional executive. The lead article in *The Evening Post* featured a picture and an enthusiastic account of how Thompson attended the Simmons School before going on to the High School of Charleston. He was a basketball standout for the Maroons of the College of Charleston. Thompson did graduate work in commerce at Princeton and Harvard. Thompson married Carmelina Sottile, lived on Rutledge Avenue and was a vestry man at St. Peter's Episcopal Church.

War reports from the Chosin Reservoir dominated each day's newspaper leading up to Christmas Day. It was clear that we were in trouble in this five-month-old conflict in Korea. The 1st Division of Marines and the 7th Infantry Division were desperate to break out of an encirclement by the enemy. MacArthur deemed the situation serious but not hopeless. He denied that the A-bomb would soon be a factor.

For those holiday merrymakers who took a few moments to inform themselves of current events, it was a bitter disappointment to Roosevelt devotees that the late president's son, James, lost the California governor's race by over a million votes. James Roosevelt was seen by many Democrats as their hope of securing the White House in the 1960s.

Pity the poor folks of Ellington township not far from Aiken. Their whole town was being condemned by the government for the building of the Savannah River Plant, a monstrous undertaking still referred to as the "bomb plant" by

Carolinians.

Other than the Korean imbroglio and the East Germans acting onerery around the Brandenburg Gate, the only other tension to blot the holiday spirit was the incessant Spanish nagging about Britain giving back Gibraltar.

The Town of Mount Pleasant noted that in the recent year there had been just $25 total property damage caused by fire. With the toll recently lifted from the Grace Memorial bridge, the traffic arteries leading into Charleston were congested between the hours of 7 and 9 a.m. and 3 to 6 p.m. The City of Charleston commissioned Smith-Dibble Traffic Engineers to conduct a ingress-egress study. After much consideration city fathers decided that a number of downtown streets would be one way in the morning and then they would reverse to be the other way in the afternoon. Woe be to the hapless motorist who got caught heading upstream at the bewitching hour of 2 p.m. when the traffic tide turned! The crosstown would be the next revolutionary idea for Charleston traffic relief, but it was still 15 years into the future, and that ultimate solution would cost nearly 200 families their homes and land by right of imminent domain.

Christmas and Hanukkah celebrants alike made the streets of Charleston ring with greetings as locals had more daily contact with their neighbors in 1950 than they do today. For one thing, the ice box refrigerator held only a fraction of the goods that our large appliance keeps cool for us today. It was necessary to go to the Big Star, or Doscher's, or the Market almost daily. Corner stores such as Bella's on Beaufain stayed open until late for the needs of the working class folks who occupied the streets north of Broad.

Big-ticket spenders headed to elite women's fashion stores such as Elza's and Mary Hawkins. It's doubtful that a shopping bag from any of the national snob-appeal stores today could summon the excitement of a female recipient the way a gift could if presented in Mary Hawkins distinctive wrapping paper. Gone are the days! Gentlemen shopped at Lesser-Tannenbaum at 335 King Street not far from the Gloria Theater. Horowitz Jewelry Store did an amazing trade during the holidays, as did Kerrison's and Condon's. At both of these locally-owned department stores it was treat to have the elevator operator, a lady wearing a suit and gloves, to ask which floor as she closed the elevator cage and whisked you to your shopping destination.

Two pharmacies, Tellis on the southwest end of King near Broad, and Gainey's on the northwest end where King intersects with Calhoun, stayed open until 11 p.m. on Christmas Eve to accommodate prescription needs and the sundry desires of last-second shoppers. Both pharmacies knew their customers by name and saw most of them several times a week. The large soda fountain at Gainey's was a gathering spot for merchants, loafers, and shoppers. "Doctor" Ernest Tillman Gainey, Jr., was a close personal friend of Congressman Mendel Rivers, and the Congressman and the pharmacist "held court" in the rear of the drug store where quite a bit of constituent service was conducted. Ellis, the delivery man, relished taking packages to the notorious "parlors of sin" on West and Fulton Streets where the madame always tipped in "Bo" dollars, a local term for silver dollars.

The downtown area was all on one telephone prefix, Raymond-4, so the two King Street pharmacies serviced most of the RA-4 district, an appellation used for downtown from World War II until the mid-1960s. Charleston subdivisions used to be referred to by ward numbers, and a century earlier, by parishes.

Charleston in December of 1950 was enjoying its last moments of seclusion and intimacy before the crush of tourism and the recreation culture would change it forever.

Columbia In 1900 As Remembered By John Andrew Rice

John Andrew Rice, Colleton County native, Rhodes Scholar, and one of the South's foremost champions of the liberal arts education, presents us with a memorable description of Columbia as he recalled it from the turn of the last century.

Because his father was a Methodist minister who pastored congregations around the state, John Andrew spent much of his boyhood along the Combahee River on his grandparents' rice plantation. When Reverend Doctor Rice became the president of Columbia College, young Rice was a precocious boy more interested in the girls boarding upstairs over the parsonage than he was in the Latin grammar school he attended in a dilapidated mansion downtown. Fifty years later Rice penned Thomas Wolfe-style his autobiography, *I Came Out Of The Eighteenth Century*, and his recollections provide a memorable picture of Columbia as our great-grandparents saw it.

Columbia in the late 1890s and early 1900s was part state capital and part farmers' market. Its reddish unpaved streets rose and fell over the three principal hills that make up downtown. Hickory, elm, oak, and pine trees shaded every street, and, unlike Charleston, there were no narrow, winding alleys. City fathers authorized loafers benches around the Capitol, and old men with white goatees and black hats chewed tobacco.

Confederate veterans, some missing an arm or leg, thronged into town on Saturdays and were seen passing the day on these benches while their womenfolk traded in the open-air market and the dry goods stores. The Panic of 1893 plagued the southern economy for five years hence and left the region with 15 percent unemployment. However, Columbia hardly noticed the sag as it was still depressed from the wartime disruptions of the Confederacy.

Young Rice, as son of a college president, was fortunate to attend a private Latin academy in a run-down antebellum mansion. The headmistress was a spinster from the Civil War. The way in which Rice describes this reduced aristocrat makes her the spirit and image of Miss Habersham in Dickens' *Great Expectations*. Rice recalled in later years how the prim old maid could be overheard in the parlor as she haggled with the creditors who endlessly dunned her. "I didn't see her likes again until I saw the Dons of Oxford," recounts Rice in his memoirs. "She was all past and no future."

In this "parlor academy" amidst the faded glory of a lost era, Rice learned grammar and writing by imitating the authors of the classics. Monotonous and repetitive as it was, this introduction to scholarship served Rice well. From Webb's boarding school in Tennessee, Rice won a scholarship to Tulane, and from there he was tapped as one of America's first Rhodes scholars.

One of his Columbia grammar school mates was the granddaughter of William Gilmore Simms. Rice describes her as an insufferable, self-centered little thing whose only claim to greatness was her kinship to the writer Simms. Even to a youngster it was evident that an agrarian aristocracy was struggling to survive against a harsher, more callous society based upon commercial fitness.

Rice's boyhood in Columbia was prior to electricity, paved roads, and the automobile. The bucolic aspects he describes of the state's largest city as it appeared 100 years ago are foreign to us, but the scenes in his autobiography were commonplace for our great-grandparents. Columbia was a red-rutted, upcountry town foreign in its ways to a boy accustomed to the tidal flow of the Combahee. Columbia had the bells of Trinity, but it also had the factory whistles of Adluh and a half-dozen cotton mills. Already a new class of "mill people," who were neither rural nor urban, was changing the way the upstate thought and voted.

The turn of the century belonged to the wool hat and one-gallus farmers who backed "pitchfork" Ben Tillman in the legislature rather than the "Bourbons" of the faded "Grey Glory" era. Columbia was a wool hat citadel in 1900, and

Baptist though it was, the temperance union was making very little headway in curbing the saloon influence.

Saturday mornings in downtown Columbia were a parade of country-come-to-town. Men in broad-brim hats and their women draped in calico rode in on flatbed wagons drawn by stubborn mules. Country squires came mounted on horseback and their ladies drove a light rig behind a team of high-stepping ponies. They were Carolina's Jacobins and Girondists and together they jockeyed for passage through Main, Gervais, and Assembly Streets in this new age of equality. The new equality did not cross the color boundary, however, as the Klan enforced unwritten Jim Crow rules that forbade any man of color to be on the streets after 8 p.m. It was all part of the fickle, three-tiered culture that prevailed in the new South. Landed gentry still prevailed over tradesmen, mill people rivaled the rural crackers, and sons of freedmen struggled against injustice.

Rice writes that the men wore blue jeans of Carolina cotton woven in New England mills. Hope was a word heard only on Sundays, and there was great poverty as far as the eye could see. Education was for the few who could afford it, and tobacco was the great unifying bond among the social orders.

In the art of tobacco chewing, there were the biters and the cutters. The cutters were definitely upper crust. A boy of twelve was in danger of falling behind his peers if he was not already adept at manipulating a plug of Brown Mule or Jay Bird tobacco into the hollow of his cheek and gum and sending an expertly directed stream of brown juice at a target six feet away. A check of the The State newspaper reveals that one of the big legislative expenditures in 1900 was an outlay for a dozen brass spittoons at $250 each for the State house. Women, even some of the social elites, dipped snuff. Cigarettes were for dandies who came down from the North. Cigars were reserved for somber occasions where expectorating was frowned upon. The graveyard, church yard, and the court house square were the only sacred "no spitting" areas in a southern town.

Columbia in John Andrew Rice's day was a southern town where the

definition of "gentleman" meant a stout fellow who'd stood with Lee and
Hampton and still looked to cotton as the soul of the South.

Charleston's Connection to Merry Old Camden

It doesn't take a historian to note the similarities between Charleston and
elegant old Camden, the Kershaw county seat. If cities could generate offspring,
then Charleston certainly fathered Camden. Conception of the idea of this
township was December 6, 1733, in the chambers of the Royal Council Hall on
Broad Street. After two-hundred and seventy-four years Charleston and Camden,
however, no longer share the close commercial and political relationship they
once mutually prospered by. Few can recall the adventurous Charlestonians who
set out to build a market town where the Great Wagon Road intersected the
Catawba Path at the bend in the Wateree.

In 1733 Georgian Britain was awash in commercial schemes involving
colonial trade and municipal development in the new world. James Oglethorpe's
first boatload of settlers briefly dropped anchor in Charleston harbor on January
13. This London aristocratic reformer envisioned a utopian city free from the
ills of gin, vice, and greed that corrupted Britain.

Oglethorpe fared better with establishing Savannah than did the Colonial
Council of Charleston in getting a trading post operating up on the "Watery," as
King George II spelled it. James St. Julien, a local surveyor, was paid the
handsome sum of £500 to lay out 1100 town lots and a grid of streets on a sloping
hillside near the river. It was a much more ambitious project than the original
plan for Charles Town in 1680. Royal Governor Robert Johnson, no slouch of a

politician, asked that the new township be named Fredericksburg in honor of the
Prince of Wales. Prince Frederick soon died from a blow to the chest of a well-
hit cricket ball, and the township named for him in Carolina never got off the
ground, literally. St. Julien laid the streets too near the swamp and fears of
malaria kept buyers away. It was 25 more years before the town they will call
Camden got its start.

In the smoke-filled, rum-laced taverns that lined Broad and East Bay in the
1750s, Joseph and Ely Kershaw, John Chesnut, William Ancrum, and Aaron
Loocock were not weighed down by lofty notions of reform as Oglethorpe had
been with Savannah. Already hundreds of Scots-Irish and a few German
immigrants were rolling into the upcountry and settling on generous King's
Grants of virgin pine forests in the Wateree basin. The Great Wagon Road, once
an Indian warpath, lured land-hungry colonists from central Pennsylvania down
through Virginia and into Carolina.

It's a safe bet that the Kershaw brothers, Joseph and Ely, along with
partners Chesnut and Ancrum didn't have a complete idea of what they were
getting into when they packed a mule train through rugged territory known earlier
as the lands of the Cofitachequi. But the Kershaws were Yorkshire gentlemen,
and they had friends at Whitehall in London. These Hanoverian monarchs, such
as George I and II, attracted a more commercial-minded coterie than did their
predecessors, the Stuarts. The Kershaws and Ancrums had lines of credit from
London bankers, and they were determined to profit from the mistakes of the
failed Fredericksburg developers twenty years earlier.

William Ancrum, a wealthy Charleston importer, paid to have 150 acres on
the Wateree resurveyed in June 1758 for a settlement to be named Pine Top Hill.
Ancrum was foremost of the investors in the Kershaws' store incorporated under
Ancrum, Loocock, Lance, and Kershaw. Joseph and Ely Kershaw managed the
upcountry end of the business while the rest of the partners dealt with the import-
export venture in Charles Town. John Chesnut, E.B. Cantey, And J. West

accompanied the Kershaw brothers in building a log store and warehouses in the vicinity of where the Kershaw-Cornwallis House stands in Camden today.

For several decades this partnership prospered in a thriving settlement that was called Pine Top, or sometimes referred to as Log Town. In the American Revolution the British commanders Cornwallis and Tarleton used both names, Camden and Log Town, to refer to this strategic upcountry town.

Kershaw and Ancrum laid out Market, Church, Broad, Bull, Laurens, and Boundary Streets just as Charles Town had. Broad Street coincided with the ancient Catawba Path that eventually made its way to the Lowcountry. The town lots were situated higher up the Hobkirk Hill and away from the damp bottoms of the river basin.

About a hundred and fifty Pennsylvania Quakers had descended on the Wateree in the early 1750s, as had an equal number of Scots-Irish from Virginia. Oddly, none of these newcomers had attempted to form any kind of community before William Ancrum and Joseph Kershaw laid out lots and streets with the blessing of Charleston's Royal Council and the Lords of Whitehall in London. With that kind of clout the venture was destined to succeed.

Numerous property deeds in Charles Town bore the names of Aaron Loocock and William Ancrum. Those gentlemen rubbed shoulders with the Gadsdens and Laurens factions and were formidable men of trade. It's just speculation until proven, but it's reasonable to think that Ancrum and Loocock had a high-placed backer at Whitehall and that his name was Lord Charles Pratt, 1st Earl of Camden.

Pratt, an old Etonian and Kings College, Cambridge man, was an eminent barrister who was then pioneering some of the earliest case law in libel suits and illegal search and search and seizure situations. By the 1770s it was customary in the North American colonies to name settlements and streets after political figures in London who championed the colonists' causes of representation and lower taxes. William Pitt, the Earl of Camden, John Wilkes, Isaac Barre, and a host of others friendly to the colonists' point of view were honored with place names. But it's easy to assume that a closer relationship between Ancrum, Loocock, and Pratt (Lord Camden) existed in the cozy dealings between London bankers and gentlemen's clubs along Pall Mall.

The Camden of the Kershaws, Chesnuts, Canteys, and Wests prospered as a center for cultivated people to enjoy the arts in an opera house and a private library society. The Episcopal Church established St. Matthew's parish. Baron de Kalb, Lafayette, Tarleton, Cornwallis, Gates, Greene, and Washington knew the place well and mentioned it in dispatches or memoirs. Their old homes resemble our Ansonborough, and like Charleston, the names of the founders are still to be found on property deeds today!

Edgar Brown Was Among The Last Of The Southern Statesmen

Edgar Allen Brown never signed up for the examination that could have resulted in him winning a full scholarship to The Citadel, the school that his father wanted him to attend in 1905. Brown never even finished high school, but the issue is moot, for this Cicero of the State Senate read law while serving as a court reporter. Edgar Brown represents the climax of that grand era of one party rule in South Carolina. One of the most interesting political biographies you'll ever read is that of Edgar A. Brown, written by the late editor of *The State*, W.D. Workman, a book he entitled *The Bishop From Barnwell* (R. L. Bryan & C0., 1963).

Throughout Brown's half-century of public life "the cookie crumbled" his way most of the time, but Brown will forever remain famous as the 1954

Democratic candidate for the U.S. Senate that Strom Thurmond beat with a write-in campaign.

It hasn't been many years since Edgar Brown, Sol Blatt, and Winchester Smith of the immortal 'Barnwell Ring" dominated South Carolina's General Assembly. In retrospect, their political cronyism turned out to be in the state's best interest. Brown and Blatt secured our "AAA" bond credit rating, watched over the interstate highway building, pioneered educational public television, and improved public education. All was achieved under Brown's leadership and "the Barnwell Ring's" domination of Carolina politics.

Identifying anyone in South Carolina as being a champion of public education opens an avenue for ridicule, as everyone knows that our system ranks at or near the bottom in many measures. However, South Carolina's peculiar circumstances, not the least of which is a high incidence of poverty, require politicians with wisdom. Edgar Brown's own education was a lifelong manifestation of his loving to read. He was mostly self-taught after age fifteen, but several teachers inspired him with a passion for learning.

Edgar Brown was the darling of his older siblings, and coming along late in his parents' lives they all doted on him. He was called "Eck" by family members and even a few intimate friends. It was for Eck's education that Gus Brown left the Shiloh Springs community and moved into Graniteville township. Big sister, Minnie Brown, age 17, was Edgar's first grade teacher, and she made sure that her little brother was front-row center every day in the one room school.

Almost every great man admits somewhere in his life that it was a high school English teacher who set him straight on the course of clear, concise writing and speaking, and this was very much the case with Edgar Brown. Miss Anna Hard, formerly of Charleston, took an interest in this eager farm boy who worked afternoons and weekends in the Graniteville Mill. Hard introduced him to the *News and Courier* and bade him to read it from cover to cover every day. The Charleston newspaper became a daily lesson in style and syntax as well as a political primer. And Edgar Brown, later to be one of the three most politically powerful men in the state, was a devotee to the *News and Courier* the rest of his life. He and editor Thomas Waring got into a wrangle over Waring's support of Thurmond as a write-in candidate versus Brown in the U.S. Senate race in 1954.

Miss Anna Hard and headmaster Graves Knight wanted Edgar Brown to take a scholarship examination for The Citadel in 1905, but to their dismay the boy dropped out of school and enrolled in Augusta's Osborne Business College's shorthand class. Perhaps Brown was aware that Governor "Pitchfork" Ben Tillman was no fan of The Citadel and referred to it as a "dude factory." Consequently, in later years Edgar Brown served on the Clemson Board of Trustees at a time when just the mention of his name was all that it took to get legislation passed in Columbia.

Brown copied another South Carolinian of humble origins when he pursued court reporting as a profession. James F. Byrnes of Charleston, the fatherless lad who was a runner for the law firm of Hagood, Mordecai, and Rutledge on Broad Street. Byrnes later became FDR's right hand man in the U.S. Senate, a supreme court justice, Truman's secretary of state, and governor of S.C. Byrnes encouraged Brown to learn shorthand as a way to get ahead. He was Brown's mentor, his best man in his wedding, and his friend until Byrnes supported Strom Thurmond in the bitter Senate race 1954. However, it was Byrnes who confided in Brown that the Atomic Energy Commission would build a huge facility between Aiken and Barnwell. Brown was the only South Carolinian entrusted with that top-secret knowledge for over a year.

From being a court stenographer in Aiken to passing the law exam in Columbia was a mere three year process for this highly ambitious man. Brown's law career began, strangely enough, when a debt defaulter was hauled into court without legal counsel. Sensing an opportunity, Brown, then serving as court reporter, informed Judge Aldrich that he'd serve as legal counsel! With less than 30 minutes to prepare his case, Brown secured a debt waiver for his client. In later years when Edgar A. Brown of Barnwell was one of the state's foremost legal minds, he loved to regale listeners with his "country-boy logic."

While still a young man, Edgar Brown contracted a severe case of tonsillitis. Doctor Bethune Patterson did an emergency operation in the back of Deason's Aiken drug store. On the way home Brown collapsed and nearly bleed to death. Years later Patterson was was state senator from Aiken and in a heated altercation with Edgar Brown, Doctor Bethune Patterson pulled a derringer and shot at him from inside the House chamber! Brown survived that encounter, plus a fist-fight with yet another House member. He lived through a small-plane crash in Virginia, and a automobile flip-over on Edisto Island. However, Edgar contracted Tuberculosis while he was a young man and this nearly ended his political career. Brown attributed his remarkable recovery to the fact that he spent three months a year for 10 years living in a tent on Lake Junaluska. For a look at southern politics when political bosses governed the state from their vest pocket, and did it well, read William D. Workman's *The Bishop From Barnwell*.

Jackson-Benton Quarrel Typical of Early Southern Politics

We've witnessed quite a few political wrangles in this season of primary politics. Politicians tear into each other with reckless charges and harmful insinuations. At least it's just words that they are hurling at each other! One of the most dramatic and colorful, yet tragic-comic, dustups in the broad scope of American politics occurred in 1813 between Andrew Jackson and Thomas Hart Benton, and in Nashville at least, they're still talking about it 195 years later!

In the early days of the republic, it would have been hard to find two men in Tennessee more allied with each other's interests than Andrew Jackson and Thomas Hart Benton. Each had Scotch-Irish ancestry with roots in Whig party

259

beliefs. They were the original Tennessee Democrats. Jackson and Benton were Indian fighters who saw the opening of the West as the ultimate fulfillment of the American Dream -- the shaking off of the last remnants of kings, aristocrats, and bishops. They were Tennesseans, yet each had a Charleston connection. Old Jack's mother lies buried in an unmarked grave on the College of Charleston's campus. Benton's father-in-law, John C. Fremont, grew up in a boarding house on Charleston's east side.

Major General Andrew Jackson, age 46, came into his glory as a Nashville lawyer, planter, and militia general by the War of 1812. When the British in Pensacola provoked the Creek Indians to attack the Mississippi settlements, Jackson marched the Tennessee militia, 2000 strong, overland to Natchez. One of his regimental commanders was Colonel Thomas Hart Benton, age 31. Another impressive officer that Jackson promoted to brigade staff was Captain William Carroll, age 25.

Not much fighting occurred on this campaign. Meanwhile soldiers sickened and suffered from a lack of supplies. Old Jack disobeyed orders of the secretary of war to turn his command over to General Wilkinson in New Orleans. He marched his poorly provisioned men back to Nashville signing promissory notes all the way on his own account. Since the government had never officially ordered Jackson to Natchez, it was reluctant to reimburse his out-of-pocket expenditures.

Upon return to Nashville, Benton departed for Washington, D.C., seeking a regular army commission and to plead for reimbursement for Jackson's out-of-pocket expenses. While Benton was on his trip, Jackson retired to his plantation, The Hermitage. A few miles away in Nashville, Jackson's staff officer, Captain Carroll, opened a hardware store, part of a chain of stores that his father in Pennsylvania owned with prominent politician, Albert Gallatin. Gallatin was Jefferson's secretary of the treasury and later, the representative who devised the House Ways and Means Committee. It was to Gallatin that Benton was applying for funds to reimburse Jackson.

Jealousy over promotion led to Thomas Hart Benton's younger brother Jesse taking a dislike to William Carroll. Benton ridiculed Carroll's highfalutin' connections with Jackson, Gallatin, and Eastern politicians. Jesse Benton insulted Carroll in such a way as to ensure that a duel would follow.

Jackson was naturally pained that two of his junior officers had become enemies, but he was mortified to be asked to stand as second to Carroll in the duel against Jesse Benton. The duel took place on June 14, 1813, with Carroll getting a piece of his thumb shot off and Jesse Benton receiving a grazing wound across his rump. The hilarity of Benton's discomfiture spread all over Tennessee. Benton was the butt of many crude jokes, jokes that reached the ears of Thomas Hart Benton as he returned from Washington. Thomas Benton could not believe it when told that his friend Jackson had backed Carroll against Jesse Benton. In every tavern he stopped in on his way to Nashville, Thomas Hart Benton swore violent oaths of revenge against the villainous Jackson.

General Jackson, thin as a rail, weathered and sinewy, heard that the Bentons were looking for him. "Old Jack" promised to horsewhip the lot of 'em if they set foot near Nashville. What a turnaround of events for Thomas Hart Benton who'd successfully negotiated the controversial repayment of Jackson for the unauthorized Natchez campaign.

All summer of 1813, amidst talk of war with Britain, two of America's great Tennesseans waged a bellicose campaign of their own. The most profane oaths imaginable were uttered by Benton and Jackson and a showdown was imminent.

On September 3, 1813, Jackson, horsewhip in hand, along with friend, Colonel Coffey, walked by the City Hotel in Nashville. To no one's surprise, Thomas Hart Benton and son Jesse, stood with arms folded glaring at them from the porch. Suddenly Jackson whirled about with the horsewhip and yelled to Benton, "Now, you d-----d rascal, I am going to punish you!" Jackson lunged at

Thomas Benton as Jesse pulled a pistol loaded with ball and buckshot. Jesse Benton fired pointblank at Jackson's back, piercing him just below the shoulder blade. Jackson crumpled as he fired at Benton but the shot missed.

Coffey shoved Thomas Benton backward down a flight of stairs as another Jackson supporter stabbed Benton with a sword. A brass button deflected a would-be fatal wound. Several other shots were fired, but in less than a minute the fracas was over. The critically wounded Jackson was taken to a hotel across the street.

Thomas Hart Benton, along with Jesse, and a host of Benton drunken backers whooped in the street outside Jackson's window as doctors worked to save his life. Benton broke Jackson's sword in half and loudly denounced "Old Hickory" as a villain.

Of course Andrew Jackson was up and in the saddle leading troops into battle with the British less than a year after this bloody encounter. Jackson and Benton mended their grievances and became strong political allies. Thomas Hart Benton moved on to St. Louis and championed the cause of "Manifest Destiny." "I had a fight with General Jackson," said Benton. "One was hardly fashionable who didn't."

The bloody scuffle occurred because Jackson and Benton partisans called for blood. Benton barked, "I never quarrel, sir, but I do fight, sir, and when I fight, sir, a funeral follows, sir." As an aside to the incident at the City Hotel, one of the errant bullets fired that morning passed close to an infant in an upstairs room. The child was John C. Fremont, the future son-in-law of Thomas Hart Benton!

Excerpts Regarding Charleston From Bishop's Asbury's Journal

Thursday, March 5. [Charleston 1795] "I left this seat of wickedness, not without both grief and joy. I never saw so great a prospect here, and doubt if there hath been such an one since the place was first settled. We crossed Ashley River about ten miles from town. Here was a bridge of value, which was so damaged by the worms and barnacles, that it stood only two years. Sister G., her family, and a wagon were on it when it gave way; it sunk with them into the water, but they received no injury." Thus departed Bishop Francis Asbury from this city that he despaired more for than any other place he preached in America!

While packing his saddle bags at the parsonage of Bethel Methodist Church Asbury confided to his journal: "I am now about packing up in order to take my leave of this city. I am sure faithful preaching will be blest. I have effectually worn myself out, and I feared we should not have strength to ride over the barren sands. If the people are prudent and the preachers faithful, we shall have a work in this place. The poor Africans brought their blessings, and wishes, and prayers. Dear souls! May the Lord provide them pastors after his own heart!"

The self-educated Birmingham, England son of a blacksmith who almost single-handedly established the Methodist faith in America kept a travel journal of his horseback ministry in the cities, boroughs, and frontier of early America. As a young Englishman this pious convert to evangelical Christianity heard John Wesley pleading, "Our brethren in America call aloud for help. Who are willing to go over and help them?" "Send me," the youthful Asbury responded to the bewilderment of his mother.

"Who will answer God's call? Who will bring the Gospel to the American frontier? I felt a jolt. Our movement was spreading like wildfire through England, but in 1771, the American frontier was an untamed land full of danger."

Francis Asbury's journal begins in January 1794 and continues through

1816. A year before Asbury recorded his dismal dismissal of Charleston, he recorded a more pleasant appraisal: [Monday, 20. 1794] "I reached the city of Charleston. Here I began to rest: my cold grew better. Doctor [David] Ramsey directed me to the use of laudanum, nitre and bark, after cleansing the stomach with an emetic."   Asbury wore out three horses, Jane, Fox, and Spark, in his estimated 300,000 miles of travel over muddy, sometimes frozen roads in order to preach the gospel in barns, cabins, or rustic churches. He preached in the wilderness where he competed with liquor stills, card games, and licentious frolic. Asbury preached in the open pastures in weather so chilly that skeptics would say that "only the crows and the Methodists are stirring."

Bishop Asbury was 44 years of age when he rode a horse named Fox into Charleston in 1794. He preached at Bethel Methodist and lived in the nearby parsonage, so his sojourn here was among his most comfortable lodgings. However, what Charleston possessed in ambiance it lacked in spiritual development. Of the dedicated churchgoers in Charleston Asbury commented sadly upon their rivalry and apparent devotion to frivolous things. "I preached in Cumberland street in the morning and at Bethel in the afternoon.. . There is a holy strife between its [Bethel ?] members and the Episcopalians, who shall have the highest steeple; but I believe there is no contention about who shall have the most souls converted to God."

During the Revolution Asbury had to dodge both the American and the British armies to remain neutral. As soon as the war was concluded, Asbury set out to rekindle a religious fervor in this raucous and often lawless land.

Upon departing Charleston for week in Georgetown Asbury remarks: "Out tomorrow for Georgetown. I doubt if in Charleston we have joined more than one hundred and seventy-eight members of the fair skin in twenty years; and seldom are there more than fifty or sixty annually returned: death, desertion, backsliding: poor fickle souls, unstable as water, light as air, bodies and minds!"

This tireless evangelist who is credited with keeping the flames of

Methodism alive after George Whitefield, Thomas Coke, and John Wesley returned to England actually delivered over 16,000 sermons and ordained or commissioned 4000 ministers and missionaries. He often despaired for the spiritually shallow souls that he encountered on his treks through the Carolina backcountry, but it was Charleston that fired his ire.

"I heard part of a discourse by Mr. Furman on partial and total backsliding: I thought he spoke well, and that it was an excellent sermon; I doubt if he had more than seventy white hearers. A vast number in the city do not attend to the worship of God anywhere. . . . The desperate wickedness of this people grieves and distresses my soul, so. . . . Charleston is, to me, one of the most serious places I ever was in. . . . I was insulted on the pavement with some as horrible sayings as could come out of a creature's mouth on this side of hell. . . . The unparalleled wickedness of the people of this place, and the spirit of contention among the professors of religion, most severely agitate my mind."

As a parting comment Asbury records, " I was deeply dejected. I have been lately more subject to melancholy than for many years past; and how can I help it: the white and worldly people are intolerably ignorant of God; playing, dancing, swearing, racing; these are their common practices and pursuits. Our few male members do not attend preaching; and I fear there is hardly one who walks with God: the women and Africans attend our meetings, and some few strangers also."

On several occasions Francis Asbury wrote of the sweet peace he felt in Charleston when the brothers and sisters lived in harmony. His frustrations could be overcome quickly when a sinner turned to the Lord. If Francis Asbury sometimes despaired of our ancestors' spirituality, then he'd be overjoyed to know that we're the "buckle of the Bible belt" today!

When Francis Asbury was buried in Baltimore on March 31, 1816, over ten-thousand people attended his funeral. There were memorials in many cities and contemporaries referred to him as an American founding father along with Jefferson and Franklin!

Lee's Letters To His Wife The First Year Of The War

No gentleman reads another man's letters to his wife. There's still a shred of decency remaining with what the public recoils at. However, if the letters were penned by Robert E. Lee, the noblest knight of the Confederacy, and historians as creditable as Clifford Dowdey and Louis Manarin edited them . . . well, then it's the grandest insight into the private life of the southern hero we could imagine.

Robert E. Lee is best known for his brilliant defense of Richmond between 1862 and 1864, but his military career spans thirty years. He commanded men in the Mexican War, fought Indians in the Wild West, and served as superintendent at West Point before taking command at age 55 of the newly formed Army of Northern Virginia. Lee and his wife Mary were often apart due to his years of remote military postings. Her rheumatism made ease of movement a trial for her, and throughout the War Lee was distracted with concern for her well-being.

Dowdey and Manarin's book, *The Wartime Papers of Lee,* very much broadens our appreciation of the historical, stoic General Lee. No longer solely the warrior chieftain, Lee through his letters is revealed as the worried husband of an invalid wife, as the father of unmarried daughters who doted on their father, and as Lee the deeply religious man. Clifford Dowdey's publication of Lee's wartime correspondence gives a vivid contrast of the taciturn, militarily-aggressive Lee with the tenderhearted Virginia patrician who despaired for his beloved homeland.

The first Lee letter to Mary is postmarked from the Spotswood Hotel in Richmond to her at Arlington. The date is April 25, 1861, and the firing on Fort Sumter was just a few weeks past. Lee's status as a Virginia militia officer or Confederate general was still up in the air. He tells Mary of his resignation letter to U.S. Secretary of War Cameron, and Lee fears that the United States will dream up various unusual deductions from his final paycheck. It's obvious that the Lees depend upon his monthly check to make ends meet. He has socks and shirts aplenty, but in his haste to get to Richmond Lee left the wire collar rank and epaulet loops that allow him to fasten his new Confederate rank on his uniform coat.

Thus begins a reference to a trifling concern that dogged the South for four years, the inability to produce even basics such as sewing needles, uniform parts, and shoe eyelets. Ever the concerned family man, Lee sends Mary a check for $500. In today's figures, the check would be worth 20 times that amount.

A week later Robert Lee is still very much a citizen of Virginia with loyalty only to the governor and not yet an officer of the larger Confederacy. He sends Mary instructions for their farm foreman, Mister Maguire. Throughout the war, Lee tried to keep his and his wife's lands under production with cotton for the Army's consumption. Mary, with arthritic fingers, darned yarn socks for the men in his command. Lee distributed socks almost weekly to poor soldiers who were gratified at getting fresh items darned by the granddaughter of George and Martha Washington, the wife of their beloved commander!

For her part, Mary was reluctant to leave Arlington, the Custis family home. Lee had to cajole her again and again as hostilities increased around Washington. Mary wrote her husband in an angry tone that if only the rest of the nation had ignored South Carolina and let her go on on her out of the Union, then this whole war would have been unnecessary. As she abandoned her home on the Potomac as well as the town house in Alexandria Mary left sharp notes tacked to the door reminding the Federals that this was property of George Washington's heirs and to show proper respect!

In Richmond, Lee attended services at the Episcopal Cathedral and commented on how the Bishop's homily brought tears to his eyes. Every letter that Lee writes to Mary, and he averages two weekly, ends with a phrase about

God's will being done. In his early letters Lee expresses concern that this war may actually be God's divine retribution upon an arrogant South.

By May, 1861, Lee plans to take to the field and asks Mary to send him utensils for his mess, which he refers to in a more chivalrous tone as his "banquet." Lee family slaves Perry and Billy serve the General as butler and cook.

An early revelation in the Robert-to-Mary correspondence is how poor the new southern mail service is. In fact, it's totally unreliable, even in the city of Richmond before the start of hostilities. Lee sent to Mary checks drawn on Richmond banks in letters that never arrived. When she tried sending checks to him drawn from Fairfax banks, the Richmond banks refused to honor them, accusing those banks of collusion with the Federals across the Potomac! To make matters more tense, he tells Mary not to write about specific things because all correspondence is opened and censored, even though that fact was not broadcast to the public.

The first death of the war to trouble the Lees privately was that of Colonel John Washington, killed on reconnaissance north of Charlottesville as he accompanied Lee's son, Major Fitzhugh Lee. This genteel relative of George Washington was one of the very first to fall in defense of the new southern nation.

Rumors of every kind swirl around invasions, but the most troubling one for the Lees was the scandal mongers in Richmond whispering that Robert and Mary Lee were estranged in their marriage and actually had separated! Lee directs Mary to quell that pernicious, groundless gossip immediately.

The tenderest words from Lee's pen are reserved for his daughters Annie and Agnes. He relates how he thinks often of them as he dines at sundown from his banquet in the field. He's solicitous about their comfort, safety, and their financial status. Robert Lee also delights in hearing from Charlotte Wickham, his beautiful daughter-in-law who married son Rooney.

When placed next to the formal orders to field commanders and his diplomatic exchanges with Confederate bureaucrats in Richmond, the Lee's personal letters reveal his gentler nature, even amidst the horrors of war.

Why We Wanted Willie Magnum For President in 1836

How refreshing that democracy with its marketplace of ideas is alive and combative after 208 years and 54 quadrennial elections. As one of the original 20 states to vote in the world's first national election in 1796, South Carolina has backed a winner 30 times, supported a loser on 22 occasions, and owns 3 other oddball contests where the outcome was decided by pistols, chicanery, and breaches to the rule of law. Excepting 1876, the mother of all election debacles -- the one that ousted carpetbagger rule from Columbia -- our weirdest Carolina electoral outcome involved our fascination with North Carolina's Willie Mangum in that brawling presidential contest of 1836.

Willie Person Mangum of Red Mountain, North Carolina, is not a name that resonates through time eternal as one worthy of a few drops of a historian's ink. Who knows, but 170 years from now, Hillary, Barack, or John Sidney may also have been relegated to the dustbin of historical trivia. Willie Mangum was the frontier, log-cabin-born son of a young revolutionary war veteran and his red-haired Irish bride. The year was 1792 and George Washington had just passed through neighboring Hillsboro in his 1791 Tour of the South.

Mangum exemplified all of the virtues of the young republic and the ideal of New World meritocracy. Farm money paid his tuition at Hillsboro Academy, one of the best classical schools in the South. The studious Willie Mangum graduated at the top of his class at UNC in Chapel Hill at the time when America was concluding the Treaty of Ghent ending the War of 1812. He read law and had a legal practice in Red Mountain, a community halfway between Raleigh and Roxboro. As a staunch Jackson man, Mangum was elected first to Congress and then to the U.S. Senate where he came under the sway of titan politico John Caldwell Calhoun. When, in 1828, Jackson and Calhoun became president and vice-president, respectively, the veep intrigued to get Mangum the chairmanship of the then powerful naval Affairs Committee. Mangum hitched his proverbial wagon to Calhoun. When the feud over tariffs and nullification split Old Jack's cabinet in two, Willie Mangum was staunchly a Calhoun Nullifier and Jackson opponent.

Unfortunately for Willie, his political clout would have been greater had he remained loyal to the Unionists, but that was not the passion of his region. On a whim and a push from Calhoun, back-woods-lawyer Willie Person Mangum offered himself as candidate for president in the politically raucous year of 1836. Calhoun opposed the candidacy of Free-Soiler Martin Van Buren and Whigs William Henry Harrison, Dan Webster, and Hugh White. Thus, Mangum received South Carolina's 11 electoral votes. In those days state senators controlled the electoral college. Calhoun's refusal in making a deal with Van Buren or Clay was a "fire-bell in the night," a harbinger of the union-splitting politics headed our way a generation later. Even Mangum's home state voted for Van Buren. Tennessee and Georgia cut deals with Whig candidate Hugh White. Never before or since has our state been so much in the vice-grip of one, albeit brilliant, political mind as it was in the hey day of Calhoun. Cotton may have been our King, but Calhoun was our Emperor!

On occasion we allow ourselves to think that we alone live amidst the turbulent times, that we alone face the unsolvable social and economic problems. The historical reality is that we have it mild compared to the voters of 170 years ago. The continuation of that grand political union with its mishmash of Montesquieu, Locke, and Rousseau so intriguing to the founding fathers was touch-and-go for a hundred years after George Washington. No matter what happens in Election 2008, no one seriously believes that democracy as we know it will cease to exist.

South Carolina served notice to the Union in 1787 that it'd play hardball on every issue. That "three-fifths compromise" negotiated by Carolina delegates in Philadelphia regarding slaves counting for electoral representation was the opening shot across the bow that our state plays an atypical role in the political process. Excepting 1796 when South Carolina supported Jefferson and broke with the majority of states who backed John Adams, our state worked for building national consensus. The Jefferson, Madison, Monroe years were a time that saw our state in league with the north and the midwest. Things came unglued in 1824, and by 1836 South Carolina had established herself as the maverick playing trendsetter, or upsetter in national politics. A thread of that old spirit remains alive as our recent "First in The South Primaries" attests.

The 1836 election that saw South Carolina cast her 11 electoral votes for U.S. Senator Willie Mangum (N.C) was a watershed year both in national and state politics. In that year regionalism was temporarily extinguished. Southern, northern, and midwestern states cast electoral votes for five different candidates on election day. It took several weeks to settle the outcome, though Martin Van Buren out polled Clay, Webster, White, and our state's favorite, Willie Mangum.

The 1876 presidential election was by-far the ugliest in our country's history. Compared to the razor-thin margin in the 2000 election with Florida's Broward and Dade counties, 1876's election turmoil came perilously close to shattering the Union for good. The Democrats nominated Sam Tilden, a New York trust lawyer who had made his reputation fighting corruption in Tammany Hall.

Tilden, hopeful that the white democrat vote in S.C. would be counted, was bamboozled by the Hampton faction. South Carolina's ex-confederate democrats cleverly bargained with Republican Rutherford B. Hayes to exchange electoral votes for a pledge to end radical reconstruction in the state. The bitter election of 1876 took nine months to settle, and South Carolina, Florida, and Louisiana were central to the squeaky-close Republican electoral victory. White democrats in the three southern states, ex-confederates all, did what they felt they had to do to bring an end to the harsh conditions imposed by the Union following the Civil War.

Did South Carolina throw its electoral votes away on Willie Mangum in 1836? From a states-rights point-of-view, absolutely not, because it was clear to Calhoun that support of the Democrat Van Buren, or either of the three Whig candidates, would have signaled "buckling under" to northern interests.

SC Conservatives Say Adios To Democratic Party In 1964

Liberal northeastern republicans never saw subtle humor in the phenomenon of southern conservative democrats jumping the fence during a leap year to wrestle the Grand Old Party from New England's heritors of privilege. The reform-minded party of Lincoln and Teddy Roosevelt had morphed into the party of Wall Street bankers and CEO's during Ike's era. These powerful titans of the military-industrial-complex never counted on an Arizona department store mogul wooing over millions of rural southerners and executing an ideological makeover of the GOP!

That year 1964 was a watershed in American politics as it witnessed the birth of the southern conservative wing of the republican party as the South drifted away from its traditional Jefferson-Jackson-Wilson roots.

Goldwater's nomination over the establishment candidate Scranton was cinched on the first roll-call ballot. But it was not until 10:32 p.m. after much delegate floor wrangling when South Carolina's J. Drake Edens hoarsely shouted into the microphone: "Mister Chairman. Mister Chairman." The convention delegates and observers on the upper deck went wild. No one could hear what Edens was saying. Convention chairman Thruston Morton banged the gavel repeatedly shouting for order. Pennsylvania and Rhode Island had abstained from casting their delegate vote. Each of those states had split delegations, but with a majority for Scranton their executive committees didn't want their delegation to be the one to advance Goldwater over the top.

After repeated gaveling, Morton calmed the crowd for a moment and a hoarse J. Drake Edens, Columbia real estate executive, with voice cracking, "Mister Chairman, South Carolina humbly grateful to be able to do this for America, casts 16 votes for Barry Goldwater." The sound of Eden's voice over the radio and his excited image on the black and white tv screen are indelible memories to many middle-aged South Carolinians who watched transfixed that hot July night as the republican party changed hands.

The flip chart on the podium turned to 662 and the nomination battle was over! There was dancing and cheering as delegates hugged and screamed their delight. Scranton supporters stood quietly as their party's platform and candidate took flight in a southwesterly direction!

Nine days prior to the dramatic roll call that repositioned republican ideology, the *News and Courier* carried the story of W.W. "Duck" Wannamaker, III, of Orangeburg and Dr. Charles H. Zemp of Camden departing Columbia for San Francisco and the important platform committee showdown. Platform warriors for contenders Goldwater, Scranton, Rockefeller, Lodge, and Margaret Chase Smith prepared to do battle for the soul of the party. Mrs. Norman C. Armitage of Spartanburg and Drake Edens of Columbia were already there.

High atop the Jack Tar Hotel in downtown San Francisco the nation's top republican national committee members fought behind closed doors.

Scranton's forces had a different position on everything from the Viet Nam War's escalation to civil rights to nuclear proliferation. Never before had the industrial interests of the northeast been checkmated at every turn. The henchmen of Henry Cabot Lodge, Jr. -- Harold Stassen, Nelson Rockefeller, and Milton Eisenhower -- tried everything to block Goldwater's bid, including a desperate attempt to nominate the old war horse, Dwight Eisenhower, then a patient in Walter Reed hospital. Constitutional lawyers were trotted out to remind party faithfuls that the 22nd Amendment would not stand in the way of Ike's renomination. But it was to no avail, the delegate polls favored the Arizona maverick.

Henry Cabot Lodge, Jr., resigned as LBJ's ambassador to Saigon so that he could come back and derail the Goldwater candidacy. For a few weeks it looked as if the northeastern establishment would block the upstart conservative. Nelson Rockefeller won the Oregon republican primary on May 26th and momentarily blunted the inevitability of the AuH2O express, as the chemical symbols for gold and water suddenly popped up everywhere. On July 2 Californians gave an overwhelming boost to the Arizonan and nipped Rockefeller's and Scranton's hopes. California favorite son Richard Nixon received 3 delegates. But Republican patriarch Alf Landon of Kansas predicted a Goldwater nomination on the first ballot.

The front-page political news shared space with the British phenomenon of four shaggy-headed youths shouting "I wanna hold you hand." An anti-segregation rally threatened violence in St. Augustine, and South Carolina's senior democrat senator threw fellow senator Ralph Yarborough to the floor in a heated dispute outside the senate cloakroom. Capitol police seized photographers' film in an attempt to quash the story on one of the senate's ugliest scenes since Preston Brooks of S.C. caned Charles Sumner of Massachusetts.

Charlestonians were not all of one accord on Goldwater in the spring of '64. The state republican party was in its infancy. *News and Courier* editor Tom

Waring praised the wisdom and integrity of Barry Goldwater numerous times from his masthead editorials. Apart from a couple of oral surgeons, a few realtors, and a quiet contingent of housewives, much of old Charleston remained that curious anomaly "southern conservative democrat." The state, though traditionally democratic since the age of Jefferson, struggled with its political loyalties in 1964's presidential election. Not everyone was willing to abandon allegiance to the democrats. Steven Steinert, a sophomore at the University of Virginia, told the newspaper of visiting Luci Baines Johnson, LBJ's teenage daughter, numerous times in the presidential quarters of the White House while he served as a Capitol page and planned to greet Luci at a hootenanny held in her honor at South Windemere.

South Carolina delegates to the 1964 Republican National Convention made history that July evening by casting their votes for the southwestern conservative. Floyd Spence of Lexington and Arthur Ravenel of Charleston were two of the young delegates who'd later carry the party banner into Congress.

Much behind-the-scenes scrapping occurred in san Franciso between the conservative and liberal wings of the republican party. Scranton's liberal colleagues in the Senate -- Clifford Case of New Jersey, Kenneth Keating of New York, and Hugh Scott of Pennsylvania -- railed against their conservative Arizona colleague's quote from his acceptance speech "Extremism in defense of liberty is no vice, and moderation in the pursuit of justice is no virtue." They turned the phrase against Goldwater and his followers by labeling them "extremists." Barry Goldwater lost the election in a landslide to Johnson, but his triumph was the rebirth of the republican party in the South.

Confederacy's Hopes Ended 144 Years Ago In North Georgia

Grant called it "dropping the hammer." Tecumseh Sherman referred to the Union's war-ending Operation Anaconda as " the tightening of the noose." "I'll make 'em [southerners] howl!" Tecumseh said. Military historians as far away as Oxford look upon Sherman's famed march to the sea as a classic strategic maneuver in the world's first modern war. The Virginia battlefields are pilgrimages for southerners because valiant boys wearing butternut and gray held off three times their number of bluecoated assailants in twenty-some-odd desperate battles. But the ultimate gallantry of the southern military occurred in a forgotten northwestern corner of Georgia with terrain so rugged that today's Army utilizes it for ranger training. If you haven't driven the scenic, but bitter, bloodstained 90 miles of Georgia road from Ringgold through Dalton and Resaca to Cartersville, down to Kennesaw Mountain, then you haven't yet sensed the savagery of the struggle between the blue and the gray.

Somewhere between northwest Dug Gap and Ezra Church the gloves came off for both the blue and the gray as rough, desperate bare-knuckled men brandished rifle butts and bowie knives in contesting every foot of the red clay route to Atlanta. Ohioans, Iowans, and Michiganders lie buried in shallow graves in a hundred lonely fields. No "Johnny Comes Marching Home Hoorahs" greeted the ears of these martyrs -- just the crack of a .57 Enfield from a distant cornfield.

In November 1863, shortly after Lincoln settled upon Grant as his supreme commander, General Sherman received a telegram directing him to begin planning for the severing of the South into two parts. Winfield Scott proposed this bold strategy almost as soon as the war had broken out. Now Grant had complete authority to conduct a ruthless campaign designed to strangle the rebellious south in the same way that a big snake constricts its prey.

The troubling fact for Lincoln was that George B. McClellan had resigned his union general's commission to run for president. This new twist had much to do with the decisiveness with which the War Department now acted. McClellan's "peace party" gave southerners hope to hold out a little longer. Antiwar riots across the North and widespread substitution of Irish and German immigrants for those conscripted led the Confederate congress to conclude that a favorable settlement could be won.

However, Sherman and Grant coordinated a military strategy for 1864 that rivaled the Lee and Jackson one of 1862 in effect if not in brilliance. The combined result of Operation Anaconda was the salvation of the Union and the Lincoln administration's legacy.

Yet from March through September 1864 the fate of the Confederacy bore most heavily upon ranks of teenage Johnny Rebs marching barefoot across Georgia. CSA General Joseph E. Johnston was called the "Ace of Spades" as his 54,000 men grimly dug in on ridges blocking every thoroughfare to Sherman. Union subalterns were George "Slow Trot" Thomas, who'd distinguished himself as "the Rock of Chickamauga" and as "The Sledge of Nashville," and James McPherson, a hero of the battles of Fort Donelson and Shiloh.

"Fightin' Joe" Johnston, was the general who some say rivaled Lee in military instinct. Johnston was the southern reincarnation of the Roman commander, Lucius Quinctius Cincinnatus, who won many victories by feigning retreat. President Davis was under the influence in 1864 of his military aide, the bitter, discredited Braxton Bragg.

Johnston was outnumbered two to one by a Union commander who actually knew the Georgia terrain better than he did. Sherman, as a young lieutenant, had been a part of a surveying team in this Georgia wilderness. From March to May of 1864 Union forces muscled their way as far south as Dalton. There they met the steely-eyed, square-jawed men of Johnston and Wheeler, Hardee, Polk, Cheatham, and Charleston's Arthur Middleton Manigault.

At Dug's Gap, near Dalton, Union General McPherson outnumbered Confederates by ten to one, but his men took a whipping by Confederates who rolled huge boulders down upon them -- sending the union invaders into a panic.

Johnston withdrew from Dug's Gap and repositioned in an almost impregnable fortress at Resaca, not far from Dalton. The steep hills look like an endless washboard stretching north to the Tennessee River. Resaca, a log-cabin village, still had octogenarians living there in 1864 who recalled the days of Indian scalpings.

Charleston blue-blood, Brigadier General Arthur Middleton Manigault, was shot from his horse while leading the 28th Alabama Regiment at Resaca. This able commander, College of Charleston alum and former Charleston merchant banker, continued to lead his regiment for another two weeks through the bloody fighting, temporarily relinquishing command after the battle at Ezra Church. Manigault is depicted fighting gallantly on the magnificent Cyclorama mural at Grant Park.

Again Joe Johnston withdrew, stealthily moving his forces at night after a feigned advance. Each retreat was designed to place his numerically inferior force into a stronger defensive posture than the preceding one. And yanks were dying in droves along the so-called 'Cracker Line," not just from rebel marksmanship, but from the terrible heat and drought which set in that summer of '64.

Telegraph wires were cut and dispatches rarely got out from Johnston's army, but rumors leaked out that the South was being cut asunder by Sherman's plundering blue coats. Alex Stephens, vice-president of the Confederacy and a resident of Crawfordsville, Georgia, recorded his own private fears for the South as he heard the dismal reports. Around Richmond the talk centered upon Jefferson Davis's controversial firing of Johnston and replacing him with John Bell Hood, an attack-oriented fighter.

Hood was reluctant to take the command from his friend Joe Johnston, partly because Hood realized that Davis and Bragg had a personal dislike of

Johnston, but more importantly because Hood realized that Johnston's defensive strategy had been a sound plan. None-the-less, John Bell Hood came out swinging with an offensive at Peach Tree Creek, just north of Atlanta, today in the midst of the prestigious Buckhead area. The attack was uncoordinated, mistimed, and caused another southern withdrawal. Confederate General Hood received word that his old West Point roommate, General James McPherson, had been killed in an engagement with Hood's forces northeast of Atlanta. Both the Confederate and the union commander went into mourning, but the fighting continued until September 3rd, when Sherman wired Lincoln "Atlanta is ours, and fairly won."

Hard Shell Baptists Of The The PeeDee Basin's Welsh Neck

We Carolinians are known for many things, our abundant peach crop, our colorful old-time tobacco auctions, spirited shag dancing contests, and a dozen other oddities. Yet what outsiders talk most about is our religious fundamentalism. Have you noticed the increasing tendency to refer to Greenville as the "Buckle of the Bible Belt?" Not so. Greenville's place on that divine strap is two notches shy of the Thanksgiving dinner notch. The absolute buckle of the old-fashioned Bible belt has forever been centered on the upper reaches of the PeeDee River on land cleared by 18th century Welsh dissenters.

Furman grads may have heard of Professor Harvey Toliver Cook, one of the graybeards of wisdom at that fine institution around the turn of the 20th century. Cook, with his confidante, Major James Lied Cooker, co-authored a wonderful but forgotten book of Carolinian entitled *Rambles In The PeeDee Basin, Carolina* (1926, The State).

Professor Cook realized over three generations ago the unusual influence that the Welsh dissenters had upon the developing culture of the Carolinas. Lost amidst the 20th century's rush to sameness is the story of this religious sect from Wales, driven from pillar to post in their quest to worship in an ancient Christian tradition that predates even the Church of Rome in early Britain.

Early historians of the Welsh in America refer to them as Anabaptists with the "Ana-" Greek prefix signifying "re-" as in rebaptism. Cook's history of the Welsh people of the PeeDee basin tells of their struggles such as being driven out of Delaware, but he doesn't shed much light upon the origin of the Welsh religious stubbornness. They opposed the more modern practice of infant baptism as well as quite a few other doctrines held by the Christians in Rome.

In Davis and Hogan's *Early History of the Welsh Baptists* (Pittsburgh: 1871) we find that there's a church tradition of Christianity in Wales dating from approximately 60 A.M. According to these scholars, the Roman legions failed to conquer Wales so they negotiated a truce and dwelt there among them as neighbors rather than as conquerers. A legionnaire named Cesura employed a Welsh couple named Pudenda and Claudia to work in his household. When Cesura returned to his native Rome, he carried Pudenda and Claudia with him as his servants.

According to tradition, Claudia came under the influence of the teachings of the Apostle Paul who was under house arrest in Rome. The Welsh Baptists believe that it was Claudia, with a little help from Pudenda, who established the Christian faith in Wales. It was the simple faith of the heart unadorned by creeds, vestments, rituals, and hierarchy -- the unadorned essence of St. Paul's teachings from his house of incarceration in Rome.

For our purposes the story does not end here. The Welsh people maintain that their good King Lucas was the world's first monarch to embrace Christianity, 180 A.M. The early Baptists endured a pagan Druid majority in Wales and in 300 A.M. Emperor Diocesan of Rome vowed to purge all Christians from his far flung empire. The bonfires of the Welsh martyrs sent spirals of smoke from a thousand biers. But the Welsh Baptist tradition survived. Their tradition claims that the mother of Emperor Constantine was a Welsh Christian and that this pious woman, much like St. Augustness mother, prevailed upon her dutiful son to embrace the soul-changing message of Christianity.

With all of this bold tradition on their side it's obvious that these western Britons would not get along well with Anglo-Catholicism, or its successor, Anglicanism. And that's when many Welsh Baptists fled Anglican church persecution during a "time of troubles" in the 17th century. Regrettably, their arrival in New England wasn't cordial, and as various stern sects of Christianity foisted their worship demands on outsiders, numerous Baptist refugees headed south on the Great Wagon Road from Pennsylvania down through Mecklenburg in North Carolina.

Hearing that abundant land was theirs for the claiming in Craven County (now Marlboro and Hoary), the Welsh found their New Cannon at the bend of the PeeDee River and named the place Welsh Neck. We know it as Society Hill, and its environs are just west of the Great PeeDee River swamp.
Society Hill, a prosperous community today and home to former Governor David Beastly, is the epicenter along the southern Baptist fault line. Baptists fleeing New England persecution had already settled Fort Dorchester on the upper reaches of the Ashley, not feeling welcome in Charleston. However, the steady flow of newcomers seeking cheap land and religious freedom rolled in on the Great Wagon Road to Welsh Neck.

An essay by Hoarse Friseur Redistill on the history of Arlington mentions that the earliest known resident in this Welsh Neck area was one Murphy, a claim stacker on the PeeDee near present-day Pocket Landing. Soon the surnames of James, Evens, Harry, Wilds, Nixon, and Jones appear on deeds. Hog farming was their forte and Chew bacon was the delicacy of Charlestonians throughout the 18th and 19th centuries.

281

The Charleston Ashley River Baptist alliance rode circuit in the PeeDee basin for decades and 21-year-old Richard Furman traveled from here to preach in the Welsh Neck Church that dates back to 1756. The Baptist denomination took criticism in the 18th and 19th century because it did not have a strict educational policy for ordination. Some of the early clerics, Woodmason being one, sent out by the London-based Society For The Propagation of the Gospel (SPG) reported that ignorance, licentiousness, and sloth were rife in the backwoods areas populated by these so-called dissenters.

Perhaps there was some backsliding of the frontier where daily raids by Indians took a toll and the scourge of untreated diseases occasionally caused the settlers to forget their roots. However, up on Welsh Neck the Baptists established their log church and then they built St. David's Academy, a fine educational institution that was an ornament to Society Hill for many decades. The Library Society of Society Hill was patterned after the fine one that already existed in Charleston. Rudisill's essay points out that this inland Welsh Baptist village possessed a cultured aspect that made it a nexus of intellectual exchange -- this Bible belt was a far different image of the back country descriptions rendered by the Englishman Woodmason.

Unlocking The Mysterious Historical Date Codes of 9-11 and 3-15

Time measurement fascinates high-achievers the world over. Everyone from Steve Spurrier to Stephen Hawking wrestles with time as a fundamental quantity. From history's viewpoint, time is measured best by what has become the bane of every high school history student -- dates. What's the essence of a calendar date? Is the calendar date just a numeric reminder in a formulaic fashion of time measurement that we commonly know as the Gregorian calendar?

We tear off a day or a month from a wall calendar and mutter something about so much to do, so little time. But there's both a science and a philosophy of time as measurement of human existence. Aloysius Lilius was a Naples-educated physician in the mid-16th century as well as being one of the great thinkers of his day. He practiced the healing art in Calabria, the toe of the boot that forms the Italian peninsula. In that Mediterranean latitude he could study the stars distinctly just as Arab and Hebrew scholars had done for centuries just across the sea.

Aloysius believed that the alignment of the stars along predictable calendar dates provided a spiritual insight into a patient's medical prognosis. It was Aloysius who is credited with the deep analysis of time measurement that we refer to today as the Gregorian calendar. From the detached perspective of a historian, the Gregorian method resembles a horizontal card file with 365 slots, each slot having an assigned value, such as 1 equals January 1, etc. Since time began some offbeat thinkers have held that some of these "values" have more "historical implication" than others. For example, two dates that appear to be "loaded" with historical implication are 9-11 and 3-15, each stacked unusually high with earth-changing events.

The good doctor Aloysius of Calabria attributed much of his medical prognoses to the alignment of the stars. And because superstition was not extinguished by the 16th century Aloysius naturally blamed Clio, the muse of history, for the heavy-handedness in which the gods ladled out good and evil over the course of a year. And for a Roman no date loomed more somber than did March 15.

"Beware the ides of March," a line that echoes from Shakespeare's *Julius Caesar*, refers to the *Idus Martiae*, or the 15th of March, May, July, and October and the 13th of all other months. Julius Caesar had a bad day that day, and so did Rome. Today the the term *Ides of March* has a Gregorian-sized knot of conspiracy theorists as well as alienated heavy-metal music artists manipulating the term's mysterious synergy.

But to Muslims the Ides of March marks the violent expulsion of the Moriscos of Valencia, or the purging of the Muslims from Spain -- a date not lost upon today's devotees to radical Muslim beliefs. Does the cadence of time really carry out its themes in some prearranged, divinely-ordered fashion?

The scholars influencing Aloysius -- Tacitus, Thucydides and Maimonides -- were aware that September 11, 9 A.D., marked the Battle of Teutoburg Forest. To them it was the battle where Roman legions commanded by Quinctilius Varus were annihilated by savage Germanics. As a consequence, Rome's influence waned north and west of the Rhine.

The British have long forgotten that March 15, 1776, was the date of South Carolina's secession from its colonial relationship with Britain. That's a lost fact that should have caused Lincoln some concern in 1860.

Ancient Scots perpetuate 9-11 because of William Wallace's slaughter of the English at Stirling Bridge in 1297.

Compare the gravitas of 3-15 to 9-11 and once again the historian is mystified at the unusual number of coinciding events. In the card file of time this date looms tallest of all. The date is indelible in our minds for its connection with the twin towers and pentagon terror incidents. However, Chileans use the phrase "el once" as slang for the CIA-backed coup d etat that assassinated Marxist Salvador Allende in favor of Augusto Pinochet. The string of political upsets and reversals occurring on 9-11 is frightening.

In 1683 the Muslim attempt to subdue Vienna for Muhammed was thwarted by the arrival of Polish King Jan Sobieski and his army on 9-11. Catholic Christianity secured southern Europe with this victory.

Add to the drama of the date the founding of the Jewish Colonization Association by Bavarian Baron Maurice de Hirsch in 1891 for the expressed purpose of finding a permanent homeland for the much persecuted Jewish race.

In 1978 on this date Jimmy Carter met with Anwar Sadat of Egypt and Prime Minister Begin of Israel for the historic Camp David Summit.

Measure that event with 2005's September 11 where the State of Israel completed its unilateral disengagement from the Gaza Strip. There's reason to speculate that September 11 is one of the two "heaviest" dates in the Gregorian calendar measurement of time.

On this date in 1941 FDR ordered the U.S. Navy to attack German U-Boats. This act of war predates Pearl Harbor's attack by the Japanese by nearly three months. Astute Americans took this bellicose statement by our government a *de facto* declaration of war. The date of 9-11 has the most serious implications for Middle Easterners, though.

On September 11, 1982, on the heels of Israel's invasion of Lebanon, the Lebanese Christian Philangists -- Pierre Gemayel's freedom fighters -- butchered over a thousand Palestinian refugees corralled in a detention camp near West Beirut. In the Mideast the event is referred to as the Sabra-Shatila Massacre. Hundreds of thousands of Israelis demonstrated in Tel Aviv to protest the brutal killings that occurred in Beirut while their army occupied the area. Oddly, no Arab nations protested. It was just another grisly event in the horrendous Lebanese Civil War.

Eastern Europeans think of 9-11-1989 as the glorious date that the Communist guard gates went unmanned and thousands of Hungarians fled to freedom in Austria. This event helped propel the financially troubled cable station CNN into a much-watched news source. And on 9-11-1990 George H. W. Bush used the Hungarian border opening to deliver his now famous "new world order" speech. So beware the ides and stay tuned to cable news alerts on 9-11!

Strolling About Charles Town In 1732

Everyone talks of the baby boomers these days and the society they've created for themselves. The theory of conspicuous consumption has a plus ultra illustration with our postwar generation. The phenomena of bumper baby years has much historical precedence. In our fair city, the first settlers of 1670 came as family units -- quite unlike the Spaniards and French who also attempted colonies in North America prior to the 17th century. By 1672 there were toddlers crawling the ramparts of Old Town on the Ashley. What kind of society did the first-ever Charleston baby boomers enjoy 60 years later in 1732?

Foremost, these early Carolinians were formerly Englishmen, Scots, Irish, and Europeans at large. Their accents or brogues belied their origin and parentage. A true set of distinctly American accents did not mature here until the mid-18th century. It took 60 years to establish a newspaper here and ten years before a church, St. Philip's, was erected. Almost everything that terrified us was local and most of what fascinated us was foreign. In appearance, early Charles Town was a jumble of hip-roofs, half-timbered stuccoed walls, and a few brick and plaster structures similar to what any sailor would find in Bristol, Poole, Ostend, or the Hanseatic ports. No doubt our wharfs, called bridges by the colonials, were colorful hubs of international commerce with colorful bolts of broadcloth, osnabruck, cambric, and satin marketed right from the boat.

As remote as we were from the European hubs of intellectualism, culture, and civility, the continual coming and going of maritime trade kept us abreast of the latest thoughts and trends. Two-hundred and seventy-six years ago, or approximately 10 generations, our culture was shaped from powerful forces abroad. Yet, we did enjoy some indigenous culinary delights such as squash, pumpkin, and corn. And the dusky color of two-thirds of the colony's thirty-thousand inhabitants was not a sight ever seen on the streets of London.

In 1732 Londoners flocked to the new Covent Garden Opera House, a sign that those cosmopolitans were making inroads into cultural advantage long held by Italian and Austrian rivals. In 1732 a traveling troupe of London performers produced a play for the first time on a New York stage. However, theater in a "Church Colony" such as Carolina was still a generation away in 1732. It took David Garrick lighting up the West End in London to popularize the dramatic art here. Colonial historians agree that Charles Town's Bay Street ale houses were lively enough places that vignettes of the bawdier scene from Shakespeare and Chaucer were cleverly acted for pub entertainment.

Promenading along the waterfront -- there was no Battery in 1732 -- was quite the social diversion on sunny afternoons in here. But even that innocent pastime elicited male scoldings for the fairer sex who wandered out unattended. *The South Carolina Gazette*, a partnership between local Thomas Whitmarsh and Benjamin Franklin of Philadelphia, carried numerous catty comments on page one deriding the ladies for wandering about the wharf unescorted by gentlemen.

The Gazette was a four-page paper published fortnightly from its offices on Church Street, and much of the news was reprinted from Franklin's paper in Philadelphia. However, one column that occupied half of the front page entitled *The Papers of the Meddler's Club,* contained anonymous pungent remarks designed to provoke debate and no-doubt promote newspaper sales. The thinly veiled jibes must have cut their targets deeply and stirred the sentiments of the thousand free citizens of the city.

At a time when Europe was contesting the Pragmatic Sanction which gave ascendancy to the Habsburg throne to a woman, Maria Theresa, Charles Town fretted over whether unchaperoned ladies should be allowed to take fresh air on the waterfront!

Our seaport town was a pawn in a much larger scheme of commercial empire in 1732, and colonists were captivated with developing news of the megacorporations then forming in Europe -- the Ostend Company, The Swedish East-India Company, The Dutch East-India Company, etc. These trade giants were combines of royal and private investors who wielded more power and accumulated more wealth than had ever before been imagined by subjects in Europe. Savvy merchants on Bay, Broad, and Church Streets began to seek illicit trade opportunities with the French and the Dutch at rendezvous in the Caribbean. This breach of mercantilism much angered London bankers.

The political talk of 1732 related to the Hanoverians who'd succeeded to the English throne a few years earlier. George II's consort was Caroline of Brandenburg-Ansbach. She was a shrew and the George was a philanderer, so the Empire was largely in the hands of Prime Minister Robert Walpole. Walpole's distant American cousins occupied enormous land holdings south of Charles Town.

Whitmarsh's *South Carolina Gazette* carried news from Vienna that the Duke of Lorraine would soon be declared the governor of the Austrian Netherlands. Every fortnight a new installment appeared detailing the Duke's royal progress enroute to his cousin's palace at Potsdam. Judging from the positioning of the story, it must have been a compelling read over here.

The year 1732 also saw Voltaire's *Zaire*, a play of 5 acts, produced on the London stage. In Charles Town our forebears were literary-minded enough to denounce Arouet, the man behind the pen name "Voltaire," as having copied Shakespeare's *Othello* and given it a French twist. The locals preferred Addison, Swift, and Steele to Voltaire.

The ventures that summoned our investments then were earthy things such as the building of a salt works and the enlarging of warehouses for importing Jamaican rum. When a ship arrived from Madeira, Holland, or England large advertisements lured buyers to Adger's and Boyce's wharfs to purchase casks of port wine and bolts of silk or lace.

In 1732 Pope Clement XII renewed a series of anti-Jewish regulations in

Rome, yet four thousand miles away Jews were well-treated in Charles Town. Catholics, Jews, and Protestants tolerated each other's beliefs to a greater extent in Charles Town than in any other city in the western world in 1732. In his book, The Jews of Colonial and Antebellum Charleston (University of Alabama Press, 1993), author James William Hagy tells of numerous Jewish families in Charleston in the early colonial days. Alexander, DePass, and Valentine were well-known Jewish merchants here. Examining their culture, it's easy to conclude that Charleston's earliest baby-boomers were visionaries .

Remembering The Tams And Art's Seaside at IOP in the 1960s

Maybe you can recall a place at the IOP Pavilion called Art's Seaside. There was an "old side" and a "new side." This juke joint wasn't much more than a barn with a huge door that opened out onto a volleyball net strung up on the beach. A rickety bar served frothy beer and soft drinks. The sound was always shaggin' beach music, and never was it better at Art's Seaside than when the legendary Tams with vocalists Joe and Charlie Pope were clapping, singing, and swaying to the awesome sound of Old School, the best horn section in the South.

Harmonizers Robert Lee Smith and Horace Kay did their choreographed shuffle as the rich-baritone chorus. Those were carefree days of beach music, madras, khakis, and Weejuns. Today a lot of Charlestonians have a serious case of nostalgia. There's no way of recapturing the magic of that long ago time when Joe Pope's and Robert Lee Smith's raspy tenor voices mellowed out into the night with "There's a ramshackle shack down in ol' Carolina, and it's calling me back to that girlfriend of mine . . . . "

Before soldiers were dying in rice paddies, before a president waved and assured us that he wasn't a crook, long before the rat race world became a 24/7, we had Art's Seaside and beach bands. Special summer evenings were partied late with Joe Pope and The Tams at some southern coastal spot.

The Pope brothers, backed up by Robert and Horace, swayed to the throbbing guitars and wailing horns as they belted out "What Kinda Fool Do You Think I Am?" If you didn't get there between 1962 and 1969 then you probably can't picture the innocence of the Charleston teen and college culture back then. Summer here meant sand, music, and a ball game called half-rubber, and this idyllic life stretched from Edisto Beach to Folly, to Sullivan's, and IOP, O.D. -- reluctantly renamed North Myrtle, all the way to Wrightsville Beach.

The raspy-mellow soul sound of the Tams originated in Atlanta's east side with the Pope brothers, Joe and Charles, during the late the 1950s Doo Wop craze. Joe Pope grew up not far from where the Martin Luther King Center is located today. Like street buskers the world over they played for coins tossed into a hat -- in their case, the hat was a knitted navy-blue tam. The story recounted by Charles was that they were too poor to buy nice matching outfits for their performances. All they could afford was blue tams and red sweaters.

From these humble beginnings the Tams became a legend from Daytona to Virginia Beach, from Charleston to Charlottesville and Oxford, Mississippi, they played frat parties and to sold out concerts at every beach pavilion on the coast.

Stories are told of how the Tams' great customized touring bus with their name, logo, and "The Sound of The South" emblazoned on the sides would sweep past motorists on the interstate and soon, pied piper style, fans would be trailing them in a caravan just to see where they were playing that night!

Maybe there was irony that the smooth lyrics so beloved in the '60s South celebrated poor black, tenant farming folks in those crooning blues melodies. Black groups dominated the music scene down south. Jerry Butler, Percy Sledge, Ben E. King, The Drifters, The Platters and host of others played gigs at IOP's

Seaside, the Old Folly Pier, and County Hall on King Street. Playing for the fabulous Citadel Senior Parties was a bread and butter staple for big name soul bands such as The Tams. But music tastes, dancing styles, and drinking laws have distanced college students from those sun, sand, beach music and beer days of the '60s.

In 1964 when The Tams recorded "Hey Girl, Don't Bother Me," little did they know that a military DJ would soon be blasting that sound through GI hooches all over South Viet Nam. Even Lyndon Johnson's teen daughter Luci knew every word of this magical group's tunes. The music recalls timeless themes of teen romantic angst.

ROTC was and still is a popular thing on southern campuses, and in 1962 college boys returned home from their Army or Air Force summer camp prior to commissioning. They let boys keep their ROTC uniforms, and invariably the "1505 khaki" trousers made it all the way to casual wear. Before that time there was not much khaki seen around Charleston. At first the distinctive khaki trousers were indicative of the ROTC boys, but manufacturers could see a trend developing. Today the khaki culture and beach music groups such as The Tams are as much a part of Charleston as is the palmetto tree and those big guns on the Battery.

Joe Pope, the lead singer, died in 1996, and younger brother Charles, now in his 70s, has taken over the group. New talent has come aboard to continue the deep tradition that began in Atlanta 50 years ago. Albert Cottle, otherwise known as "Lil Redd, the fastest feet in show business," is the star performer today, and the band occasionally tours with Jimmy Buffet as a way to keep the soul music tradition alive. But mostly it's the nostalgia sufferers who turn out -- still wanting to shuffle across a beer-stained floor shag-dancing to the carefree tune "I've Been Hurt," as they recall their "bulletproof" youth.

How many wedding receptions has Charleston had in the last decade where the bride and her father dance the shag to the soulful sound of a generation back.

There are a hundred groups today that imitate the unique sound of The Tams, and an unconfirmed rumor has it that there are actually two separate bands performing using the Tams name -- similar to what happened with The Drifters. Also, quite a few vocalists have been part of the band's mix, notably Joe Jones and Robert Arnold.

The next time there's a Carolina moon and the breeze rattles the palmettos, take a walk on the IOP, and if you turn your head into the wind you can still hear the smooth notes of Joe Pope's "Be Young. Be Foolish. But Be Happy!" Just for a moment you'll be at Art's Seaside with the "Remember Bannockburn 1314" flag over the bar, and the memories come rushing back!

Segregated Charleston As Remembered By Mamie Garvin Fields

Coming to terms with Charleston's 300 years of segregated past is just a part of what goes on inside The Avery Research Center on Bull Street. Avery is one of the nation's premier black history research meccas. Even with sophisticated, cross-referenced research techniques of the 21st century it's no small accomplishment to gather accurate information on the daily life of colonial and antebellum blacks. Fortunately we've been blessed with some precious memoirs culled by some very gifted grandchildren of the "Jubilee Generation" -- the descendants of the liberated slaves. Those early 20th century African-Americans are the fruit of the 13th Amendment.

We Charlestonians bask in the glory of the prominent role played by the Pinckneys, Lynches, Middletons, Rutledges, Draytons, and other famous surnames of our celebrated past. But until recently few Americans bothered to read the life stories of the black men and women who, though present at every step, were relegated to the back seat of society. Let Karen Fields, Ph.D., the great-granddaughter of Middleton family slaves, tell you her memories of that wonderful Charlestonian, Mamie Garvin Fields.

Furthermore, if you seek a page-turner of a book that reveals a seldom-seen slice of Charleston's past, then you must get a copy of *Lemon Swamp And Other Places: A Carolina Memoir by Mamie Garvin Fields with Karen Fields* (1983: The Free Press, A division of Macmillan, Inc.). Many schools across the USA use this little treasure to help with presenting a more balanced look at the times between the 13th Amendment in 1865 and the 1964 Civil Rights Act.

Just how the great-granddaughter of Charleston slaves breaks out of a three-century ordeal of captivity, poverty, and illiteracy is its own fascinating story, but Brandeis University professor Karen Fields chooses instead to recount a local history using the words of her grandmother, Mamie G. Fields, whom the state of South Carolina saw fit in 1971 to name "SC Senior Citizen of the year."

For Charlestonians Karen Fields' book is a much better primer on African-American culture than is the more famous *Roots* by Alex Haley. Mamie Garvin Fields' recollections touch us deeply with stories of people, places, and events that are seldom mentioned in books lauding our local heritage.

Most of us who have a hankering for history know nothing of a place called Lemon Swamp, the title of Karen Fields' book about her Grandmother Mamie's memoirs. Lemon Swamp is a dismal bog southeast of Bamberg and it bordered the plot of land given to Mamie Fields' grandparents by the Freedmen's Bureau in 1866. In February of 1865 there were tens of thousands of former slaves milling around the coastal south with no idea of how to begin life as free citizens.

A great American diaspora resulted from the Civil War's chaotic aftermath. Freed men wandered far from their accustomed plantations. It appeared that the Federal government had made no plans for following-up the victory that was certain to be theirs. The Washington government seized rebel property throughout the area and the Freedmen's Bureau resettled the ex-slaves, giving them 20 acres of confiscated land and a mule. The Fields, formerly slaves of the Middletons, were transplanted miles away from an area they were familiar with.

Karen Fields, narrating her grandmother's recollections, reveals the pathetic story of an elderly and illiterate black woman friend of the family begging her grandmother Mamie to write letters in a vain attempt to locate her loved ones. This story recalled a time long ago when Mamie was a young school teacher. The poor woman was dying and wanted to be buried with her kin, but the confusion of the 1860s separated them.

The Freedom Jubilee of 1865 was bitter sweet because the struggle for self-sufficiency was made even more brutal by the lack of education coupled with the resentment that existed between the races. Even the occupying Federal troops attempted to round up the freedmen and move them back to their old plantations as day laborers. Lemon Swamp near Bamberg was a hideout for black men fleeing Federals who seemed bent on revoking their freedom. Mamie G. Fields, ancestors of the Fields and Fieldings, taught these lessons to young blacks at Miss Izzards' School downtown.

The Fields were always an educated family it appears. Even during the colonial era they had training and skills reserved for the most trusted of the servants. One distant relative of Mamie Garvin Fields accompanied the Middleton boys to Oxford University in the 1700s. He attended lectures and tutorials, and even learned Greek and Hebrew as he waited upon his young masters! A direct line of descendants from this unique black man has yielded South Carolina leaders in the legislature, legal and judicial arenas, as well as academia and business. Many American success stories chronicle rags to riches -- Carnegie style, but you're not likely to see another story like this one.

All those years that Karen Fields listened to her granny, Mamie Fields, she filed away the stories pledging some day to write them down, if for nothing else than to perpetuate the memory of her family's triumph over adversity.

There are so many stories here, some quite humorous, that reveal the
subtleties of culture existing between the races throughout the era of segregation.
In the early 20th century South many of the master carpenters, bricklayers, and
metal workers were descendants of former slaves who'd learned their art on the
great plantations. When these skilled black men moved up north in the 1920s they
often encountered white resistance, for in the North the master craftsmen were
white men.

In 1924 Charleston celebrated a labor day decades before there was a
national labor holiday. The white guilds, forerunners of unions, sauntered along
in random fashion waving nonchalantly at the crowd, but bringing up the rear
were the black men's craft unions colorfully outfitted according to their trade,
stepping out smartly to the omm-pah-pah sound of the Jenkins Orphanage Band!
According to Mamie's memoirs the white craftsmen thought that their "black
brothers" had gone too far to outshine them, so that was the last labor day march
in Charleston!

Mamie Garvin Fields' memoirs span the years 1890 through the 1940s, and
this book, *Lemon Swamp and Other Places*, is an oral history of these parts unlike
any other you'll ever read.

How Daufuskie's Bloody Point Got Its Name in 1715

Worst violence in our state's history is how historians describe the
Yemassee War of 1715. Though it has been 283 years since bloodcurdling
screams were heard on that terrible night as war-painted Yemassees wreaked
vengeance upon white settlers. In the opinion of the Yemassees, settlers had
cheated them and violated their women. Though the terror stretched from Cape

Fear to the Congaree to the Ogeechee River in Georgia, the hot zone of hate and revenge was localized in a triangle encompassing Pocotaligo, Beaufort, and Daufuskie Island.

Aside from a few oystermen and forty-some-odd island dwellers, there's not one South Carolinian in ten-thousand who has ever been to Daufuskie, a remoter barrier island lying southwest of Hilton Head.

Beaufort townsmen remember back to the early 1970s when Pat Conroy moved over to the inaccessible island to teach twenty poor children who lived there amidst the moss-draped oaks that time had forgotten. Years later the delicious prospect of several hundred acres of island highland situated above the historic flood level was too much for real estate developers to resist. That's when Savannah entrepreneur Ted Turner put forth his controversial plan to buy most of the island and forever maintain it as a wildlife preserve.

Conroy got a book, *The River is Wide*, and a movie, *Conrack*, from his experience on Daufuskie. All Turner got was a huge legal bill and a nightmarish lesson is the tangled rights of heirs property in coastal South Carolina.

As Hilton Head prepares to receive the world's greatest golfer at the Heritage Tournament, a small cannon will boom a shot across Harbour Town's Calibogue Sound and a smoke ring will drift lazily across to Bloody Point on Daufuskie Island. As the golfers tee it up, at least one spectator will daydream back to the desperate days of spring 1715 when the largest Indian coalition ever to strike a lethal blow rained down fire and destruction upon our colony.

In the Creek Indian language, daufuskie translates to "land point." From the marina at Harbour Towne you can see across Calibogue Sound to the land point that Indians knew as a rendezvous point for 4000 years. Archaeological evidence reveals that native Americans feasted and worshipped there at a barrier cove sheltered by dense forests.

David Mongin was the first settler history associates with Daufuskie. However, the high land cut by numerous freshwater creeks lured Spanish,

Portuguese, Dutch, French, English, and renegade pirate ships seeking fresh water. Mongin Creek is the southern geographic feature of Daufukie. Seven miles of sandy beach can be seen at a sweep from the air on this island shaped curiously like a hog's tooth. And the sharp tip of that hog's tooth known as Bloody Point, conceals some of the most colorful history of our coastal region.

Mongin was a Calvinist Switzer to use the language of the 18th century. He was a follower of Jean Pierre Purry, a Swiss protestant of Neufchatel, and with 500 other religious refugees. Morrat, Brabant, Fraur, Winkler, and Robart are a few of the other surnames associated with this Swiss settlement that reached to the Savannah River.

At least three bloody skirmishes were fought against the Indians on the southeastern tip of Daufuskie before the American Revolution.

The first industry around Daufuskie and Hilton Head was the Indian trade for deer, beaver, and otter skins. The Indians had no concept of numbers; they lived happily with but two concepts -- scarcity and plenty. The traders made out like the bandits they were, obtaining hundreds of skins for a few yards of dyed cloth. Before long the natives grew distrustful, and the traders violated colonial rules by adding cheap rum and firearms to the one-sided deals.

On Good Friday, April 15, 1715 all torment broke loose, beginning with a ghoulish massacre around Pocotaligo and spreading compass-like in every direction for 75 miles. The licensed traders of the 1715 era were Samuel Hilden, Nicholas Day, Thomas Nairne, James Cockran, and John Wright. Ribbons, threads, beads, glass, blankets, rum, and baskets were the inexpensive stock from which these men made huge fortunes as they shipped fur pelts to England. The Indians were kept in debt and then manipulated into even worse financial disadvantage, and often their squaws became part of the bargain.

Thomas Nairne and John Cockran met several chiefs at Pocotaligo for a routine *parley* and a peace pipe. That night, April 14, 1715 all parties turned in for a good night's sleep. But before dawn the piercing screams of men being

scalped alive could be heard, and then columns of smoke could be seen from
settler's homes as the ten-thousand warriors systematically destroyed everything
the colonists had built.

Cockran was tortured for several days before he was burned alive by
Pocotaligo Creek. The Indians preferred to club their victims to death rather than
waste precious gunpowder in their newfangled firearms. On Huspa Creek the
home of John Bull was burned and all of his family was slaughtered while he was
away on business in Charleston. The communion silver used at St. Helena's
Episcopal Church in Beaufort is Bull's bequest given in memory of his family.

Colonial homes in Beaufort still retain the musket gun ports where settlers
blazed away at vermillion-painted savages intent upon eradicating them. Over on
Daufuskie a Yemassee war party heading back to St. Augustine with their loot
decided to celebrate their grand fortune a bit too early.

Captain John Palmer and his heavily-armed rangers stalked this fleeing band
of marauding Indians to Dauuskie and slipped up on them just as the warriors
prepared a grand victory feast. The official report to Governor Craven in
Charleston says in crisp military style that every Indian was slain by Palmer and
his men firing large-caliber swivel guns. There were two more Indian skirmishes
at Bloody Point, and the Indians avenged their earlier losses by annihilating the
white men. During the Revolution Daufuskie was Tory base that carried on a
lively Indigo trade with Britain despite Carolina's association with the Patriot
cause. Frequent assassinations of tories and patriots occurred there.

Today, as our great men swing clubs and whoop over Calibogue Sound and
shoot birdies and eagles, they can recall that hundreds of years ago the
Yemassee's great men also swung clubs and whooped as they shot birdies, eagles,
and colonists nearby!

How else would well-heeled foreigners know about Charleston other than by reading the travel diaries of their acquaintances? Imagine a time when there was no Travel Channel, no bed and breakfast on-line guide, and no trip-tik to guide one effortlessly on his journey. A century and a half ago foreign travel was more of an adventure than one bargained for. Much of what was known was word of mouth. No *Conde-Nast* glossy magazine proclaimed Charleston's charms. Not even the innovative, Leipzig-based Baedeker Guide mentions Charleston until the year 1900. Fortunately, almost all educated folks kept a journal. Personal travel journals made for lively reading in the 19th century, and thankfully a number of the English diaries survive. And they reveal quite a bit about Charleston before the War of 1861.

Historians have resorted to old diaries for candid observations of everything from the climate and cuisine to the architecture and the sophistication of the locals.

The best collection of British travel diary excerpts relating to antebellum Charleston belongs to Ivan D. Steen, professor of history at State University of New York in Albany. Steen is one of the leading authorities when it comes to understanding the European influence upon early American urban centers. Philadelphia, Boston, New York, Cincinnati -- Steen has published accounts of foreigners' impressions of these cities as they existed at the time when the age of steam was shrinking distance and travel time.

In January, 1970, Ivan Steen published an essay on English travel impressions of Charleston in the *South Carolina Historical Quarterly*. In this piece he uncovers some little-known aspects of antebellum Charleston culture, and he relates anecdotes that English visitors communicated to friends back home about our ancestors.

Most readers agree that Charleston remains a charming and cosmopolitan seaport with a distinctive Barbadian, or Bermudan charm. In the 1850s visitors who were fortunate to be invited into the walled gardens and double piazza homes all concurred that, not only was there refined hospitality on a grand scale equal to the gentry of Old England, but there was stimulating conversation abounding at our social gatherings.

The 1850s was the time of the world-renown John E. Holbrook, M.D., as chief lecturer at the Medical College. Holbrook married into the Rutledge family and their Tradd Street residence and country seat, Hollow Tree (near the navy base), became well-known for visitations from world famous thinkers such as zoologist Jean Louis Rodolphe Agassiz and his equally famous educator wife, Elizabeth Cabot Cary Agassiz. Holbrook hosted the Swedish novelist and pioneer feminist Frederika Bremer and *Atlantic Monthly Magazine* editor, James Russell Lowell who a relative of the Gilmans here. And these travelers noted the excellent discussions and entertainments they experienced in Charleston among the planter elite and their scholarly New England guests!

A notable topic of discussion among foreigners was Charleston's declining population in the decade prior to the War. The census of 1850 puts Charleston's white population at 49,985. Yet by 1860 the city count had diminished by 19% to just above 40,000. Was Charleston in economic decline as it plunged headlong into war? Visitors note that the commercial district here appeared tatty as one wandered east or west of the commerically vibrant Meeting and King Streets.

Walter Thornbury, an Englishman, writes (1852) that Charleston possesses two of the finest hotels anywhere on the continent -- the Mills House and the Charleston Hotel, both situated on Meeting Street. He labeled the Mills House "a noble palace of a hotel where could be had all the fineries" one could command in Europe. Amelia Murray, a genteel English woman, remarks that the Mills House is finer than the Willard in Washington. Jane and Marion Turnbull, noted world travelers from Britain, exclaimed that the table set by the Mills was the finest they'd encountered in America!

Eyre Crowe accompanied William Thackery on his USA tour in the 1850s and records that The Charleston Hotel on Meeting Street was a majestic building possessing an enormous reception hall where steamship trunks were stacked so high that hotel guests had to maneuver around a maze of incoming luggage. Other trunks awaited transport to the waterfront. Celebrities such as Thackery, Jenny Lind, the Booth acting family, and politicians frequented The Charleston Hotel.

The *New York Times* published correspondence received from Thackery involving a friend named Rankin who was with him in Charleston. Rankin had a mishap at the Charleston Hotel where he was robbed of $20, a large slice his ready cash. Elegantly upholstered benches lined the lobby at the Charleston Hotel and gentleman loungers, or loafers, congregated there daily to smoke cigars, ogle the ladies, and savor the seaport's international flavor.

Foreign visitors noted that Charleston streets had more in common in appearance with European streets than any city in America, except for New Orleans. As far as port activity goes, foreigners commented that our waterfront bustled, but that the shipping activity didn't appear as organized as ports in New York or New Orleans. Cotton bales bound for Manchester, Glasgow, or Bristol were piled a mile along Cooper River wharves. Bales were open to the weather and stacked haphazardly to mountainous height as overflowing warehouses dominated the eastern side of the city -- jamming right up to the old Exchange Building.

Visitors were stunned by the overwhelming number of Africans they saw on the streets, most of whom were slaves. The odd thing for Englishmen to grasp was that their notion of slavery included chains and an overseer with a bull whip. Here in Charleston, slaves strolled freely carrying bundles on their heads and wearing the most colorful attire seen on anyone in the states. The irony was that they were free to travel the streets on errands, but the sidewalk was forbidden and no person of color could be out and about after 9 P.M. The bells of St. Michael's were rung promptly at 9 to announce the patrol of the horse guards who kept nightly vigilance, less there be another slave insurrection such as the one planned by Denmark Vesey in 1822.

Reading accounts of old Charleston from the travel diaries of foreigners reaffirms our quaint notion that Charleston has charmed sightseers in every decade of its 340 year existence. Next week *History's Lost Moments* will share some of the humorous tidbits recorded by English diarists.

The Captivating Mrs. Holland And Other Tales Of 1850

Few women in Charleston, few women anywhere for that matter, have been so celebrated for their classical good looks, elegant simplicity, and apparent effortless ease in entertaining as has Jane Holland of 77 Tradd Street in 1850s Charleston.   Mrs. St. Julien Ravenel's book *Charleston, The Place and The People* (1912) provides us with a sentimental, descriptive portrait of one of the most beguiling belles ever to grace this southern city. The magnetizing Mrs. Holland, bewitching in her beauty, come-hither with her charm -- was the *doyen* of Charleston society through the 1840s and '50s. Though her rented two-room apartment on Tradd dimmed in comparison to the mansions inhabited by her friends, it was Holland's party invitations that were prized above all others!

The story of fair Holland reveals as much about pre-war Charlestonians and their appreciation for what was genuine as it reveals about Mrs. Holland and her ability to move in aristocratic circles despite reduced circumstances. Obviously antebellum Charleston was not exclusively chandeliers, ballrooms, and magnolias.

The world-famous John Holbrook, M.D., lived a stone's throw to the west at the corner of Tradd and King. Through the portals of his 101 Tradd passed the famous luminaries of the 19th century, be they scientific, literary, or political. Often the next evening found the same social set sipping lemonade and biting into sweet wafers at "Mrs. Holland's Salon" -- a noble tribute to the two rooms she occupied at 77 Tradd Street.

Mrs. Holland was a close friend, perhaps a relative, of Robert J. Turnbull who lived at 12 Logan Street. He served as a sort of *charge d'affaires* for widow Holland. Turnbull, an English-educated lawyer, was the intellectual behind the principle of nullification before John C. Calhoun assumed the mantle. Turnbull's polemics, published in *The Mercury*, were republished in hardcopy entitled *The Crisis*. That collection of speeches and essays influenced every politician south of the Mason-Dixon line.

So, the political talk that sizzled from 12 Logan through 101 and 77 Tradd Street equaled in political intensity and consequences to anything uttered in the drawing rooms of Madame de Stael or Emilie du Chatelet prior to the French Revolution!

Jane Holland, Harriott Pinckney (Rutledge) Holbrook, and Caroline Howard Gilman, poet and wife of Unitarian minister Samuel Gilman, were Charleston ladies whose political opinions were valued by gentlemen merchants, bankers, and planters. And the forty-years of continual social discourse on disunion refutes the popular notion that Charleston's secessionists were all impetuous hotheads and fire eaters.

The alluring Mrs. Holland dressed always in a flowing white drape of a dress of a fine material, perhaps satin, that was as beautiful as it was simple. The wide sleeves draped open to reveal her lovely arms, and in the summer her shoulders were daringly bare, and her graceful neck never was adorned by jewels or pearls. Yet, amidst the finery of the lowcountry elite she shown forth like the evening star.

We have no known portrait of the divine Mrs. Wallace save for the flowery

303

description rendered by Harriott Ravenel -- who remembered the elegant woman whom neither wealth nor poverty could corrupt. Harriott Ravenel (Mrs. St. Julien Ravenel) lived at 126 Tradd until the early 20th century and remembered "Mrs. W." from earlier times.

For the woman who reigned unrivaled over fashionable antebellum Charleston, Mrs. Holland entertained congressmen, senators, millionaire planters, and foreign visitors in a two room apartment of a large dwelling that she rented from a friend. Everything about Mrs. Holland's person and apartment was spontaneous and unrestrained.

Her black-braided hair was set off by a gold chain "fillet" around her pulled-back hair. A multifaceted jewel dangled from the chain in the center of her forehead -- giving her the air of a European princess. She greeted each guest warmly by the hand and led him or her into her cozy abode -- small rooms of merry laughter that spilled into the adjoining flower garden.

Where other hostesses had chamber music playing on the veranda, Mrs. Holland strummed her guitar and sang Italian or French songs in her soft, sweet voice. Occasionally her songs went up tempo into Greek melodies, making everyone wonder just whether this stunning Athena was truly a goddess, or just posing as one for the evening.

Holland's tiny bedroom was transformed in a trice to a lovely withdrawing room by placing several colorful shawls over a small day bed and disposing of her wardrobe and vanity. One rather clumsy, or tipsy, Charleston gentleman bumped into a screen that concealed her hanging clothes. Without missing a chord of her song, Mrs. Holland strolled troubadour style to the scene of her admirer's *faux pas* and deftly righted the partition.

Men adored her and women were drawn to her. Her gatherings attracted so many admirers that park benches were dragged over and even wooden packing crates were brought to her garden for partygoers to rest between songs and impromptu quadrilles, reels, and contra dances.

One exceedingly wealthy Charlestonian who'd been living abroad in Italy left a *soiree* of Mrs.' Holland's in the company of a fellow townsman and as each walked Tradd Street one said to the other, "Do you know on what you have been sitting?" "No," stated the other. "On the edge of a packing box with 'soap' branded on the bottom." To this astonishing fact the expatriate exclaimed, " My dear Sir I would sit on St. Laurence's gridiron to have the pleasure of spending the evening with Mrs. Holland."

The inimitable Mrs. Holland was part of that tapestry of downtowners that included Judge Prioleau and his literary society noted for excellent late night dinners where some attendees literally forgot to eat. Out-of-towners such as Charles Lyell (Darwin's professor at Cambridge), Louis Agassiz, noted Harvard lecturer, Commodore Maury, the world-famous cartographer, William Bache, grand nephew of Franklin, and many, many others gathered in the garden of Mrs. Holland to savor the finest of southern hospitality. Let it be remarked that antebellum Charlestonians valued the content of a person's character and his or her ebullient individualism as super incumbent to crass displays of wealth.

Mrs. Holland died with no heirs, but her legacy is a an elegant simplicity that few others than southerners and Europeans achieve. Holland had that "come hell or high-water" mien that Charlestonians remember in their women long after their men are forgotten.

Blackwater: Soldiers of Fortune, or Security Agents For Sale?

It was week three of the 2007 college football season. The Gamecocks were hosting S.C. State in what was being erroneously billed as an intrastate thriller. The Tigers entertained Furman in Death Valley -- both games were snoozers; Cocks and Tigers, each three and oh, settled in to what fans expected would be the mother lode of college football glory.

The Sunday newspapers reported the lopsided scores on the sports pages, but the international section barely reported what turned out to be the news scoop of the weekend -- the deadly shooting of 17 Iraqi citizens by Blackwater International security guards in Baghdad, a story that unfolded 6700 miles and several civilizations away from Williams-Brice stadium's Cockabooses.

When the page four story broke we were focused instead on "Air Spurrier's" invasion of Baton-Rouge and the coming SEC battle with LSU.

Similarly, few paid attention to the regrettable air mishap three years earlier where a Presidential Airways contract plane carrying three Army personnel smacked into a mountainside. The crash of the civilian CASA-212 turboprop cargo plane into a rock-walled canyon in Afghanistan caused a titter at the water coolers in Washington, D.C. All of a sudden political insiders were wondering out loud just what role this so-called private security agency was up to half a world away.

Eyebrows arched and lips pursed wider when the Congressional Committee on Oversight summoned Erik D. Prince, the 38 year-old CEO of Blackwater International, to testify as to the nature of Blackwater's operations in Iraq and Afghanistan. The public grilling of the highly secretive Prince is now a part of the Congressional Record for October 2, 2007.

The notion of private paramilitary organizations maneuvering inside countries hostile to the USA angers some Americans. The average fellow who gets his news in sound-bites from the AM shows is confused as to why we tolerate private gunmen running loose around Baghdad and Kabul. Howbeit, the use of civilian toughs to take care of the "loose ends" of empire is certainly nothing new in the western world. And what a difference the profit incentive can make.

Remember Elizabeth I, that most cunning of monarchs? Not much escaped her hawk-like senses. There was that graceless matter of the *Madre de Deuce* in 1592. *The Deuce*, as historians refer to the ship, was a Portuguese East India frigate taken in the Solent by English privateers. Laden with the wealth of the Orient, the ship was towed into Dartmouth. But when nightfall came, townsmen rowed out and *Deuce* was plucked of its wealth as a chicken is of its feathers.

Good Queen Bess was furious that her one-third share of loot was pilfered. And if she sent her horse guards to recover it, then it'd look exactly like the act of international aggression that it was. So Elizabeth sent swashbuckler Walter Raleigh overland with his trained band. 'If I meet any of them coming up," Raleigh swore, "if it be upon the wildest heath in all the way, I mean to strip them as naked as ever they were born, for her majesty has been robbed and that of the most rare things." The amount recovered equaled a half-million pounds sterling, half of what was currently in the English exchequer! Raleigh privately managed Elizabeth's "loose ends."

Those incommoding loose ends of America's foreign and domestic interests began to surface in the earliest days of the Lincoln administration. Old Abe had heard of Allan Pinkerton, the railroad detective, long before the election of 1860. Pinkerton, a Scotsman from Glasgow, single-handedly pioneered modern security guard methods. He was so adept at sleuthing that Lincoln relied on him even when it came to checking up on Union generals. Allan Pinkerton handled many special assignments for Lincoln. But Congress switched Lincoln's personal security over to the U.S. Army in 1865. Abe was shot down at Ford's Theater soon thereafter. Pinkerton was disgusted at the laxity of the Army in its protection of the President. Pinkerton's logo was "the eye that never sleeps."

Today the Pinkerton Security Company has been sold to Securitas AB, a Swiss security outfit that has clients in over two dozen nations. Securitas AB is a rival of Blackwater Worldwide, the primary security service operating inside Iraq and Afghanistan. There are others consisting mostly of soldiers of fortune, companies such as Aegis or Loomis, but Erik Prince is the personal choice of top brass when it comes to "tying up the loose ends" of international political expediency.

Security dons are seldom eager to publicize personal information, but what is believed to be true of Erik Prince is that he is a Michigan native, son of a billionaire, and Naval Academy dropout. He finished the small liberal arts Hillsdale College and qualified at Coronado as a Navy Seal in the 1980s. Prince is believed to be passionate about patriotism, evangelical causes, and the Catholic Church.

The published accounts of Prince's family list his sister as being married to billionaire Richard DeVos, son of the founder of Amway. Prince plunked down a lot of cash for 6000 acres of Dismal Swamp in the northeastern quadrant of North Carolina. There he supervises the training of a commando-styled security force made up of very well-paid former special forces soldiers. The arsenal of this private army includes a fleet of fixed-wing aircraft, armed helicopters, armored vehicles, and automatic weapons galore. The burly men who wear the big dog paw emblem of Blackwater have a no-nonsense demeanor. Judging from the number of consonants in their names, it's evident that not all the agents are Anglo-Saxons.

Some unexplainable and perhaps inexcusable violent acts have been reported involving Blackwater guards. Yet look at what the USA seeks to do in Iraq and Afghanistan. The Pentagon is engaged, not only in defeating a wily foe, but also in rebuilding and realigning the infrastructure. That means hundreds of foreign contractors moving in and around the urban areas, and these fellows are prime targets of Al Qaeda. Winning the hearts and minds of the Iraqi people is the first measure of establishing lasting democracy. Contractors crawl all over Baghdad, and they feel secure with the Big Dog Paw riding alongside. If lasting democracy is achieved, then we will owe Blackwater boys much more credit for tending to the "loose ends" than they've gotten thus far.

Cooper, Priestley, and Ayers: Controversial Professors With USC Connections

The age-old problem with professors is that they are given to professing.
Frequently it's an idea whose time has not yet come. In America there can be a
double-barreled repercussion when university's academic freedom clashes with 1st
Amendment protection, especially if the intended outcome is to excite " young
and dangerous minds." Thomas Jefferson, no slouch when it came to defending
free speech -- he coined the 1st amendment, had to wince when Professor
Thomas Cooper's blatherings on Deism at Charlottesville sounded too much like
blasphemy to Virginia clergymen. The enlightened Jefferson was forced to sever
his association with the esteemed Cooper. Thomas Cooper wound up at South
Carolina College (now USC), initially as a chemistry professor, later as president
of the institution. That magnificent Thomas Cooper library, ranked in the top 50
of America's 2000-plus research libraries, is the 20th century tribute to an
outspoken, highly controversial academician.

Cooper came of age in England during the turmoil of the French
Revolution. At Oxford, Cooper dallied between natural philosophy and moral
philosophy with the consequence that he wracked up a lot of coursework, but no
degree. He hoped to be both a medical doctor and a lawyer, and he finally did
qualify in law, but Cooper was driven out of England for his political views. The
man who would be the most internationally-known academic in USC's history
was thought of as a dangerous man by the likes of William Pitt and Edmund
Burke.

Cooper and his liberal-thinking inventor friend, James Watt, drifted to Paris
during the 1792 Jacobin upheaval. Applauding the rise of the Parisian National
Assembly and Sieyes' *Rights of Man*, Cooper was humiliated in a bitter debate
with the shrill Robespierre.

In London The Royal Society jerked Cooper's application for membership when
his anti-royal views became known. Having his application endorsed by the
ultraist Joseph Priestly sealed Cooper's doom in England -- he could leave
voluntarily, or be transported as an undesirable. He and Priestley fled to America
and fell in with like-minded leftists such as Jefferson, John Stone, Constant
Volny, and Thomas Paine's Philadelphia backers. Deism, free speech, and
republicanism were the uniting threads of these intellectual nomads. They were
the refuse of the enlightenment spewed upon these shores.

Thomas Cooper managed to get imprisoned for his violent denunciation of
the alien and sedition acts, the very first homeland security bill, and He was fired
from Dickinson College for espousing Deism in that Calvinistic institution.

Cooper was of the Joseph Priestley stamp of philosophical thought;
therefore, he qualifies as a direct link of to the enlightenment. Priestley was the
near genius whose profound mind encompassed science, theology, philosophy,
politics, and pedagogy. Evicted from England by George III, Priestley and his
sympathizers, notably Cooper, sought refuge in America.

Having been accused of planning riots to destabilize the monarchy and
organizing a French-styled revolution in the streets of London, Priestley was a
dangerous man indeed. In his home laboratory it was discovered that he'd
isolated oxygen, and there's no telling what damage could have resulted from this
devilish scheme.

Joseph Priestley, a founder of the Unitarian Church, befriended the Deist
Jefferson. Soon Priestley's publications in this country became an embarrassment
for Jefferson.

Cooper, Priestley, and a dozen freethinking luminaries of two continents
organized a society for the exchange of progressive thinking in science, politics,
architecture, and literature. William Withering, the physician who discovered the
beneficial uses of digitalis from the foxglove plant, was a Lunar Society
cofounder, as was James Watt, Erasmus Darwin, and poetess, Anna Seward.

Jefferson and Ben Franklin received Lunar Society correspondence.

In the paranoia of the French Revolution, Britain's crown and parliament suspected this new thinking of being subversive -- and in many respects it was. America rejected new thinking also. Unbridled criticism against government, church, and against conventional mores was considered unpatriotic, or treasonous. But, Locke and Rousseau, also Voltaire and Hume had already opened the door to free thinking. Were they dangerous revolutionaries, or limp-writed academics whose rage derived from the rejection of their unconventional beliefs about man, society, and religion? Fast-forward to the present.

One of the candidates in the 2008 presidential nomination struggle has gotten himself embroiled with the outspoken scholar, Bill Ayers, distinguished professor of education at the University of Illinois. Perhaps the candidate didn't know that Ayers had been on the FBI's most wanted list in the 1970s for participating in the Weather Underground terror movement. Bill Ayers was pardoned and now ranks as one of the country's leading professors of pedagogy. He views educational theory as linked with political theory. Ayers, in keeping with the tradition begun there by Thomas Cooper, maintains close connection with the University of South Carolina's College of Education.

Ayers grew up in Glen Ellyn, an upper-class borough of Chicago. His father was the CEO of Commonwealth Edison. "Radical Bill" prepped at Lake Forest Academy, an elite private school for the children of Chicago millionaires.

The '60s culture of civil rights, antiwar protests, and sexual liberation seeped into college culture. When Ayers went to the University of Michigan he joined the radical youth group Students For A democratic Society. He met a girl there named Diane Oughton, an education major. Together they started the Children's Center at Ann Arbor. It was a project to encourage a less-structured educational philosophy similar to experimental, Rousseauist-based approaches then being attempted in a few schools in Britain.

From a Bob Dylan song Ayers got the idea to name their violent attention-getting scheme 'The Weathermen." This group of privileged radicals dropped out and moved to Greenwich Village. Oughton and two other Weather Underground members accidentally blew themselves up while making nail bombs. The remaining Weathermen scattered and focused their bomb blasts on army recruitment centers and buildings in Washington, D.C. Most were apprehended and did prison time.

Ayers married fellow Weather underground fugitive and felon, Bernardine Dohrn. She's currently a law professor at Northwestern University and counsel for child advocacy groups.

The message for advocates of violence for social change is beware -- it's a slippery slope. Unless your radical view prevails you're are branded as a felon. Politicians will disavow and renounce you. However, if the revolutionary notion prevails, as happened with Priestley, Voltaire, Rousseau, and USC's Thomas Cooper, then expect to find yourself lauded as a visionary!

Making Sense Of 16,000 Years Of Civilization in Carolina

One thing that can be said about history is that it's a sure fire cure for delusion and conceit. Sometimes history can bring a helpful dose of humility. It's definitely human nature to believe that no age can equal ours in accomplishments. Just as we declare the supremacy of our culture to all other civilizations, archaeologists confound us with news of the 10th, 11th, and 12th wonders of the ancient world. Historians today are having to give way to mud-spattered, sunburned archaeologists and a host of other scientists to interpret the mysteries of the past. Those soil sleuthing archaeologists can cull a hundred pages worth of historical data from barely a cubic yard of dirt.

In South Carolina it's the archaeologists not the archive-loving historians who are rewriting the history books. We used to believe that the first humans dwelled here 8,000 years ago. Now, thanks to Albert Goodyear, Ph.D., and the USC Institute of Archaeology, we have strong evidence of a Paleo-American community near Allendale that dates back approximately 16,000 years. That's 4000 years earlier than humans were thought to exist in North America!

We also know that the Spaniard Francisco de Gordillo cruised off our shore in 1521. His squadron leader, de Allyon, set up an outpost on Winyah Bay in 1526 -- 144 years before the English settlement at Albemarle Point.

Simple arithmetic reveals that Europeans have prevailed in our region for 487 years. With Professor Goodyear's discovery of the Topper Site we must conclude that European settlers have called the shots around here for just a miniscule 1/32nd fraction of this region's human civilization! Maybe we're not the greatest, just the latest!

Professor Goodyear's Topper Site reveals startling discoveries about a Carolina settlement existing during the ice age. These early "Carolinians" were part of the Clovis Culture, the Asiatic ancestors of the native Americans. Clovis Man migrated across a frozen land bridge in the Bering Straits 13 centuries ago -- so archaeologists believed. However, the USC Topper Site is causing textbook writers to correct the 13,000 years of known human existence in this hemisphere to 16,000 years instead. Often what we learn about these long- lost cultures enables us to understand our own existence upon these coastal plains and piedmont hills.

The Carolina that we know is approximately 32,000 square miles of land surface. That's roughly the size of Austria, Ireland, and Lake Superior. The native-Americans who dwelled here were extensions of larger native tribes that covered areas equal to the size of France or Germany.

Just as the native-Americans dwelt along rivers, we have the same tendency today. The Savannah River that was home to the Clovis culture 16,000 years ago has 238 miles of Carolina riverbank. In the 18th century the colonials dotted that river with little towns named after European cities -- Vienna, St. Petersburg, South Hampton, and New Bordeaux. The new world sites replaced Indian towns -- Yuchi, Oakfuskee, Westoe, and Oconee. Today, practically all traces of the native and colonial era villages have vanished.

One estimate of SC Indian population during the era of Spanish exploration tallies as high as 4000 men, women, and children in six dozen villages ranging from the mountains to the coast. The Indians around Mount Pleasant were the SeeWee, a part of the Sioux nation, and their village of Avendaughbough passes down to us as Awendaw today. The SeeWee were the natural enemies of the Iroquois, so between the hostilities of the English settlers and their centuries-old struggle with the Iroquois, the SeeWees have disappeared.

Population density for the native-Americans inhabiting what we know as South Carolina was one person per 8 square miles. Our population density today is 132 persons per square mile. Their native villages appear to have been organized in concentric circles of huts facing a common community center. From the air some of our subdivisions have a similar appearance.

So far, archaeology has not revealed that the Indians were anything but urbanites -- preferring their communal village life rather than living isolated. In South Carolina today, census figures reveal that 76% of us are urban or suburban, whereas 24% of us prefer to live in the rural settings.

The social make-up of an Indian village reveals an interesting lifestyle. Apparently the day-to-day life was regulated by a council of women. Matriarchs organized the food preparation and many of the daily rituals and ceremonies. Males were either warrior / hunters, or they were food harvesters. We can only assume that much status was associated with the warrior / hunters, and that their elite band possessed privileges and obligations not experienced by the others.

In our culture today we are alarmed by the statistic of 23.7% of SC's adults have not completed a basic high school education. And, according to the 2000 census, 15.6% of us are living below the poverty level. In the Indian villages everyone had a job, from the nut and berry gatherers to the corn meal grinders, bakers and hunters. There was no such thing as an unemployed, or laid-off Indian.

The native-American era that we identify most with is known as the Mississippi Era, 1000 A.D. to 1700 A.D. These industrious inhabitants of our region cleared fields and planted pumpkins, beans, and maize. Their acorn-cornbread was a wonderful-tasting treat for the earliest English arrivals. If a SeeWee Indian could roam about the Mount Pleasant Farmers' Market, he'd see many items that reminded him of the old days, from shellfish to squash to scantilly-clad squaws.

Judging from the numerous artifacts found in the archaeology sites, the earliest inhabitants of our area liked to deer hunt, eat oysters on the half shell, dance half-naked, and race down the waterways in sleek canoes. The historian is us makes us wonder if there's something in the water or the soil that perpetuates these same habits and desires in locals today.

Back in 1540 when de Soto met the beautiful Indian princess Cofitachequi by the banks of the Wateree River near Camden, that beautiful woman's face was decorated with red paint composed of kaolin that the Indians were mining nearby. Today kaolin is being mined in Kershaw county and a major kaolin use is for women's lipstick. Maybe we do continue the dream of the earliest inhabitants, from Clovis Man to Colonial Man -- right down to the Cable Man.

The Charleston Anglican (Free) School, 1712- c.1777

Charleston, like all of America's colonial seaports, abounds in eyewitness descriptions of its storied past. One significant, but little-known feature of old Charles Town a half-century before the Revolution is the story of its first formal school, the Charleston Anglican (Free) School. Though known locally and in London by many names, the Charleston Free School, Saint Philip's School, Reverend Guy's School, etc., the Anglican-affiliated foundation is the tap root of all free and private schools in Charleston.

Most certainly there were occasional grammar schools and informal latin academies tucked away on side-street piazzas and church back-pews, but there's scant evidence of any educational institution here preceding this two-story brick building on the periphery of Charles Town in 1712.

The notion of a school in the southern colonies belongs to the London-based Society For The Propagation of The Gospels To Foreign Parts (S.P.G.). That pious organization, made up largely of London clerics, prayed for the souls of the settlers and especially for the primitive natives of the American colonies. Within the S.P.G. there was a splinter-group of intellectuals, mostly graduates of All Souls College, Oxford, who organized the Society For The Propagation of Knowledge, the S.P.K.. The young Anglican priest of All Souls who was the spark of the S.P.K. was Thomas Bray. His mission was to send over a classical and theological library for each parish in America. Hence, Bray's Libraries were the beginning of the American Anglican schools, especially in the southern colonies.

The Bishop of London who had a burden upon his heart to keep the colonials connected to their faith was Henry Compton. Though he died unexpectedly in 1713, he was responsible for putting these two missionary societies, the S.P.G. and the S.P.K. into being.

Compton had been a major player in British politics as he was one of the "Immortal Seven." These were the bold ones who risked inviting William III of Holland to invade England in 1688 when James II aligned himself with the Roman Catholic faith. The Stuart princesses Anne and Mary, were entrusted to

Henry Compton for their education. Later both women would wear the protestant crown of England. Such was the resume of the man who sponsored the earliest Anglican school in Charles Town. Though the Bishop of London exercised broad oversight, the close supervision fell to Thomas Bray of the S.P.K.

The founding fathers of Charles Town's Anglican Free School included such worthies as Thomas Broughton, Arthur Middleton, William Rhett, Ralph Izard, and George Logan. These influential men put up money for land and the construction of a two-story recitation hall. Not all of these men, however, sent their sons to the local school, for going abroad was still the educational choice of those who could afford it. It's interesting to ponder what might have been the outcome of this early school if the colonial elites had put their money and their sons into the new establishment. In Boston and Philadelphia the dissenters were in the majority and they sought to educate their sons in colonial schools.

Where was the Charleston Free School? Judging from correspondence between school officials and the S.P.G. in London, the school was situated a half mile north of the original St. Philip's, then located at Broad and Meeting Streets. Charles Town of the 1720s was known to be a lusty, bawdy, rum-drenched port where buccaneers sold their stolen loot directly from the wharves. Locating the school on the fringe of the walled town was a way to remove the lads from the seamy side of colonial life -- the auctioning of slaves, drunken sailors carousing with tavern wenches, and the relentless butchering of livestock and poultry in the slaughter pens. Still, the young scholars complained about the distance they had to traverse in order to reach convocation at the church.

It couldn't have been much fun attending this school, but school back then wasn't supposed to be fun. Discipline was severe, and the curriculum was tediously classical -- Latin and Greek. They translated and memorized lengthy selections of Homer or Tacitus. School operated through the hot summer months. Thomas Morritt writes the S.P.G. in London to complain about student lethargy during the summer. Students had Saturday afternoons unscheduled. On Sundays they were catechized by Alexander Garden, rector of St. Philip's.

Schoolmasters were Englishmen sent out as missionaries by the Bishop of London. One social benefit of this English-style boarding school in the midst of colonial Carolina was that it maintained a proper English accent among the colonials.

William Guy resigned from the school to become the vicar for St. Helena's Parish, however, the Yemassee Indian uprising scorched the earth from the Combahee to the Ogeechee and Guy narrowly escaped with his life.

Excerpts of Thomas Morritt's letters to London can be found in the SCHQ, Vol. 32, (1931). In 1725 he writes excitedly that the school has reached out to the natives and soon expects the enrollment of the 12-year-old son of a Creek Indian chieftain. Morritt boasts 52 students, 10 of whom were charity boys, and 2 were mulattos.

Thomas Morritt's wife ran the boarding school's laundry and catering with the aid of an English domestic and six slaves. He complained that the townsmen sent their sons as day students yet expected the school to feed them as if they were boarding students.

Charleston Anglican Free School suffered from numerous disruptions in its year-round schedule in the 1720s. On two occasions the school was suspended indefinitely because fires ravaged Charles Town. Tropical rains flooded the peninsula and made the outlying countryside inaccessible. Yellow fever and smallpox forced parents to withdraw their sons for months at a time.

The greatest disaster to befall the school was the drowning of headmaster, Gideon Johnston, when the sloop he was sailing in capsized in 1716. Another faculty member died later from exposure experienced during this same tragic incident. The capsizing was witnessed by many from the waterfront.

In 1770 the Anglican School was an isolated Tory institution amidst growing Whig opposition. By 1776 numerous Charlestonians were dissenters and their sons attended rival schools such as Reverend Furman's Baptist School on

Church Street. The school ceased to exist because of the Revolution. Ninety years elapsed before Reverend Anthony Porter opened The Institute of the Church of the Holy Communion, Charleston's next Episcopal School.

Forty-Five Mile House and Markley's Old Field At Black Oak

It's been a hundred and fifty years since anyone has mentioned the muster ground at Markley's Old Field, Black Oak community, St. John's Parish. Quaint as the appellation is, today's unimaginative road map refers to this historically romantic spot merely as the intersection of Highways 6 and 311. And nary a marker tells the motorist what wondrous things occurred long ago in this vicinity.

In days gone, make that 250 to 300 years ago, the roads leading out of here were few and nearly impassable. The most-travelled route was the Old Cherokee Path that follows present-day Highway 52 through Moncks Corner and then becomes Highway 6. As early as the Revolution this Cherokee path was thought to be ancient. It followed the Santee and Congaree to the state boundary where the Cherokee towns were.

By the 1720s the settlers had pushed the tribes back and made the Cherokee Path their own commercial road. And they built taverns every 10 miles or so to provide a safe haven from the thieves who roamed the roads after dark.

The Forty-Five Mile House was the most famous of the roadhouses along this northwest to southeast route and it went by various other names such as Martin's Tavern and Barnett's Inn. The only description we have of the old place was the late 19th century recollection of Professor Francis A. Porcher, "a long, two-story frame house kept by Mr. Faust." Today the actual site of Old 45 Mile

House is a hundred yards out in Lake Moultrie. When the Lake dried up recently some vestiges of the foundation could be spotted.

Should you drive up Highway 6 expect nothing but the murmur of oaks and pines to recount the legends. But near the intersection of Number 6 and Highway 311 there once was a bustle of activity from colonial times continuing beyond reconstruction. This area called Black Oak community was the uppermost reach of St. John's Parish. Parishioners had a wooden chapel of ease known as The Church of The Holy Trinity. The priest conducted a free school here for the plantation overseers' sons. Families who desired more their sons than the fundamentals could boarding and instruction at the Charleston Anglican Free School.

When the stagecoach rumbled through Black Oak community twice weekly, wealthy 18th century sportsmen received mail addressed to them at the St. John's Hunting Club, especially during deer season when gentlemen habitually staged three and four day hunts.

The 45 Mile House was a meeting place for the Black Oak Agricultural Society to discuss the advantages of long versus short-staple cotton and New England versus old England markets. Just a few minutes ride upon a cantering horse and a guest at this inn and tavern could be at the gates of Wantoot Plantation, Chapel Hill, or Pooshee.

Less than three miles from here was Thomas Sumter's General Store. The man who became known as the Gamecock of the Revolution began his great career as a sergeant in the militia and as a hardware dealer for the region lying between Wassamassaw, Eutaw, and the High Hills of Santee. This section of St. John's was known then as the English Santee to distinguish it from lower French Santee.

This newly cleared area was a beehive of rumbling wagons moving to and from Lenud's and Nelson's Ferries crossing over the Santee River. Cargo such as pelts and barrels of pitch went down river by barge. Young men made fortunes sweating under a broiling Carolina sun cultivating cotton and supervising the constant flow of wagons and bateaux moving along road and river -- all in the vicinity of 45 Mile House. Residing here were Ravenels, Gourdines, Porchers, Marions, Gaillards, Simons, Canteys, and a dozen other surnames now enameled into our state's storied past.

During the Revolution the 45 Mile House was a rendezvous for Marion's men. Francis Marion's Belle Isle Plantation was just a couple of miles from 45 Mile House, then known then as Barnet's Tavern. Marion's men had dozens of rendezvous spots and the patriot ladies left a handkerchief on the porch to signal if the area was free from tories. There reportedly were kidnappings, lynchings, and assassinations by both sides in the Revolution along the route we call Highway 6. Every major leader in the southern sector of the Revolution passed by this haunting spot.

Tarleton's Legion swept up the road on several occasions and so did Lee's. Lord Rawdon lost many a convoy wagon to patriot raiders, and once his pay wagon with 700 gold coins was purloined by Marion's partisan band.

General Nathaniel Greene fell back to 45 Mile House following the Battle of Eutaw Springs in September, 1781. Though the British camped on the battlefield and claimed the victory, it was a pyrhic one and Conwallis realized he'd have abandon South Carolina as too costly to hold. On September 11, 1781, a swift rider departed 45 Mile House in a cloud of dust with dispatches for the Continental Congress telling them of the Battle of Eutaw Springs.

Wounded patriot and British soldiers were left to die on the porch and inside the 45 Mile House. Their burial mounds were seen near the inn until the area was flooded in 1941 to make way for the Santee-Cooper Project.

Located adjacent to the 45 Mile House was Markley's Old Field, a rather large acreage that served as a track for thoroughbred racing and as a muster field for the beat company of militia volunteers. During emergencies such as the Nullification Crisis, the War of 1812, and the Confederate War the locals mustered here and drilled in a unit known for generations as the Eutaw Company. They drilled mounted and on foot and were a formidable force in three wars. Military parades were part of the festivities when dignitaries visited Black Oak. One poor boy, a militia private from upstate guarding Charleston in the war of 1812, succumbed from illness at this spot and was buried between the big house and the Cherokee Road.

No one ever mentioned luxurious accommodations at 45 Mile House -- just the essentials for man and beast. Only the breeze in the pine tops remains the same. Today Highway 6 is a lonely road leading to the bait shops and boat landings that make up a community called Cross.

Racing Legend Tiny Lund Made Town of Cross Famous

Dewayne Louis Lund was anything but tiny. When he kedged his 6 foot 6 inch, 280-pound frame inside the roll cage of a souped-up stock car, the man they called "Tiny Lund" intimidated racing's hard chargers from Daytona all the way to the Summerville Speedway. The gentle giant with the Elvis sneer and slicked back hair understood torque and horsepower in a way that even the professors of M.I.T. will never know. Call it Cracker Culture or Red Neck History, but stock car racin' is as much a part of Southern culture as fried chicken and fresh-baked biscuits. This Iowa-born race driver brought NASCAR fame to the tiny community of Cross. Lund also built a first-rate fish camp on Lake Moultrie and captured the world's record for flathead catfish!

When Tiny Lund was killed in a fiery crash at Talledega in 1975, he had begun to fade into the exhaust-tinged haze of stock car lore. He was an "independent" when factory-backed drivers such as A.J. Foyt, Bobby Unser, and Juan Fangio raked in the big bucks with factory sponsors.

Money flowed through Tiny Lund's hands quicker than gasoline filters through a carburetor. His total winnings amounted to less than a quarter of a million, but back in the 1960s that was extravagance for a Iowa farm boy who holed up in a fish camp on Lake Moultrie!

As a teenager Tiny saw service in the Korean War. He'd raced go-carts, motorcycles, and had done a bit of drag racing, but he'd never raced professionally until he took his new '55 Chevy to Lehi, Arkansas. His sponsor was seat belt pioneer, Carl Rupert. Rupert hadn't started making the belts out of parachute webbing yet and Tiny's girth snapped the belt in two resulting in a badly broken arm on lap 65. Race number two was the Columbia Speedway.

Gastonia, Hillsboro, Blainey Drag Strip, Darlington -- it didn't matter to Tiny as long as he was racing. Getting sponsorship was easy when fuel cost 29 cents a gallon and shade-tree mechanics could tweak and tune a race car. Black's Fish Camp of Moncks Corner was emblazoned on one side of his red number 55 car with Southern Music Shop of Orangeburg was on the other side.

Lund ran short on funds when he began qualifying for the bigger races. Time after time he would be near the front of the pack when an axle would break or a clutch would go out. Other racers had deep pocket sponsors and lots of parts. But Lund's hard charging, gritty "run-it-til-it-breaks" attitude brought Lund and Lee Petty together. Petty Enterprises was racing Oldsmobiles and getting corporate sponsorships. During the 1960s Tiny raced with Petty, or Holman-Moody, or with the Wood Racing Team--wherever he could get the fastest and best-prepped car.

With Lund in the pit area there was always a radio blaring and Jerry Lee Lewis would be belting out "There's A Whole Lotta Shakin' Going On." Lund's mountainous frame would shake rhythmically with the beat as he sang along.

It was no singing matter in 1963 down in Daytona when Marvin Panch's

race car hit the wall. Disregarding his own safety, Tiny ran out on the track
amidst oncoming cars and dragged Panch out of the burning wreck. For his
heroism he received the Carnegie Medal of Honor.

Lund raced that day with severe burns on his hands. It became his biggest
ever race day as he managed to slip past Fireball Roberts and coast across the
finish line. Even though his gas tank was running just on fumes, Ned Jarrett
drafting behind Lund, actually bumped Tiny across the finish line!

Stock car drivers have temper tantrums on asphalt tracks approaching 120
degrees. Tiny and teammate Lee Petty had hot words in the pit and soon Tiny had
Petty in a headlock with Lee's pit crew pounding away on Lund's flanks. Out of
nowhere "Ma" Petty slammed her handbag against Tiny's forehead and he went
reeling. legend has it that Ma carried a handgun in her bag for protection and the
effect was like brass knuckles against Tiny's temple.

Lund, Joe Weatherly, and a former Marine-turned-racer named Larry Frank
loved nothing better than to start a bar room brawl after a few late-night beers.
Despite his fisticuffs, Tiny was an overgrown teddy-bear. Truth be known, Lund
loved a good practical joke better than he loved Elvis impersonating or destroying
bar furniture.

Leave it to Cale Yarborough to get one up on Tiny in the pranks
competition. Yarborough loved rattlesnakes and used to get a kick intimidating
his racing buddies by seizing a rattler from a cage and milking the venom right
there in the pit area with terrified bystanders watching in awe. One afternoon
before qualifying trials Yarborough waited until Lund got his immense torso
strapped into the car and then Cale walked over and threw a live rattlesnake inside
Tiny's tight racing cockpit. Of course the snake had been milked and defanged
but Tiny nearly tore the car apart and cursed a blue-streak in getting out of there!

Lund managed the last laugh by slipping some of his wife's most intimate
lingerie into Yarborough's motel room just before Mrs. Yarborough was to arrive.

Ever the romantic, this gear-head racer won the future Mrs. Lund's heart when, after some banter with a girl outside the pit area he said, " "You've got a short memory. I just met you last Thursday night. So remember my name, Tiny Lund. I'm going to marry you." The girl told him, "My momma would kill me if I dragged something like you home."

Lund the Legend was killed in a senseless mishap at Talledaga in 1975. He was first alternate on the qualifying roster and had not expected to race there. Instead, he was at the Summerville Speedway and then at Myrtle Beach when he learned that he'd made the cut. Bobby Allison sent his private plane to fetch Tiny to the Alabama track. Several cars knotted together and a rookie driver slammed into Tiny's driver's side. Two recently discharged Viet Nam vets jumped the restraining wall and tried in vain to get the big man out of the fiery inferno. The most colorful and best-liked NASCAR racer was dead. His beloved fish camp at Cross still stands.

SC Air Guard "Swamp Foxes" First Over Baghdad Gulf War I

Forty years ago the National Guard had the reputation, probably undeservedly, as a safe haven for the sons of privilege and a respectable dodge of the draft in war time. If that ever was the case, the times have certainly changed now. And the South Carolina Air National Guard's (SCANG) 157th Fighter Squadron, nicknamed "the Swamp Foxes," is ranked as the number one air guard unit in the united States.

At precisely 3 a.m. Saudi time on January 17, 1991, F-16 Strike Eagles of the elite 157th Squadron, the famed Swamp Fox unit, became the first fighters over Baghdad as they drew the enemy fire and jammed the radar of Saddam's ground batteries. Their "First Over Baghdad" honor is just one more proof of the

"Semper Primus," always first, motto of the elite 157th, the most combat-experienced squadron in the Air Force.

If the names Lt. Col. Scott "Cleetus" Bridges, Colonel Dean "D-Dawg" Pennington, Lt. Col. Michael "Crab" Manning, and Lt. Col. David "Oscar" Meyer are not household names in this state, they probably should be. They're the elite "Top Guns" of the SCANG F-16 Block 52 Viper. The airmen are lawyers, stockbrokers, corporate executives, and airline pilots in their regular lives, but on weekends and recall they don the desert flight suit with the swamp fox patch on one shoulder and their coveted 1000 hour or 2000 hour air patch on the other. Then it's hatch down and thumbs up as the thunderous jets roar into harm's way. One woman is a fighter pilot with the 157th, Captain Tally Parham, a practicing attorney in her "other life."

Except for the ultra new F-22 Raptor, the aircraft flown by the SC Guard is the most sophisticated fighter in the Air Force arsenal. Just two Air national Guard units fly this version of the F-16 -- SC's 157th and the Syracuse's 174th FS NYANG "Rockateers." Both of these red hot units saw action in Gulf War I and II.

McEntire Air National Guard Base is located 16 miles southwest of Columbia. The runway was known as Congaree Air Field in 1942 and Army Air Corps pilots learned to fly the P-47 Thunderbolt "Flying Milk Jug" or the P-38 Lightning, a twin-tailed, fast pursuit fighter. Marine Corps aviators trained in F-4 Corsairs got Congaree Field in 1943 to train in F-4 Corsairs.

Congaree Field might have become a private airport after the war had it not been for Truman's Cold War buildup. The Berlin Airlift of 1947 was a bold reminder that we needed a seasoned corps of military airmen and technicians in reserve.

The first general to command the South Carolina Air National Guard was Brigadier General B.B. "Barnie" McIntire, Jr., a colorful air combat veteran of World War II. Barnie learned to fly as a teenager and flew cargo planes in the war as a teenager! He became the youngest general in the history of the state's national guard. McIntire "augured in" his F-104 fighter in the Susquehanna River when it flamed out after take off from Olmstead A.F.B. Rather than bailing out, General McIntire stayed with the powerless craft guiding it into the rocky river bed rather than letting it crash into heavily populated Harrisburg. That was May, 1961, and during Governor Fritz Holling's term, the Congaree Air Base was renamed in McIntire's honor.

Former state treasurer and distinguished World War II fighter pilot, Grady Patterson, is one of numerous distinguished South Carolinians to have commanded the famed SC Air Guard. Patterson was associated with the air base for more than 40 years. The legislature made him a three star general upon his retirement.

More recently the SC ANG has been commanded by Brigadier General Timothy R. Rush, a highly-decorated fighter pilot and 1974 Citadel graduate. In Gun Smoke '80 Rush won the Top Gun award for Air Force fighter jocks and was chosen to be the F-16 demonstration pilot for air shows around the world.

On three occasions our citizen warriors of the SCANG have been called to extended active duty. The first time was in 1950 when the flyers from Congaree Field went to Korea where they flew the F-80 "Shooting Star." In 1961 our boys deployed to Spain in support of the Berlin crisis. In 1990 the 157th covered itself with glory as its air assets were chosen to go in first, fast, and low over Baghdad to draw the enemy's fire. Remember that January 17, 1991 evening when broadcasters interrupted the nightly news to say that the war had begun and that "our boys were in the air?" The Swamp Fox emblem roared all over Baghdad that hellatious night. It took us just a few hours to gain complete air superiority over Iraq.

For days and days there was round-the-clock bombing against land targets. On February 5th of 1991 South Carolina's 157th Squadron deployed all of its F-16s from Al Kharj Air Base in Saudi Arabia on search and destroy pinpoint annihilation sorties. Pilots destroyed 5 Iraqi tanks and one truck. The aircraft crew chiefs and mechanics and all support personnel performed round-the-clock maintenance on these " war birds," thus insuring that aircraft rearmament and engine overhaul was performed in record time. The heat and constant blowing sand presented problems never before experienced back home. But air guardsmen greeted each other cheerily with "Semper Pri."

One Airman of the 157th remarks, "As members of the South Carolina Air National Guard, we are proud of many "firsts". We were the first Air National Guard Unit to fly the F-16 Fighting Falcon. We were the first F-16 fighter unit to deploy in Operation Desert Storm, and we are the first guard unit to be assigned with the High Speed Anti-Radiation Missile (HARM). These are a few extraordinary achievements!"

In 2005 the Base Realignment Committee (BRAC) saw fit to close Mountain Home AFB in Idaho and reassign 9 of its F-16s to McIntire, another testimony to the proven combat readiness of our state's national guard.

The next time you see Iraqis holding a purple index finger proudly in the air, or a nightly news segment of girls going to school in Mosul, recall that our SCANG played a huge role in the cause of freedom!

Mount Parnassus Best Epitomizes The Old South

Close your eyes and recall Tara, that tarted-up Hollywood version of Margaret Mitchell's fictional plantation mansion in Gone With The Wind, or GWTW as it's referred to by the the smart set. Mitchell chose to represent the demise of the Old South with a family whose fortune and roots ran shallow at just two generations of prominence. However, that southern literary lion did much of her research for GWTW here in Charleston, yet she deliberately set the scene for the demise of the Old South myth in the upstart rail town of Atlanta -- playing up those concocted red clay and cotton O'Hara parvenus.

Mitchell's cycloramic literary epic is now of such importance to the southern psyche that there's no second doubting the wise woman's motives. But it's certainly intriguing to mull over what GWTW might have been like had Mitchell chronicled a genuine southern family with a cypress-sided, low-country mansion -- sodden with lore from ten illustrious generations already illustrious by 1860.

Such could have been the case if she'd chosen to memorialize long-forgotten Mount Parnassus plantation and the interconnected families that owned the oak and pine crested bluff over the centuries. Mount Parnassus, or Parnassus as it was shortened through usage, is located on the Back River, a tributary of the western branch of the Cooper, a bit north of the Naval Weapons Station.

Ride up U.S. Highway 52 and just beyond the area they call Mt. Holly, before you reach Moncks Corner, look to your right. Across those railroad tracks you are gazing upon the land that Zachariah Villeponteaux established his country seat, Mount Parnassus, in the 1720s.
Villeponteaux was a Huguenot lawyer who made his way to Charleston after practicing law briefly in New York. He made a fortune here from indigo, but his brick yard earned him lasting fame in this region. Brick fired at Parnassus was used exclusively for building St. Michael's Church as well as St. Stephen's Parish, the Chapel of Ease at Pompion Hill, and Charles Pinckney's townhouse in Charleston.

In colonial Charleston, Zachariah Villeponteaux was one of the wealthiest men around. His Parnassus plantation backed up to Foster's Creek, and the grey marl of that specific area became the distinctive Charleston grey brick noted by outsiders as a dull and unexceptional. Today the brick yard is the site of the MenRiv Housing project for the Naval Weapons Station.

It's difficult from the ruins of Parnassus to discern what the big house looked like, but ornate bricks are all that remain after Hurricane Hugo's final

329

blow to the old mansion. We do know that it was renowned for architectural beauty and for its twice weekly deer drives!

Louisa Cheves Stoney added notes in 1932 to a reprinting of Dr. John Beaufain Irving's 1842 book, A Day On Cooper River. She tells of her friend, Laura Tennent, then an old lady, who reminisced about growing up at Parnassus before the Confederate War.

Laura Tennent's recollections are of a great hall on the river with an avenue of oaks a mile long leading south toward Goose Creek. Charles Tennent was the owner of Parnassus by 1860 and he extended the oak avenue another one and one-half miles with young trees. In April of 1861 the firing on Fort Sumter could be distinctly heard at Parnassus, over 20 miles from the scene of the action. Very soon Tennent was called to be a surgeon in the Confederacy and the women were left in the care of an overseer and a hundred slaves.

Like all Charleston-area plantations, Parnassus barged staples down river to aid the Confederate army. The war seemed far away until the awful February in 1865 when the defenders of Fort Sumter nailed their biggest garrison flag to the flag pole and spiked their guns. When the CSA withdrew from Charleston at night on February 16 and 17, the army passed by Parnassus on their way to rail stations that took them on to North Carolina.

In a few days the advance units of the northern army made up of former slaves led by white officers began sacking the outlying plantations. Rowdy invaders burst in upon Mrs. Tennent and demanded that she fix supper for them. After taking what they wanted they swore that they'd come back the next night "to dance with the girls." With fear and trembling, Laura Tennent and her mother were rowed across to Cote Bas plantation where they watched the systematic looting of the homes on both sides of the river.

Stoney recounts Tennent's pathetic recollection of going back to Parnassus and all was gone -- everything except a paper doll trodden on her bedroom floor. In the slave quarters there was no one except an elderly man whose family had left to die. Everything was gone, but old Parnassus house was still there. However, in 1866 the deserted mansion caught fire and burned to the ground leaving nothing but brick columns that stood until Hugo.

Parnassus and nearby plantation, The Oaks, were bought after World War I by wealthy New Yorkers to use as hunting preserves.

Edwin Parsons, the chairman of the board of several railroads bought The Oaks and much of the land that was Parnassus sometime prior to 1908. He married Mary B. Whitehead, of an old Savannah family and their son, Edwin, later a rear admiral, was a fighter pilot Ace in the famed Lafayette Escadrille flying corps in Word War I.

Charleston writer John Bennett published his novel, The Lost Treasure of Peyre Gaillard in 1906. It's a yarn about a prominent Charleston family who never recovered their silver after it was buried in a forest during the Revolution. The novel included a cryptic message that was a key to finding the lost treasure. When sleuths cracked the coded message, it led to Parnassus and to the shaded area of a huge old oak. Many Charlestonians of the 19th century maintained that John Bennett's story was true!

One night a hundred years ago some treasure hunters set off dynamite near the tree in an effort to locate the silver. That was the last time Parnassus was in the news until it was sold to the U.S. government for use by the naval base. To Charlestonians, Parnassus represents all that Margaret Mitchell expressed in GWTW -- and more!